C000100842

1,000,000 Books

are available to read at

---◆---

www.ForgottenBooks.com

---◆---

Read online
Download PDF
Purchase in print

ISBN 978-0-428-60423-3
PIBN 11301980

English
Français
Deutsche
Italiano
Español
Português

www.forgottenbooks.com

Mythology Photography **Fiction**
Fishing Christianity **Art** Cooking
Essays Buddhism Freemasonry
Medicine **Biology** Music **Ancient**
Egypt Evolution Carpentry Physics
Dance Geology **Mathematics** Fitness
Shakespeare **Folklore** Yoga Marketing
Confidence Immortality Biographies
Poetry **Psychology** Witchcraft
Electronics Chemistry History **Law**
Accounting **Philosophy** Anthropology
Alchemy Drama Quantum Mechanics
Atheism Sexual Health **Ancient History**
Entrepreneurship Languages Sport
Paleontology Needlework Islam
Metaphysics Investment Archaeology
Parenting Statistics Criminology
Motivational

PREFATORY NOTE

The following scheme is based upon "America: history and geography; preliminary and provisional scheme of classification, January, 1901," prepared by Charles Martel, Chief Classifier, whose counsel has been at my disposal throughout the revision.

In the course of the past 13 years, during which I have had entire charge of Americana, the collection has considerably more than doubled in size—from transfers and new accessions; and it has been found necessary to expand certain sections and make extensive alterations in others.

In the preparation of this edition copious explanations and references have been added. They are not exhaustive, and not designed to teach history; but are merely given as illustrating the usage of this library and as a guide to the location of related material in other classes.

CHARLES A. FLAGG

HERBERT PUTNAM
Librarian of Congress
Washington, March 1, 1913

CONTENTS.

OUTLINE.

AMERICA.

UNITED STATES. GENERAL.

UNITED STATES. LOCAL.

F

F

851	Pacific States. Pacific coast.
852–853	Pacific Northwest. Columbia River and Valley.
854	Northwest boundary since 1846.
856–870	California.
871–885	Oregon.
886–900	Washington (State).
901–915	Alaska.
. 931	Klondike region.
951	Bering Sea and Aleutian Islands.
970	Insular possessions as a whole.

AMERICA (EXCLUSIVE OF UNITED STATES).

1001–1035	British North America. Canada.
1035.8	Maritime provinces. Atlantic coast.
1036–1039	Nova Scotia.
1041–1044	New Brunswick.
1046–1049	Prince Edward Island.
1050	St. Lawrence River and Valley.
1051–1054	Quebec.
1056–1059	Ontario.
1060	Canadian Northwest. Northwest territories.
1061–1064	Manitoba.
1071	Saskatchewan.
1076	Alberta.
1086–1089	British Columbia.
1090	Rocky Mountains of Canada.
1091	Yukon.
1096	Mackenzie.
1101	Franklin.
1106	Keewatin.
1111	Ungava.
1121–1124	Newfoundland.
1136–1139	Labrador.
1140	The Labrador peninsula.
1170	St. Pierre and Miquelon.
1201–1391	Mexico.
1401–1418	Spanish America.
1421–1440	Central America.
1441–1457	British Honduras.
1461–1477	Guatemala.
1481–1497	Salvador.
1501–1517	Honduras.
1521–1537	Nicaragua.
1541–1557	Costa Rica.
1561–1577	Panama.
1601–1623	West Indies.
1631–1639	Bermudas.
1651–1659	Bahamas.
1741	Greater Antilles.
1751–1849	Cuba.
1861–1891	Jamaica.

F	West Indies—Continued.
	Greater Antilles—Continued.
1901–1911	Haiti.
1921–1929	Haiti (Republic).
1931–1939	Dominican Republic.
1951–1981	Porto Rico.
2001–2129	Lesser Antilles.
2131	British West Indies.
2136	Danish West Indies.
2141	Dutch West Indies.
2151	French West Indies.
2161–2171	Spanish Main. Buccaneers.
2201–2239	South America.
2251–2299	Colombia.
2301–2349	Venezuela.
2351	Guiana.
2361–2390	British Guiana.
2401–2430	Dutch Guiana.
2441–2470	French Guiana.
2501–2659	Brazil.
2661–2699	Paraguay.
2701–2799	Uruguay.
2801–3021	Argentine Republic.
3031–3040	Falkland Islands.
3051–3285	Chile.
3301–3349	Bolivia.
3401–3615	Peru.
3701–3899	Ecuador.

GENERAL ORDER OF FORM AND OTHER SUBDIVISIONS

It is seldom that all are needed in one place; at times two or more are united, as a, b. and c; and a modified or special scheme is sometimes preferred. The special scheme for states of the United States is given at the beginning of F.

The letters (a, b, c, etc.) prefixed do not form part of the notation; they are merely given to facilitate reference.

a   Periodicals.

b   Societies.

c   Collections.

d   Collected works, or papers and essays of individual authors.

e   Dictionaries. Gazetteers. Encyclopedic works.

f   Biography. Genealogy.
> Collected works only; individual biography in subdivision "n" or "p" (except where special subdivisions are provided for individual biography in the schedules); history of a single family in CS. Cf. footnote, p. 85.

g   Comprehensive works. (Works emphasizing the economic conditions are classified in HC.)

h   Guide books. Handbooks.

i   Miscellaneous.

j   Travel and description. Social conditions. National characteristics.

k   Period subdivisions.

l   Antiquities.

m   Indians.
> (This subdivision applies under Latin American countries only).

n   History.

o   Historical miscellany.

p   Period subdivisions.
> Boundary disputes (q) usually contain much on earliest period.

q   Regional. States. Provinces. Boundaries.
> Works treating of all the boundaries or boundary disputes of a country are placed here. Usually a boundary dispute between two countries or states might be equally well classed with either; sometimes it clearly belongs with one rather than with the other. In cases of this kind it has been indicated with which country the boundary lines and controversies relating thereto have been classed, reference being made from the other.

r   Cities and towns.
> 1. Metropolis, or chief city.
> 2. Other cities and towns.

s   Topics not within the scope of the preceding divisions.

E

11   Periodicals. Societies.
      International American conferences F 1405.
13   Collections. Collected works of authors.
14   Dictionaries. Gazetteers.
17   Biography.
18   Comprehensive works. History.
      Surveys, General GA 55-63.
                Geological QE 71-251.
                Hydrographic VK 597.
      Cartography. Maps GA 201-775.
      Physical geography GB 111-170.
      Hydrography GB 701-719.
      Anthropogeography GF.
      Anthropology and Ethnology GN.
19   Miscellaneous.
      Description and travel.
      Travels around the world and itineraries including America and other
          countries, G 420-503. Polar discoveries, G 575-890.
      Before 1607   E 141.
      Discovery and exploration   E 101-135.
      1607-1810   E 143.
27   1810-
      Cf. G 470-480.
29   Topics. Foreign elements.
      .F8 French.   .J5 Jews.
      .I8 Italians.

NORTH AMERICA E 31-50.

31   Periodicals. Societies. Collections.
35   Gazetteers.
36   Biography.
38   Comprehensive works.
39   Miscellaneous.
41   Description and travel.
      Most works of travel in North America treat largely of the U. S. and are
          classed in E 162-168.
45   History.
      Discovery E 101-135.
      History of Spanish America F 1410.

ABORIGINAL AMERICA—THE INDIANS   E 51–99.

> All material on the American Indians is classified here, except language
> PM, and the special works referred to in note under E 65.
>
> Cf. Anthropology and Ethnology, GN.

51   Periodicals.   Societies.   Collections.

> (e. g. Archaeological institute of America; International congress of
> Americanists; Société des Américanistes de Paris; U. S. *Bureau of
> American ethnology.* But American antiquarian society E 172.A.)

56   Museums.   Exhibitions.   Collections of antiquities.

57   Theory.   Methods of investigation.   Biographies: Jones, William; etc.

58   General works on the aboriginal inhabitants of the Americas.

59   Topics.

.C2 Canoes and boats.	.M8 Mortuary customs.
.D9 Dwellings.	.P8 Pottery.
.F6 Folk-lore. Legends.	.W9 Writing.

61   Origin of the Indians.   Prehistoric archaeology.   Cliff dwellings in America.

> Atlantis   GN 751.
> Cliff dwellings in the Southwest.   E 78.S7.

65   South and Central America, West Indies, and Mexico.

> General works on this group, only. Special go in local history, usually
> under the country; in special cases with state or province, e. g. F 1219;
> F 1434; F 1529. M9; F 2229; F 3126, etc.
> Spanish treatment of the Indians   F 1411.

71   North America (north of Mexico).

> General works on the aborigines. If relating to Indians only, class in E 77.

73   Mound builders.   Mounds.

74   Local.   By state or region, alphabetically,

> e. g.: Mounds in Franklin County, Ohio: E 74.O3.

.A3 Alabama.	.M6 Mississippi Valley.
.A7 Arkansas.	.M65 Missouri.
.F6 Florida.	.N5 New York.
.G3 Georgia.	.O3 Ohio.
.I2 Illinois.	.S7 South Carolina.
.I3 Indiana.	.T2 Tennessee.
.I6 Iowa.	.V5 Vermont.
.K3 Kentucky.	.V8 Virginia.
.M3 Manitoba.	.W5 West Virginia.
.M5 Minnesota.	.W8 Wisconsin.
.M55 Mississippi.	

THE INDIANS OF NORTH AMERICA   E 77-99.

77   General works.   Periodicals.   Collections, etc.

Zeisberger, David   E 98.M6Z.

78   Local.   Indian antiquities.

States, provinces, and regions of U. S. and Canada, alphabetically.
(Indian reservations are classed here under state, unless held by a
single tribe, when they are classed in E 99.)

.A28	Alabama.		.N7	New York.
.A3	Alaska.		.N74	North Carolina.
.A7	Arizona.		.N76	Northwest, Old.
.A8	Arkansas.		.N77	Northwest, Pacific.
.B9	British Columbia.		.N8	Northwestern states.
.C15	California.		.N9	Nova Scotia.
.C2	Canada.		.O3	Ohio.
	Cf. E 78.B9, .N9,			Zeisberger, David
	.O5, .U5; E 92.			E 98.M6Z.
.C6	Colorado.		.O4	Ohio Valley.
.C7	Connecticut.		.O45	Oklahoma.
	Dakota E 78.S63.			Cf. E 78.I5.
.D3	Delaware.		.O5	Ontario.
.D6	District of Columbia.		.O6	Oregon.
.F6	Florida.		.P2	Pacific coast.
.G3	Georgia.		.P4	Pennsylvania.
.I18	Idaho.			Zeisberger, David
.I3	Illinois.			E 98.M6Z.
.I5	Indian Territory, Old (The		.R4	Rhode Island.
	five civilized tribes).		.S6	South Carolina.
	Cf. E 78.O45.		.S63	South Dakota.
.I53	Indiana.		.S7	Southwest, New. Cliff
.I6	Iowa.			dwellings.
.K16	Kansas.		.S8	Southwest, Old.
.K3	Kentucky.		.T3	Tennessee.
.L8	Louisiana.		.T4	Texas.
.M4	Massachusetts.		.U5	Ungava.
.M6	Michigan.		.U55	Utah.
.M7	Minnesota.		.V5	Vermont.
.M8	Missouri.		.V7	Virginia.
.M9	Montana.		.W3	Washington (State).
.N3	Nebraska.		.W5	The West.
.N5	New England.		.W6	West Virginia.
.N6	New Jersey.		.W8	Wisconsin.
.N65	New Mexico.			

81   Indian wars.

Boone, Daniel   F 454.B.
Wetzel, Lewis   F 517.W.
Carson, Christopher   F 592.C.

82   Indian wars of the colonial period.   General works.

83   Special wars, chronologically.

83.63   Pequot war, 1636–1638.

.655   New York Indian uprising, 1655.

.663   Esopus Indian war, 1663–1664.

INDIANS OF NORTH AMERICA.

Indian wars.
    Special wars, chronologically—Continued.
83. 67   King Philip's war, 1675–1676.
         Denison, Daniel F 67.D
       King William's war, 1689–1697 E 196.
       Queen Anne's war, 1702–1713 E 197.
  .71   Tuscarora war, 1711–1713.
  .716   War with the Natchez Indians, 1716.
  .72   Wars with the eastern Indians, 1722–1726. Rasles.
  .739   Chickasaw war, 1739–1740.
       King George's war, 1744–1748 E 198.
       French and Indian war, 1755–1763 E 199.
  .759   Cherokee war, 1759–1761.
  .76   Pontiac's conspiracy, 1763–1765. Henry Bouquet
         Bradstreet, John E 199.B.
  .77   Dunmore's war, 1774. Battle of Point Pleasant
  .775   Indian wars, 1775–1783.
         Boone, Daniel F 454.B.
       Campaigns of the revolution E 230–239.
       Wyoming and Cherry Valley massacres, 1778 E 234.
       Sullivan's Indian campaign, 1779 E 235.
       Crawford's campaign, 1782 E 238.
  .79   Wars with the northwestern Indians, 1790–1795. Expeditions of Harmar (1790), Scott, Wilkinson and St. Clair (1791), and Wayne (1793–1795).
         St. Clair, Arthur F 483.S.
  .794   Wayne's campaign, 1793–1795.
         Wayne, Anthony E 207.W35.
  .81   Tippecanoe campaign, 1811.
         Harrison, W. H. E 392.
  .812   Indian wars, 1812–1815.
       Campaigns of the war of 1812 E 355.
  .813   1st Creek war, 1813–1814.
         Jackson, Andrew E 382.
  .817   1st Seminole war, 1817–1818. Execution of Arbuthnot and Ambrister, 1818.
         Gaines, E. P. E 353.1.G14.
         Jackson, Andrew E 382.
  .83   Black Hawk war, 1832.
         Taylor, Zachary E 422.
  .835   2d Seminole war, 1835–1842.
         Gaines, E. P. E 353.1.G14.
         Harney, W. S. E 181.H.
         Scott, Winfield E 403.1.S4.
         Smith, P. F. E 403.1.S7.

Indian wars.

    Special wars, chronologically.

        2d Seminole war—Continued.

            Taylor, Zachary E 422

            Worth, W. J. E 403.1.W9.

83.836   2d Creek war, 1836. T. S. Jesup.

.84   Wars with the Pacific coast Indians, 1847–1865. (Cayuse, Rogue River, Yakima, Klikitat, Spokan, and other Indian wars)

            Cf. E 83.858.

            Wool, J. E. E 403.1.W8.

.854   Dakota Indian war, 1855–1856. "Sioux war."

            Harney, W. S. E 181.H.

.855   3d Seminole war, 1855–1857.

.857   Spirit Lake massacre, 1857.

.858   Mill Creek war, 1857–1865.

.86   Dakota Indian wars, 1862–1863.

.863   Indian wars, 1863–1865.

            Carson, Christopher F 592.C.

.866   Indian wars, 1866–1895. Massacre at Fort Phil Kearney, 1866. Biographies: Crook, George; Miles, N. A., etc.

            Howard, O. O. E 467.1.H8.

            Sheridan, P. H. E 467.1.S54.

.868   Beecher Island, 1868.

.869   Washita campaign, 1868–1869.

.87   Modoc war, 1872–1873.

            Canby, E. R. S. E 467.1.C2.

.876   Dakota Indian war, 1876.

            Custer, G. A. E 467.1.C99.

.877   Nez Percés war, 1877.

            Howard, O. O. E 467.1.H8.

.879   Ute war, 1879.

.88   Apache war, 1883–1886.

.89   Dakota Indian war, 1890–1891.

    Captivities. Indian attacks, adventures, etc. Depredations.

85   General or collected works.

87   Individual captivities.

            If of special interest in relation to a particular tribe or war classify in E 99 or E 83.

89   **Biography,** Collected. Collections of portraits.

90   Individual.

            Important historical characters with war or tribal history:

                Black Hawk E 83.83.B.

                Geronimo E 99.A6G.

                Pokagon, Simon E 99.P6P.

                Pontiac E 83.76.P.

                Sitting Bull E 99.D1S.

INDIANS OF NORTH AMERICA—Continued.

91   **Government relations.**
     (General.)

92   **Canada.**
     Cf. Indians in Canada   E 78.C2.

93   **United States.**
     The Indian question. Treatment of the Indians. U. S. *Office of Indian affairs.* U. S. *Board of Indian commissioners.* Indian rights association, etc. Reservations. (Single reservations are classed with tribe E 99, if belonging to a single tribe; otherwise, E 78.)
     Indian lands.   HD 231–234.
     Meacham, A. B.   F 881.M.

95   **Treaties. Collections.**
     Individual treaties are classed with locality E 78, with tribe E 99, or with war E 83, as the case may be.

97   **Education.**

.5   **Indian schools. Collective works.**

.6   **Special schools.**

.C2	Carlisle, Pa.	.P4	Phoenix, Ariz.
.C4	Chilocco, Okla.	.P6	Pierre, S. D.
.H3	Hampton, Va.	.R2	Rapid City, S. D.
.L3	Lawrence, Kans. Haskell Institute.	.R5	Riverside, Cal. Sherman Institute.
.M5	Moor's Indian charity school. Cf. Dartmouth college LD 1420–1445.	.S2	Santee, Nebr.
		.S5	Shawnee, Okla.
		.T4	Thomas Indian school, Iroquois, N. Y.
.M6	Morris, Minn.	.T6	Toledo, Ia.
.O8	Osage, Okla.		

98   **Other special topics.**

.A3	Agriculture.	.F6	Folk-lore. Legends.
.A6	Antiquities. Appropriations E 91–93.	.F7	Food.
.A65	Arms and armor.	.G2	Games. Government relations E 91–93.
.A7	Art.		History E 77.
.B3	Basket making. Biography E 89–90.	.I4	Implements.
.C2	Boats. Canoes. Captivities E 85–87.	.I5	Industries. Land transfers E 91–93. Languages PM 1–2711.
.C3	Census.		
.C5	Children. Citizenship E 91–93.	.L7	Liquor problem.
.C58	Claims.	.M4	Medicine.
.C7	Commerce.	.M6	Missions. General works only. Zeisberger, David. It is better to class the literature of missions as far as possible in E 99 or E 78. Jesuit missions in New France F 1030.7–.8.
.C8	Costume.		
.C9	Culture.		
.D2	Dances.		
.D6	Diseases.		
.D9	Dwellings. Education E 97.	.M7	Money. Wampum.
.E8	Esthetics.	.M8	Mortuary customs.

98 Other special topics—Continued.

.M9	Music.	.S5	Sign language.
	Cf. ML 3557.	.S6	Slavery.
.N2	Names.	.S8	Statues.
	Origin E 61.		Suffrage E 91–93.
.P5	Philosophy.	.T6	Tobacco pipes.
.P6	Picture writing.	.T7	Trails.
	Portraits E 89.		Treaties E 95.
.P8	Pottery.	.W2	Warfare.
.R3	Religion and mythology.		Wars E 81–83.
	Reservations E 91–93, 78, 99.	.W9	Writing. Cf. E 98. P6.

99 Tribes, alphabetically.

Here are included such Mexican tribes as belong to the great linguistic families of the U. S.

.A1	Abnaki Indians.	.I2	Illinois Indians.
.A28	Ahtena Indians.	.I6	Iowa Indians.
.A4	Alibamu Indians.	.I7	Iroquois Indians.
.A6	Apache Indians.	.J4	Jemez Indians.
.A7	Arapaho Indians.	.J9	Jumano Indians.
.A8	Arikara Indians.	.K2	Kansa Indians.
.B4	Beothuk Indians.	.K26	Karankawa Indians.
.B5	Biloxi Indians.	.K4	Kickapoo Indians.
.C3	Cayuga Indians.	.K5	Kiowa Indians.
.C32	Cayuse Indians.	.K7	Klamath Indians.
.C5	Cherokee Indians.	.K76	Klikitat Indians.
.C53	Cheyenne Indians.	.K9	Kwakiutl Indians.
.C55	Chickasaw Indians.	.L9	Luiseño Indians.
.C56	Chimariko Indians.	.M12	Mahican Indians.
.C57	Chinook Indians.	.M18	Maidu Indians.
.C6	Chippewa Indians.	.M19	Makah Indians.
.C7	Chitimacha Indians.	.M2	Mandan Indians.
.C8	Choctaw Indians.	.M3	Mascouten Indians
.C85	Comanche Indians.	.M4	Mashpee Indians.
.C87	Conestoga Indians.	.M44	Menominee Indians.
.C9	Creek Indians.	.M48	Miami Indians.
.C91	Croatan Indians.	.M6	Micmac Indians.
.C92	Crow Indians.	.M68	Missisauga Indians.
.D1	Dakota Indians.	.M69	Miwok Indians.
.D2	Delaware Indians.	.M7	Modoc Indians.
.E5	Erie Indians.	.M77	Mohave Indians.
.E7	Eskimos.	.M8	Mohawk Indians.
.E8	Esopus Indians.	.M9	Moravian Indians.
	Five civilized tribes E 78. I5.	.N16	Narraganset Indians.
.F7	Fox Indians.	.N2	Natchez Indians.
.G15	Gabrieleño Indians.	.N3	Navaho Indians.
.H2	Haida Indians.	.N5	Nez Percés Indians.
.H3	Havasupai Indians.	.N7	Nipmuc Indians.
.H6	Hidatsa Indians.	.O4	Omaha Indians.
.H7	Hopi Indians.	.O45	Oneida Indians.
.H78	Huichol Indians.	.O58	Onondaga Indians.
.H8	Hupa Indians.	.O8	Osage Indians.
.H9	Huron Indians (including	.O87	Oto Indians.
	Wyandot Indians).	.O9	Ottawa Indians.

INDIANS OF NORTH AMERICA.

99 Tribes, alphabetically—Continued.

.P2	Paiute Indians.	.S68	Spokan Indians.
.P23	Pamunkey Indians.	.S7	Squawmish Indians.
.P27	Passamaquoddy Indians.	.S8	Stockbridge Indians.
.P3	Pawnee Indians.	.T12	Tahltan Indians.
.P4	Pennacook Indians.	.T15	Takelma Indians.
.P5	Penobscot Indians.	.T17	Takulli Indians.
.P53	Pequot Indians.	.T2	Taos Indians.
.P58	Piegan Indians.	.T3	Tarahumare Indians.
	Pima Indians.	.T6	Tlingit Indians.
	Ponca Indians.	.T78	Tsilkotin Indians.
.P6	Potawatomi Indians.	.T8	Tsimshian Indians.
.P8	Pueblo Indians.	.T85	Tukuarika Indians.
.P98	Puyallup Indians.	.T9	Tuscarora Indians.
.Q2	Quapaw Indians.	.T96	Tutelo Indians.
.S2	Salish Indians.	.T98	Twana Indians.
.S21	Salishan Indians.	.U8	Ute Indians.
.S23	Sauk Indians.	.W2	Wampanoag Indians.
.S28	Seminole Indians.	.W5	Welsh Indians, Tradition of.
.S3	Seneca Indians.		
.S33	Shasta Indians.	.W6	Wichita Indians.
.S35	Shawnee Indians.	.W7	Winnebago Indians.
.S4	Shoshoni Indians.	.Y2	Yakima Indians.
.S5	Sia Indians.	.Y3	Yaqui Indians.
.S54	Siksika Indians.	.Y9	Yuchi Indians.
.S6	Siouan Indians.	.Z9	Zuñi Indians.

AMERICA—DISCOVERY TO 1600   E 101–135.

Discovery.

101   General works.

103   Pre-Columbian.   General.

105   Norse.   Vinland.
           Greenland   G 730–770.

109   Other (alphabetically).
           .C5   Chinese.
           .D9   Dutch.
           .I6   Irish.
           .I8   Italian (Zeno).
           .P5   Phœnician.
           .S7   Spanish.
           .W4   Welsh   (Tradition of the Welsh Indians   E 99.W5).

110   Conditions leading to, and resulting from the discovery of America.   Toscanelli.

111   **Columbus.**   General (including biography).

112   Special (Birthplace, Canonization, Family, Iconography, Landfall, Monuments, Ships, etc.)
           Bibliography of Columbus   Z 8187.

114   Collected writings of Columbus and Collections of documents concerning him.
           Alphabetically by editor.

115   Letter to Santangel (Spanish letter).
           Original issues, facsimiles, reprints, and translations, chronologically.

116   Letter to Sánchez (Latin letter).
           Subarranged like E 115.

117   Other writings.

118   Voyages, including Journal.

119   Columbus celebrations, 1892–93 (alphabetically by place)
           Chicago   T 500.
           .32   Genoa.
           .35   Madrid.
           .36   Palermo.
           .42   Rio de Janeiro.
           .5   Salem, Mass.
           .51   San Juan, Porto Rico.
           .52   Santiago, Chile.

120   Miscellaneous material on Columbus.   Poetry, Drama, Fiction.   Columbus day celebrations and programs.

121   Post-Columbian.   (Successors of Columbus to about 1607.) El Dorado.
           Polar discoveries   G 575–590.
           Search for the Northwest passage   G 640–656.
           General history of geographical discoveries and exploration G 220–306.

AMERICA.

Discovery.

    Post-Columbian—Continued.

        Spanish and Portuguese.

123   General.

                Early history of Spanish America   F 1411.

                Spanish settlement in Florida   F 314.

                Spanish settlement in Mexico   F 1230–1231.

                Spanish settlement in Peru   F 3442–3444, etc.

                General descriptive accounts of America before 1607   E 141.

                The general subject of Spanish and Portuguese discoveries
                    G 278–289.

                Cibola; Quivira   F 799.

125   Special (alphabetically).

.A15	Acosta, Gonzalo de.	.N3	Narváez, Pánfilo de.
.B2	Balboa, Vasco Núñez de.	.N6	Nizza, Marco da.
.B7	Boyl, Bernardo.	.N9	Núñez Cabeza de Vaca,
	Cabot, Sebastian		Alvar.
	E 129.C1.	.O6	Orellana, Francisco de.
.C11	Cabral, Pedro Alvares.	.O8	Ovando, Nicolás de.
.C12	Cabrillo, Juan Rodri-	.P2	Pancaldo, León.
	guez.		Peñalosa, Diego Dion-
.C2	Caminha, Pedro Vaz.		isio de F 799.P.
.C4	Casas, Bartolomé de las.	.P5	Pinzón, Martín Alonso.
	The tracts of Las	.P52	Pinzón, Vicente Yañes.
	Casas F 1411.		Pizarro, Francisco
	Colombo, Cristoforo		F 3442.
	E 111–120.	.P7	Ponce de León, Juan.
.C7	Corte-Real, João Vaz.	.S3	Schmidel, Ulrich.
	Cortés, Hernando F 1230.	.S4	Sea, Ares de.
.C8	Cosa, Juan de la.	.S7	Soto, Hernando de.
	Díaz del Castillo, Bernal	.U8	Ursúa, Pedro de.
	F 1230.	.V3	Vásquez de Coronado,
.F3	Federmann, Nikolaus.		Francisco.
.F9	Fuca, Juan de.	.V5	Vespucci, Amerigo.
.G6	Gómez, Esteban.	.V6	The name America.
.G8	Grijalva, Juan de.		
	Jiménez de Quesada, Gon-		
	zalo F 2272.J.		

        English.

127   General.

129   Special (alphabetically).

.C1	Cabot, John and Sebas-		Pring, Martin F 7.P.
	tian.	.R2	Raleigh, Sir Walter.
.D7	Drake, Sir Francis.		Cf. DA 86.22.R2;
	Cf. G 420.D7.		F 229.
.G4	Gilbert, Sir Humphrey.		Smith, John F 229.S.
	Gosnold, Bartholomew F 7.G.		Waymouth, George
.H4	Hawkins, Sir Richard.		F 7.W.
.H8	Hudson, Henry.		
	Hudson-Fulton celebra-		
	tion, 1909 F 127.H8.		

Discovery.

   Post–Columbian—Continued.

      French.

131   General.

         French colony in Florida   F 314.
         New France   F 1030.

133   Special (alphabetically).

    .C3   Cartier, Jacques.   Ribaut, Jean   F 314.
        Gourgues, Dominique de   .V5 Verrazzano, Giovanni da.
          F 314.   Villegagnon, Nicolas
        Laudonnière, René Gou-   Durand de   F 2529.
          laine de   F 314.
    .P3   Paulmier de Gonneville,
          Binot.

135   Other.

    .D9   Dutch: .I8 Italian:
        Hudson   E 129.H8.   Cabot   E 129.C1.
    .G3   German.   The Welsers.   Colombo   E 111–120.
        Federmann   E 125.F3   Verrazzano   E 133.V5.
        Schmidel   E 125.S3.   Vespucci   E 125.V5.

AMERICA—GENERAL ACCOUNTS   E 141–143.

141   Accounts of America before 1607, including 16th century travels.

        Discoveries   E 101–135.
        History of Spanish America to 1600   F 1411.

143   General accounts of America, 1607–1810.   Spanish America.

        English colonies, 1607–1765   E 162.
        New France, 1603–1763   F 1030.
        Spanish America since 1810   F 1409.
        Other local under corresponding country and period divisions in F.

UNITED STATES.

E

151 Periodicals. Societies. Collections.
> General societies for preservation of places of historic or other national
> interest.
> Geographical societies   G 3.

154 Gazetteers.

155 Geographical names.
> Indian names   E 98.N2.
> Cf. G 104–106.

157 Critical works.
> e. g. Tuckerman, America and her commentators.
> Cf. E 175.

158 Handbooks. Guide books. Directories of summer resorts,
excursions, etc.

159 Miscellaneous. Distance tables, state capitols, historic points,
mansions.
> Roads   HE 356, e. g. Cumberland road   HE 356.C3.   But historical and
> descriptive works on region traversed by road, in F, e. g. Cumberland
> road region in Pa.   F 157.C85.
> General question of location and removal of national capital   F 196.

160 National and state parks and reservations. Collected works.
> Works on particular parks under special subject or local divisions, e. g.
> E 475.81, Chickamauga and Chattanooga national military park;
> F 868.Y6, Yosemite national park.

Travel. General descriptive works by period.
> Includes works on the civilization, social life, national characteristics,
> etc. (For travel before era of settlement, see E 141.)
> Cf. regions, as, Atlantic coast, F 106; Southern states, F 206–220;
> Mississippi Valley, F 351–354; Old Northwest, F 476–485; The West,
> F 591–595.
> N. B.   A general work on travel through the country in 1785 should
> be classed in E 164, not F 106.

162 1607–1765.
> General descriptive works on the British colonies in America to be
> classified here.

163 1765–1783.

164 1783–1812.

165 1812–1845.

166 1845–1860.

167 1861–1865.
> Travels in the Confederate States   F 214.

168 1865–

25

HISTORY—GENERAL E 171–185.

171 Periodicals.

172 Societies. Historical departments of other organizations, etc.
>> Geographical societies G 3.

172.7 Patriotic hereditary societies.
>> The general subject only.
>> Special societies E 181, 182, 186, 202, etc.
>> Political and "patriotic" societies primarily devoted to social objects HS 2321–2330.

173 Collections. Collected essays, documents, etc. Sources.

174 Encyclopedias. Dictionaries.

174.5 Chronology.

Historiography.

175 General works. History.

.1 Minor. Pamphlets.

Special.

.4 Institutions. Government commissions in historical matters.
>> e. g. .C3, Carnegie institution of Washington. *Dept. of historical research.*

.5 Individual historians.
>> General criticism and biography only.
>> Criticism of particular works, with the work under period or subject.
>> Bancroft, George Cf. E 340.B2.
>> Force, Peter.
>> Sparks, Jared.

.7 Theory. Method. Comparison and criticism,

.8 Study and teaching.
>> Advanced study.
>> History teaching in the common schools LB 1530, 1581–1583, 1641–1643.

.9 Philosophy of (American) history.

176 Biography. General collections only.
>> Biography of special period E 302.5, etc.

176.1 Presidents.
>> Individual biography of each president is found under his administration E 312, 322, 332, etc.
>> Presidential inaugurations in local history: Washington, 1789 F 128.44; Washington, 1793, and Adams F 158.44; Jefferson and succeeding presidents F 197–199.
>> White house F 204.W5.

.6 Hall of fame, New York university.

178 **Comprehensive works.**

.1 Textbooks.

.2 Outlines. Questions.

.3 Juvenile works.

.4 Comic and satirical works.

.6 Addresses. Essays.

.9 Poetical works. Rhyming histories.
> General collections of American historical poems PS 595.H5.
> Collections or single poems on a particular event, with the subject; e. g. "Ballads and poems relating to the Burgoyne campaign" E 233.

179 **Miscellaneous.**
> The frontier, (A special frontier goes with region in F.)
> Flag (Heraldry) CR 113.
> Flag day JK 1761.
> Desecration of flag JC 346.

179.5 **Historical geography.**
> General works on boundaries. History of territorial expansion. Public domain.
> Cf. E 713, Expansion controversy. Imperialism, etc.
> JK 304, National territory (Constitutional theory and history).
> JK 2551-2556, Territorial government and administration.
> Special boundaries:
> Northeast E 398; F 42.B7; F 57.B7; F 127.B7.
> North F 551; F 597.
> Northwest F 880; F 854.
> Southwest F 786; F 392.B7.
> Southeast (before 1819) F 317.B7.
> Alaska F 912.B7.

181 **Military history. Battles. Military societies covering more than a single war. (Medal of honor legion of the U. S.; Military order of foreign wars; Society of American wars; Society of veterans of the regular army and navy; etc.) Biography of military leaders not readily classed with any single war: Harney, W. S.; Liscum, E. H.; etc.**
> Cf. Military history of the various wars (E 230, etc.), also Military science (U).

Crook, George E 83.866.C.	Miles, N. A. E 83.866.M.
French, S. G. E 467.1.F87.	Schofield, J. M. E 467.1.835.
Gaines, E. P. E 353.1.G14.	Scott, Winfield E 403.1.84.
Harrison, W. H. E 392.	Sheridan, P. H. E 467.1.854.
Jesup, T. S. E 83.836.J.	Sherman, W. T. E 467.1.855.
Macomb, Alexander E 353.1.M3.	Wool, J. E. E 403.1.W8.

HISTORY—Continued.

182 Naval history. Naval societies covering more than a single war (United States navy veteran association; etc.) Biography of naval leaders not readily classed with a single war: Perry, M. C.; Paulding, Hiram; Meade, R. W.; Sands, B. F.; Preble, G. H.; Macaulay, E. Y.; Evans, R. D.; etc.

> Cf. Naval history of the various wars (E 271, etc.), also Naval science (V).
>
> National association of naval veterans   E 462.5.

Bainbridge, William	E 353.1.B2.	Maffitt, J. N.	E 467.1.M35.
Biddle, James	E 353.1.B5.	Maury, D. H.	E 415.9.M3.
Conner, David	E 403.1.C7.	Morris, Charles.	E 353.1.M8.
Dahlgren, J. A.	E 467.1.D13.	Porter, David	E 353.1.P7.
Davis, C. H.	E 467.1.D24.	Rodgers, John	E 353.1.R7.
DuPont, S. F.	E 467.1.D9.	Schley, W. S.	E 714.6.S3.
Elliott, J. D.	E 353.1.E4.	Sloat, J. D.	E 403.1.S6.
Farragut, D. G.	E 467.1.F23.	Stewart, Charles	E 353.1.S8.
Hull, Isaac	E 353.1.H8.	Stockton, R. F.	E 403.1.S8.
Jouett, J. E.	E 467.1.J86.		

183 Political history.

> Cf. history of periods, and administrations (E 188, etc.), also Political science (JK).

183.7 Diplomatic history. Biographies; Marsh, G. P.; etc.

> Special with history of period and administration.
>
> Relations with Barbary states   E 335.
>
> Cf. Foreign relations (International law)   JX 1305–1599.
>> United States   JX 1405–1429.
>> International American conferences   F 1405.

184 Elements in the population. Races. Ethnography.

> Foreign elements in various regions, states, etc., are classed in F, as F 130.G4 Germans in New York (State).
>
> Voyages of discovery by various nationalities   E 105–135.

.A1	General.	.I8	Italians.
.A2	Acadians.	.J3	Japanese.
.A7	Armenians.	.J5	Jews.
	Assyrians. See Syrians.	.M8	Moravians.
.C3	Catholics.		Zeisberger, David
	The Catholic church B.		E 98.M6Z.
.C5	Chinese.		Negroes E 185, E 441–
	Danes. See Scandinavians.		453.
.D9	Dutch.	.O6	Orientals.
.E5	English.	.P7	Poles.
.F8	French.	.S2	Scandinavians.
	Cf. E 184.A2; E 184.H9.		(Danes, Norwegians,
.F85	French Canadians.		Swedes.)
.G3	Germans. Palatines.	.S3	Scotch.
	Weiser, Conrad F 152.W.	.S4	Scotch-Irish.
.G7	Greeks.	.S6	Slavs.
.H9	Huguenots.	.S9	Swiss.
.H95	Hungarians.	.S98	Syrians.
	Indians E 77–99.	.W4	Welsh.
.I6	Irish.		Cf. E 99.W5.
	Cf. E 184.S4.		

Negroes in the United States.

185   Comprehensive works. History. The general subject of free negroes before 1863.

                 Anthropology GN.
                 Slave trade HT
                 Slavery in the United States   E 441-453.
                 Emancipation   E 453.
                 Colonization   E 448.
                 Education   LC 2701-2803.

  .18   Free negroes in the South before 1863.

                 Free negroes in a particular state   E 185.93.A-.W.

  .2   1863-1877. From emancipation to the end of the reconstruction period. The negro as ward of the nation. Freedmen's bureau. Ex-slaves. Slave pensions.

         Cf. E 668, and the reconstruction period under each Southern state: F 231, etc.
                 Freedmen by state   E 185.93.A-.W.
                 Howard, O. O.   E 467.1.H8.

  .3   1877-   Historical works.

Status and development of the race since emancipation. Social, economic, and moral conditions, etc.

185. 5   Periodicals. Societies. Collections.

                 Cf. Negro secret societies in HS.

  . 6   Comprehensive works.

  . 61   Relations with white race.   Race problem.

                 Citizenship   JK 1781-1783.
                 Suffrage   JK 1921-1929.

  . 62   Intermarriage of races.   Miscegenation.

  . 63   The negro as soldier.

                 Revolution   E 269.N3.
                 Civil war   E 540.N3; E 585.N3.

  . 65   Crime.

                 Cf. Criminal ethnography   HV 6191-6197.

         Lynching.

                 Cf. Lynch law   HV 6455-6469.

  . 7   Religion. Negro churches.

                 Special sects and local churches in BN.

  . 8   Occupations.

                 Cf. Classes of labor   HD 6305.C7.

  . 82   Higher education. The professions. Art. Literature.

  . 86   Social relations. Home and family.

  . 88   Health. Physical condition.

HISTORY—Continued.

Local.   By region, state, etc.

185. 9   Negroes in the North.

. 93   States (alphabetically).

Negroes in a particular county, town, or city, in F; e. g., negroes in Fort Worth, Tex., F 394.F7; negroes in New York City, F 128.9.N3.

.A3	Alabama.	.M7	Missouri.
	Slavery in Alabama E 445.A3.		Slavery in Missouri E 445.M67.
.A8	Arkansas.	.N56	New York.
.C7	Connecticut.		Slavery in New York E 445.N56.
.G4	Georgia.		
	Slavery in Georgia E 445.G3.	.O2	Ohio.
		.P4	Pennsylvania.
.L6	Louisiana.		Slavery in Pennsylvania E 445.P3.
	Slavery in Louisiana E 445.L8.	.S7	South Carolina. Negroes in the Sea Island district, "Port Royal mission."
.M2	Maryland.		
	Slavery in Maryland E 445.M3.		Slavery in South Carolina E 445.S7.
.M3	Massachusetts.		
	Slavery in Massachusetts E 445.M4.	.V8	Virginia.
.M6	Mississippi.		Slavery in Virginia E 445.V8.
	Slavery in Mississippi E 445.M6.		

Biography.

185. 96   Collected.

. 97   Individual.

Biography of slaves   E 444.
Douglass, Frederick   E 449.D.
Paul, R. A.   F 231.P.

COLONIAL HISTORY (OF THE 13 ENGLISH COLONIES)   E 186–199.

(From earliest permanent English settlements on Atlantic Coast
to the American revolution, 1607–1775.)

186   Periodicals.   Learned societies.
Patriotic societies for the colonial period.

.3   Society of colonial wars.
.4   National society of the colonial dames of America.
.5   Colonial dames of America.
.6   Order of the founders and patriots of America.
.7   Colonial daughters of the seventeenth century.
.8   Daughters of the founders and patriots.
.99   Other societies, alphabetically.

187   Collections of monographs, essays, documents, sources, etc.
e. g. Prince society publications.

187.5 Biography, Collected. Genealogy. Comprehensive lists of immigrants.

> Biography of later colonial period, beginning with French and Indian war, E 302.5–.6; Genealogy of New England F 3, etc.
>
> General lists of immigrants of special nationality other than English, E 184.

188   Comprehensive works. History.

> British possessions in America, in general. Cf. F 1030, F 2131, F 2361, etc.
> Early explorations before 1607   E 101–135.
> General accounts of America   E 141–143.
> Huguenot colony, Port Royal, S. C., 1562   F 314.
> Raleigh's Roanoke colonies, 1584–1590   F 229.
> History of single colonies or groups of colonies   F 7, 67, etc.
> History of inland regions   F 352, 1030, etc.
> Indian wars   E 82–83.
> Travels, and colonial customs   E 162.
> Administration of the British colonies   JV1000–1099.

189   Miscellaneous. General discussion of European origin of American institutions.

BY PERIOD.

191   1607–1689.

> Virginia company of London   F 229.
> Plymouth company and Council for New England   F 7.
> Popham colony   F 22.
> Pequot war, 1636–1638   E 83.63.
> United colonies of New England, 1643   F 7.
> War with Esopus Indians, 1663–1664   E 83.663.
> King Philip's war, 1675–1676   E 83.67.
> Andros and his government   F 7.5.

195   1689–1775. Attempts at union. Albany congress, 1754. Sir William Johnson. William Shirley. Last years of colonial government, 1763–1775.

> Cf. E 211–216.
> Tuscarora war, 1711–1713   E 83.71.
> War with the Natchez Indians, 1716   E 83.716.
> Wars with the eastern Indians, 1722–1726   E 83.72.
> Wars with the Chickasaw Indians, 1739–1740   E 83.739.
> Cartagena expedition, 1741   F 2272.5.
> Franklin, Benjamin   E 302.6.F8.
> Weiser, Conrad   F 152.W.
> Zeisberger, David   E 98.M6Z.
> Ohio company   F 517.
> Pontiac's conspiracy, 1763–1765   E 83.76.
> Disputes with Great Britain   E 211–216.
> Stamp act congress, 1765   E 215.2.
> Quebec act, 1774   F 1032.

196   King William's war, 1689–1697. Destruction of Schenectady. Port Royal. Quebec expedition.

COLONIAL HISTORY.

By period. 1689–1775—Continued.

197   Queen Anne's war, 1702–1713. Destruction of Deerfield. Church's expedition to the eastward. Haverhill. Port Royal.

Cf. D 281: War of the Spanish succession.
Tuscarora war, 1711–1713   E 83.71.

198   King George's war, 1744–1748. Louisburg. Sir William Pepperrell.

Cf. D 292: War of the Austrian succession, 1740–1748.
Acadia and Cape Breton   F 1036–1039.C2.
Shirley, William   E 195.S.

199   French and Indian war, 1755–1763. Washington at Fort Necessity. Braddock's defeat. Fort William Henry. Ticonderoga and Crown Point. Louisburg. Niagara. Quebec. Biographies: Bradstreet, John; Rogers, Robert; Montcalm-Gozon, Louis Joseph de; Lévis, Francois Gaston, duc de; etc.

Cf. DD 409–412: Seven years war 1756–1763.
Albany congress, 1754   E 195.
Acadia and Cape Breton   F 1036–1039.C2.
War with the Cherokee Indians, 1759–1761   E 83.759.
Siege of Havana, 1762   F 1781.
Pontiac's conspiracy, 1763–1765   E 83.76.
Bigot, François   F 1030.B.
Bouquet, Henry   E 83.76.B.
Gridley, Richard   E 207.G94.
Johnson, Sir William   E 195.J.
Mercer, Hugh   E 207.M5.
Pepperrell, Sir William   E 198.P.
Pomeroy, Seth   E 207.P7.
Pownall, Thomas   F 67.P.
Putnam, Israel   E 207.P9
Shirley, William   E 195.S.
Stark, John   E 207.S79.
Thomas, John   E 207.T45.
Washington, George   E 312.
Wolfe, James   DA 67.1.W8.
Wooster, David   E 207.W9.

Elements in the population: Foreigners E 184.

REVOLUTION.

201   Periodicals.   Societies for research.

Organs of hereditary patriotic societies   E 202.

202   Societies, Patriotic and hereditary.

Reports, registers, etc. Collections of documents, memoirs, etc., in E 203; e.g. Publications of the Seventy-six society   E 203.S49.

.1   Society of the Cincinnati.

.2   Daughters of the Cincinnati.

.3   Sons of the American revolution.

.4   Sons of the revolution.   (Including proposals for union of S. R. and S. A. R.)

.5   Daughters of the American revolution.

.6   Daughters of the revolution.

203   Collected works.   Collections of documents, essays, letters, journals, memoirs, etc.

Collections of anecdotes   E 296.

Biography.

206   Collected.

(Especially military and naval leaders.)

Statesmen of the revolutionary period   E 302.5–.6.

Signers of the Declaration of independence   E 221.

207   Individual.

Lives of military and naval commanders and staff officers. Regimental officers and privates either with regimental histories E 263, or personal narratives E 275. Scouts and spies E 279.

.A3	Alexander, William (Lord Stirling.)	.G3	Gates, Horatio.
		.G56	Glover, John.
.A4	Allen, Ethan.	.G9	Greene, Nathanael.
	Allen, Ira F 52.A.	.G94	Gridley, Richard.
	Armstrong, John E 302.6.A7.		Hamilton, Alexander E 302.6.H2.
	Arnold, Benedict E 278.A7; E 236.	.H4	Heath, William.
		.H85	Howe, Robert.
	Barney, Joshua E 353.1.B26.		Jackson, James E 302.6.J2.
.B2	Barry, John.	.J7	Jones, John Paul.
	Boone, Daniel F 454.B.	.K14	Kalb, Jean.
.C2	Cadwalader, John.	.K74	Knox, Henry.
.C3	Campbell, William.	.K8	Kósciuszko, Tadeusz A.B.
.C5	Clark, G. R.	.L2	Lafayette, Marquis de.
	Clinton, George E 302.6.C6.		(Such lives as deal specifically with his career in America.)
.C62	Clinton, James.		Cf. DC 146.L2.
	Cobb, David F 69.C.		
	Davie, W. R. E 302.6.D2.	.L22	Lamb, John.
		.L47	Lee, Charles.
	Dearborn, Henry E 302.6.D3.	.L5	Lee, Henry.
		.L6	Lincoln, Benjamin.
	Dorchester, Guy Carleton, baron F 1032.D.		McHenry, James E 302.6.M12.
.E3	Elbert, Samuel.	.M3	Marion, Francis.
.G2	Gadsden, Christopher.	.M5	Mercer, Hugh.

REVOLUTION.

Biography.

207 Individual—Continued.

.M6	Mifflin, Thomas.		Revere, Paul F 69.R.
	Monroe, James E 372.		Rochambeau, Comte de
.M7	Montgomery, Richard.		E 265.R.
.M8	Morgan, Daniel.		St. Clair, Arthur F 483.S.
.M85	Moultrie, William.	.S3	Schuyler, Philip J.
.M9	Moylan, Stephen.		Shelby, Isaac F 455.S.
.M96	Muhlenberg, J. P. G.	.S6	Spencer, Joseph.
.N2	Nash, Francis.	.S79	Stark, John.
.O13	O'Brien, Jeremiah.	.S8	Steuben,F.W.A.H.F.von.
	Paine, Thomas	.S9	Sullivan, John.
	JC 177–178.	.S95	Sumter, Thomas.
.P2	Parsons, S. H.	.T45	Thomas, John.
.P3	Paterson, John.		Truxtun, Thomas
	Pickering, Timothy		E 323.T.
	E 302.6.P5.		Tryon, William F 257.T.
	Pinckney, C. C.	.T8	Tucker, Samuel.
	E 302.6.P55.	.W2	Ward, Artemas.
.P68	Pitcairn, John.		Warren, Joseph
.P7	Pomeroy, Seth.		E 263.M4W.
	Potts, Jonathan E 283.P.		Washington, George
.P75	Prescott, William.		E 312.
.P8	Pulaski, Kazimierz.	.W35	Wayne, Anthony.
.P9	Putnam, Israel.		Wilkinson, James
	Putnam, Rufus F 483.P.		E 353.1.W6.
	Reed, James E 263.N4R.	.W9	Wooster, David.
	Reed, Joseph E 302.6.R3.		

208 Comprehensive works.   General histories.

> Travel, manners and customs of the period   E 163.

209 Miscellaneous.

Political history.   Causes.   Controversies, 1763–1775.

> The previous controversy in a particular colony   E 263.
>   e. g. in Massachusetts   E 283.M4.

210 Modern treatises.

211 Contemporary works.

> Sermons and addresses of a general character   E 297.

215 Special questions and events.

> .1   General subject of commercial restrictions; the enforcement of trade and navigation laws.   Writs of assistance.
>
> .2   Stamp act, March, 1765.   Stamp act congress, October, 1765.
>
> .3   Townshend acts, June, 1767 (Repealed in April, 1770, save for a tax on tea)   Non-importation agreements of 1768–1769.
>
> .4   Mutiny act.   Quartering of troops in Boston.   Boston massacre, March 5, 1772.
>
> .5   Taxation and representation.
>
> .6   Gaspee affair, June, 1772.
>
> .7   Resistance to the tea tax.   Boston tea-party, December, 1773.
>
> .8   Boston port bill, 1774.
>
> .9   Mecklenburg resolutions, 1775.

216 **Other special topics.**

   Committees of correspondence and safety. Efforts to enlist aid of other British possessions, as Canada and Ireland. Sons of liberty. The Duché letter.

     War of the regulators, N. C. F 257.

     The parsons' cause, Va. F 229.

     Loyalists in the colonies E 277.

221 **Declaration of independence. Collected biography of the signers.**

230 **Military operations. Campaigns and battles. Lists of battles.**

   Orderly books are classed with campaigns E 231–239 or with military organization to which they belong E 255–268.

     Indian wars, 1775–1783 E 83.775.

230.5 **Regional military history. War in the South, operations in the Ohio Valley, etc.**

231 **Campaigns of 1775.**

   Lexington and Concord, April. Capture of Ticonderoga and Crown Point, May. Siege of Boston, May, 1775–March, 1776. Bunker Hill, June. Invasions of Canada. Events in the South.

232 **Campaigns of 1776.**

   British occupation of New York, June–August. Washington's retreat up the Hudson and through New Jersey. Trenton and Princeton. Events in the South, Charleston, etc.

233 **Campaigns of 1777.**

   Invasions from Canada, Burgoyne and St. Leger, June–September. Jane McCrea. Clinton's advance up the Hudson. Howe's occupation of Philadelphia.

     Conway cabal E 255.

234 **Campaigns of 1778.**

   British withdrawal to New York. Raids and massacres. Conquest of Georgia. Clark's expedition.

235 **Campaigns of 1779.**

   Gen. Lincoln in S. C. and Ga. British raids in Va. and Conn. Penobscot expedition. Sullivan's Indian campaign, etc.

236 **Campaigns of 1780.**

   Siege of Charleston. Cornwallis in the South. Arnold's treason.

     Arnold E 278.A7.

     André E 280.A5.

237 **Campaigns of 1781.**

   Greene and Cornwallis. Yorktown. Clark's expedition against Detroit.

     Mutiny of the Pennsylvania line E 255.

238 **Campaigns of 1782.**

   Crawford's campaign.

239 **Campaigns of 1783.**

   British evacuation of N. Y. Nov.

     Newburgh addresses E 255.

241 **(If preferred this number may be used for battles, alphabetically, rather than classing them in E 231–239.)**

REVOLUTION—Continued.

249   Diplomatic history.   Alliances.   Treaty of Paris.
       Franklin, Benjamin   E 302.6.F8.
       French auxiliaries   E 265.
       Final withdrawal of British troops from western posts   E 313.

251   Armies.   Troops.

255   American.   Registers and lists not confined to a single state.
          Pensioners.   War claims.   Conway cabal.   Mutiny of the
          Pennsylvania line.   Newburgh addresses.
       Orderly books, E 231-239, or E 259-268.
       Military pensions   UB 373.
       Lists of prisoners   E 281.

259   Continental army.   Brigades.

260   Military organizations raised by Congress directly: Com-
          mander in chief's guard, Lee's legion, etc.

263   The states in the revolution.   British American colonies.
          Each state's part in the war and previous controversy.
          Histories.   Collections.   Registers.   Regimental histo-
          ries, rolls, and orderly books; state continental line, state
          troops, militia.
       Histories of counties and towns in the war are classed in local his-
         tory. e. g. Worcester, Mass.   F 74.W9.
       American loyalists in a particular state.   E 277.
       Military operations in a state   E 230.5-239.

.C2   Canada (Province of Que-
     bec). Cf. E 216; E 263.N9.
	Delaware—Continued.
	    Rodney, Caesar

.C5 Connecticut.	E 302.6.R6.
Arnold, Benedict	.F6 Florida (East and West).
E 278.A7.	.G3 Georgia.
Ellsworth, Oliver	Elbert, Samuel E 207.E3.
E 302.6.E4.	Jackson, James
Hosmer, Titus	E 302.6.J2.
E 302.6.H8.	.M3 Maryland.
Johnson, W. S.	Carroll, Charles
E 302.6.J7.	E 302.6.C3.
Parsons, S. H. E 207.P2.	Henry, John E 302.6.H4.
Putnam, Israel E 207.P9.	Smith, Samuel
Sherman, Roger	E 302.6.S6.
E 302.6.S5.	.M4 Massachusetts (including
Spencer, Joseph	Maine). Warren, Joseph;
E 207.S6.	Quincy, Josiah (2d);
Wooster, David	Foster, Jedediah; etc.
E 207.W9.	Cf. E 215.
.D3 Delaware.	Adams, John E 322.
Bayard, J. A.	Adams, Samuel
E 302.6.B3.	E 302.6.A2.
Dickinson, John	Ames, Fisher E 302.6.A5.
E 302.6.D5.	Bernard, Sir Francis
McKean, Thomas	F 67.B
E 302.6.M13.	Brooks, John F 69.B.

Armies. Troops.
American.

263   The states in the revolution, etc.—Continued.

Massachusetts—Continued.

Cobb, David   F 69.C.
Gerry, Elbridge
     E 302.6.G37.
Glover, John   E 207.G56.
Gridley, Richard
     E 207.G94.
Hancock, John
     E 302.6.H23.
Heath, William   E 207.H4.
Hutchinson, Thomas
     F 67.H.
Knox, Henry   E 207.K74.
Lincoln, Benjamin
     E 207.L6.
O'Brien, Jeremiah
     E 207.O13.
Oliver, Peter   F 67.O.
Otis, James   E 302.6.O8.
Paterson, John   E 207.P3.
Pickering, Timothy
     E 302.6.P5.
Pomeroy, Seth   E 207.P7.
Prescott, William
     E 207.P75.
Putnam, Rufus   F 483.P.
Thomas, John   E 207.T45.
Ward, Artemas
     E 207.W2.

.N4   New Hampshire.   Reed,
     James, etc.
Bartlett, Josiah
     E 302.6.B2.
Stark, John   E 207.S79.
Sullivan, John   E 207.S9.
Whipple, William
     E 302.6.W5.

.N5   New Jersey.
Alexander, William
     E 207.A3.
Witherspoon, John
     E 302.6.W7

.N6   New York.
Clinton, George
     E 302.6.C6.
Clinton, James
     E 207.C62.
Duane, James
     E 302.6.D8.
Hamilton, Alexander
     E 302.6.H2.

New York—Continued.

Jay, John   E 302.6.J4.
Lamb, John   E 207.L22.
Lewis, Francis
     E 302.6.L6.
Livingston, Philip
     E 302.6.L7.
Livingston, R. R.
     E 302.6.L72.
Montgomery, Richard
     E 207.M7.
Morris, Gouverneur
     E 302.6.M7.
Schuyler, Philip J.
     E 207.S3.

.N8   North Carolina.
Cf. F 257 (War of the
regulators); E 215.9.
Blount, William
     E 302.6.B6.
Davie, W. R.   E 302.6.D2.
Hooper, William
     E 302.6.H7.
Howe, Robert
     E 207.H85.
Nash, Francis   E 207.N2.
Shelby, Isaac   F 455.S.

.N9   Nova Scotia (and dependencies).   Cf. E 263.C2.

.P4   Pennsylvania.   Bayard,
     John, etc.
Boudinot, Elias
     E 302.6.B7.
Cadwalader, John
     E 207.C2.
Dickinson, John
     E 302.6.D5.
Franklin, Benjamin
     E 302.6.F8.
Hillegas, Michael
     E 302.6.H6.
McKean, Thomas
     E 302.6.M13.
Mifflin, Thomas
     E 207.M6.
Morris, Robert
     E 302.6..M8
Moylan, Stephen
     E 207.M9.
Reed, Joseph
     E 302.6.R3.

REVOLUTION.

Armies. Troops.

American.

263   The states in the revolution, etc.—Continued.

        Pennsylvania—Continued.   .V8 Virginia.

          St. Clair, Arthur   Cf. E 83.77.

               F 483.8.   Campbell, William

          Wayne, Anthony   E 207.C3.

              E 207.W35.   Clark, G. R. E 207.C5.

  .R4 Rhode Island.   Gates, Horatio E 207.G3.

        Cf. E 215.6.   Henry, Patrick

        Ellery, William   E 302.6.H5.

           E 302.6.E3.   Jefferson, Thomas E 332.

        Greene, Nathanael   Lee, Charles E 207.L47.

           E 207.G9.   Lee, R. H. E 302.6.L4.

  .S7 South Carolina.   Madison, James E 342.

        Gadsden, Christopher   Mason, George

           E 207.G2.   E 302.6.M45.

        Laurens, Henry   Mercer, Hugh E 207.M5.

           E 302.6.L3.   Morgan, Daniel

        Marion, Francis   E 207.M3.

           E 207.M3.   Muhlenberg, J. P. G.

        Moultrie, William   E 207.M96.

           E 207.M95.   Randolph, Edmund

        Pinckney, C. C.   E 302.6.R18.

           E 302.6.P55.   Randolph, John

        Rutledge, John   E 302.6.R2.

           E 302.6.R9.   Washington, George

        Sumter, Thomas   E 312.

           E 207.S96. .W5 West Indies. Bermuda.

  .V5 Vermont.

        Allen, Ethan E 207.A4.

265   Auxiliaries. French participation. Histories; lists; personal
        narratives of soldiers and sailors, etc. Rochambeau.

        Lafayette, Marquis de E 207.L2.

267   English army.

        Tory regiments E 277.6

268   German mercenaries. Hessians.

        Germans in the American army E 268.G3.

269 Topics.

    .B2 Baptists.   .I6 Irish.

    .C3 Catholics.   .J5 Jews.

    .C5 Church of England.   Loyalists E 277.

      French auxiliaries E 265.   .N3 Negroes.

    .F8 Friends, Society of.   Poles.

      German mercenaries E 268.   Kósciuszko E 207.K8.

    .G3 Germans.   Pulaski E 207.P8.

      Kalb, Jean E 207.K14.   .P9 Presbyterians.

      Steuben, F. W. A. H. F.   .W4 Welsh.

        von   E 207.S8.

270   Colleges.
       .P9 Princeton.
       .Y2 Yale.

271   Naval history. Narratives of sailors. Privateers. British
       and French fleets in the West Indies.
          Lives of naval leaders E 206–207.
          Naval operations forming part of military movements E 231–239.

275   Personal narratives. Diaries.
          Narratives relating to special campaign, battle, or regiment are to be
            classed in E 231–239 or E 263; of German mercenaries E 268, of
            prisoners E 281.
          Narratives of naval service E 271.
          Cf. E 203 Collections of source material and
            E 296 Anecdotes.

277   Loyalists. Treatment of tories. Traitors.
          Loyalists in special provinces of Canada F 1036–39, 1041–44, 1056–59.

277.6 Loyalist regiments.
            Cf. English army E 267.
       .B9 Butler's rangers.
       .M2 Maryland loyalists regiment.
       .N5 New Jersey volunteers.
       .Q6 Queen's rangers.

278   Individual

.A4	Allen, Jolley.	.G4	Gilbert, Thomas.
.A7	Arnold, Benedict.	.J6	Johnson, John.
	Arnold's treason E 236.	.L5	Leonard, Daniel.
	Cartwright, Richard	.M8	Moody, James.
	F 1058.C.		Rogers, Robert E 199.R.
.C4	Chandler, John.		Ruggles, Timothy.
.C5	Christie, James.		aF 67.R.
.C7	Connolly, John.		Simcoe, J. G. F 1058.S.
.C8	Cornell, Samuel.	.S6	Smyth, J. F. D.
.C9	Curwen, Samuel.	.T9	Tuttle, Stephen.
	Franklin, William F 137.F.	.W6	Wilkins, Isaac.

279   Secret service. Spies.
280   Individual.
       .A5 André, John. His captors: Paulding, Van Wart and Williams.
       .H2 Hale, Nathan.

281   Prisons. Lists of prisoners. Prisoners' narratives. Exchanges.
283   Hospitals. Biographies: Potts, Jonathan; etc.
285   Celebrations. Anniversaries.
          Centennial celebration, Philadelphia T 825.

286   Fourth of July.
          The observance of the day. Fourth of July celebrations and ad-
            dresses of distinct local interest, especially those containing lists
            of names, etc., are classed in F. Those classed here are arranged
            by place, alphabetically.
          Patriots' day, 19th of April E 231.
          Evacuation day E 239.
          Monuments and memorials, under place in F.

REVOLUTION—Continued.

289   Museums. Trophies. Flags. Relics. Exhibitions. Illustrative material.

295   Poetry, drama, ballads, songs, etc.

296   Anecdotes. Fiction.

> Cf. E 203   Collections of source material and
>   E 275   Personal narratives.

297   Sermons, addresses.

> Classification under specific subject is to be preferred, if practicable.
> e. g. a sermon on the Boston massacre in E 215.4.

298   Miscellaneous. Humor. Caricatures. Prints.

REVOLUTION TO THE CIVIL WAR.

301   **1765–1865.** From the beginning of the revolution to the close of the civil war.

> Slavery and the anti-slavery movement   E 441–453.
> Political history of slavery   E 338–459.
> Diplomatic history, 1783–1865   E 183.7.
> Northeast boundary question   E 398.
> Northern boundary   F 551, 597.
> Northwest boundary   F 880, 854.

302   Collected works of American statesmen of the revolutionary group.

Adams, John	Jefferson, Thomas
Adams, Samuel	King, Rufus
Cobbett, William	Lee, R. H.
Dickinson, John	Madison, James
Franklin, Benjamin [1]	Monroe, James
Gallatin, Albert	Paine, Thomas JC 177–178.
Hamilton, Alexander	Pinkney, William
Jay, John	Washington, George E 312.

.1   **1765–1836.** Political history. The supremacy of the fathers of the republic.

.5   Biography, Collected.

> Signers of the Declaration of independence, collectively   E 221.
> Revolutionary leaders (especially military commanders) E 206.

---

[1] In the Library of Congress, Frankliniana are distributed as follows:

> Bibliography: Z 8313.
> Biography: E 302. 6. F8.
>   Literary biography: PS 751.
> Collected works: E 302. F.
> Autobiography (without the "Essays"): PS 747.
> Literary works ("Works consisting of Life written by himself, with the "Essays, humorous, moral, and literary"): PS 745.
> Poor Richard: PS 749.
> Other special works, with subject in B–Z.

1765–1836—Continued.

302. 6   Biography, Individual.

Adair, John
    E 353.1.A19.
Adams, John   E 322.
Adams' collected
    works in E 302.A.
Adams, John Quincy
    E 377.
.A2   Adams, Samuel.
Adams' collected
    works in E 302.A.
Allen, Ethan   E 207.A4.
.A5   Ames, Fisher.
.A7   Armstrong, John.
.B2   Bartlett, Josiah.
.B3   Bayard, J. A.
Bedinger, G. M.
    F 455.B.
.B6   Blount, William.
Boone, Daniel   F 454.B.
.B7   Boudinot, Elias.
.B9   Burr, Aaron.
Burr's conspiracy in
    E 334.
.C11   Cabot, George.
Cadwalader, John
    E 207.C2.
.C3   Carroll, Charles.
Clinton, De Witt
    E 340.C65.
.C6   Clinton, George.
.D14   Dallas, A. J.
.D2   Davie, W. R.
.D3   Dearborn, Henry.
.D5   Dickinson, John.
Dickinson's collected
    works in E 302.D.
.D8   Duane, James.
.E3   Ellery, William.
.E4   Ellsworth, Oliver.
.F56   FitzSimons, Thomas.
.F8   Franklin, Benjamin.
Franklin's collected
    works in E 302.F.
.G16   Gallatin, Albert.
Gallatin's collected
    works in E 302.G.
.G37   Gerry, Elbridge.
.H2   Hamilton, Alexander.
Hamilton's collected
    works in E 302.H.

Hamilton, James
    F 273.H.
Hampton, Wade (1st)
    E 353.1.H2.
.H23   Hancock, John.
.H29   Harper, R. G.
Harrison, W. H.   E 392.
.H4   Henry, John.
.H5   Henry, Patrick.
Hiester, Joseph
    F 153.H.
.H6   Hillegas, Michael.
.H7   Hooper, William.
.H8   Hosmer, Titus.
Houston, W. C.
    F 138.H.
.I6   Ingersoll, Jared.
.I7   Iredell, James.
Jackson, Andrew
    E 382.
.J2   Jackson, James.
.J4   Jay, John.
Jay's treaty in E 314.
Jay's collected works
    in E 302.J.
Jefferson, Thomas
    E 332.
Jefferson's collected
    works in E 302.J.
Johnson, R. M.
    E 340.J 69.
.J7   Johnson, W. S.
.K5   King, Rufus.
King's collected
    works in E 302.K.
Knox, Henry
    E 207.K74.
.L3   Laurens, Henry.
.L4   Lee, R. H.
Lee's collected works
    in E 302.L.
.L6   Lewis, Francis.
Lincoln, Benjamin
    E 207.L6.
.L7   Livingston, Philip.
.L72   Livingston, R. R.
.L9   Lyon, Matthew.
.M12   McHenry, James.
.M13   McKean, Thomas.
.M138   Maclay, Samuel.
.M14   Maclay, William.

1765–1826.

302.6   Biography, Individual—Continued.

.M17   Macon, Nathaniel.
       Madison, James
                  E 342.
       Madison's collected
         works in E 302.M.

.M4   Marshall, John. John
       Marshall day.

.M43   Mason, A. M.

.M45   Mason, George.
       Monroe, James   E 372.
       Monroe's collected
         works in E 302.M.
       Moore, Alfred   F 258.M.

.M7   Morris, Gouverneur.

.M8   Morris, Robert.

.O8   Otis, James.
       Paine, Thomas
            JC 177–178.
       Paterson, John
            E 207.P3.

.P3   Paterson, William.

.P5   Pickering, Timothy.

.P55   Pinckney, C. C.

.P57   Pinckney, Thomas.

.P6   Pinkney, William.

.P73   Plumer, William.
       Porter, P. B.
           E 353.1.P3.
       Quincy, Josiah (2d)
           E 263.M4Q.

.Q7   Quincy, Josiah (3d)

.R18   Randolph, Edmund.

.R2   Randolph, John.

.R27   Read, George.

.R3   Read, Joseph.

.R6   Rodney, Caesar.

.R8   Ross, James.
       Russell, Benjamin
             F 69.R.

.R9   Rutledge, John.
       St. Clair, Arthur
            F 483.S.

.S3   Sawyer, Lemuel.

.S45   Sevier, John.

.S5   Sherman, Roger.

.S6   Smith, Samuel.
       Strong, Caleb   F 69.S.
       Sumter, Thomas
           E 207.S95.

.T8   Tompkins, D. D.
       Warren, Joseph
           E 263.M4W.

.W15   Washington, Bushrod.
       Washington, George
             E 312.
       Washington's col-
         lected works in
         E 312.

.W2   Webster, Pelatiah.

.W5   Whipple, William.
       Wirt, William
           E 340.W79.

.W7   Witherspoon, John.
       Yancey, Bartlett
           F 258.Y.

303   1775–1789. Continental congresses. Articles of confederation. Constitution. The critical period. Foreign relations, 1783–1789.

     Revolution   E 201–298.
     Shays' rebellion, 1786–1787   F 69.
     Constitutional history   JK 111–181.

309   Territorial questions. Cession of western land claims to the general government by Mass., Conn., N. Y., Va., and N. C. Northwest ordinance, 1787.

     Old Northwest   F 476–485.
     S. C. cession, 1787   F 292.B7.
     Georgia land cessions, 1802   F 290, 336–350.

310   1789–1812.

.7   Diplomatic history.

     Cf. E 313–314, 323, 333–336, 357, etc., for diplomatic history of special periods.

311   **Washington's administrations, 1789–1797.**
> Wars with northwestern Indians.   E 83.79.
> Bank of the United States, 1791–1811   HG 2525–2529.

312   Biography of Washington.
> At present the Library of Congress does not use this number, but has a special collection of "Washingtoniana" which includes works by and about Washington.

313   Foreign relations. Neutrality proclamation of 1793. Genet. Adet. Withdrawal of British garrisons from western posts. Embargo of 1794. Treaty with Spain, 1795. Casa Yrujo.

314   Jay's treaty; signed Nov. 1794, ratified Aug. 1795.
> British right of search   E 357.2.

315   Whisky insurrection in Pennsylvania, 1794.

320   Presidential campaign of 1796.

321   **Adams' administration, 1797–1801.**
> Washington selected as capital   F 195.

322   Biography of Adams.
> Adams' collected works   E 302.

323   Troubles with France, 1796–1799. "X Y Z letters." Naval conflicts. Biographies: Decatur, Stephen, sr.; Truxtun, Thomas, etc.
> French spoliation claims before 1800   JX 238.F 74–75.
> Bainbridge, William   E 353.1.B2.
> Barron, James   E 335.B.
> Barry, John   E 207.B2.
> Dale, Richard   E 335.D.
> Stewart, Charles   E 353.1.S8.

326   Fries rebellion, 1798–1799.

327   Alien and sedition laws, 1798.

328   Kentucky and Virginia resolutions.

330   Presidential campaign of 1800.

331   **Jefferson's administrations, 1801–1809.**
> Impressment of American seamen   E 357.2.
> The "Chesapeake" affair   E 357.3.

332   Biography of Jefferson.
> Jefferson's collected works   E 302.

333   Purchase of Louisiana, 1803. Diplomatic and political aspects.
> For the region purchased, see F 366–380 and F 351–354.

.7   Presidential campaign of 1804.

334   Burr's conspiracy, 1805–1807. Wilkinson's participation.
> Mississippi Valley   F 353, 396.
> Burr, Aaron   E 302.6.B9.
> Wilkinson, James   E 353.1.W6.

Jefferson's administrations, 1801–1809—Continued.

335   War with Tripoli, 1801–1805. The general subject of relations with the Barbary states. Biographies: Barron, James; Dale, Richard; Noah, M. M.; Preble, Edward; etc.

War with Algeria, 1815   E 365.
Bainbridge, William   E 353.1.B2.
Decatur, Stephen, jr.   E 353.1.D29.
Hull, Isaac   E 353.1.H8.
Lawrence, James   E 353.1.L4.
Rodgers, John   E 353.1.R7.
Stewart, Charles   E 353.1.S8.
Truxtun, Thomas   E 323.T.

336   Neutral trade and its restrictions, 1800–1810. French spoliations since 1800.

Controversies with England, 1797–1812   E 357.
Orders in Council   HF 3505.9.
Berlin and Milan decrees. H.

.5   Embargo, Dec. 1807–Mar. 1809.

Embargo acts: text, and effects on commerce   HF 3027.1.

337   Presidential campaign of 1808.

EARLY NINETEENTH CENTURY.

337.8   Collected works of American statesmen of the period.

Adams, J. Q.   Clay, Henry.
Benton, T. H.   Corwin, Thomas.
Buchanan, James.   Everett, Edward.
Calhoun, J. C.   Webster, Daniel.
Choate, Rufus.

338   1811–1860. Slavery controversy in politics.

Slavery in the U. S. in its moral and economic aspects   E 441–453.
Anti-masonic controversy, 1827–1845   HS 525–527.

339   Biography, Collected.
340   Biography, Individual.

	Adair, John E 353.1.A19.	.C3	Cass, Lewis.
	Adams, J. Q. E 377.		Chambers, John
	Adams' collected		F 621.C.
	works in E 337.8.A.	.C4	Choate, Rufus.
.B2	Bancroft, George.		Choate's collected
	Cf. E 175.5.B.		works in E 337.8.C.
	Bell, John E 415.9.B4.	.C5	Cilley, Jonathan.
.B4	Benton, T. H.		Graves-Cilley duel.
	Benton's collected	.C6	Clay, Henry.
	works in E 337.8.B.		Clay's collected works
.B6	Birney, J. G.		in E 337.8.C.
.B8	Brockenbrough, W. H.		Clayton, A. S. F 290.C.
	Buchanan, James E 437.		Clayton, J. M.
.B9	Burges, Tristam.		E 415.9.C6.
	Butler, W. O.		Clingman, T. L.
	E 403.1.B9.		E 415.9.C63.
.C15	Calhoun, J. C.	.C65	Clinton, De Witt.
	Calhoun's collected	.C7	Cook, D. P.
	works in E 337.8.C.	.C72	Cooper, James.

1811–1860. Slavery controversy in politics.

340   Biography, Individual—Continued.

.C76	Corwin, Thomas.		Johnson, Joseph
	Corwin's collected		F 230.J.
	works in E 337.8.C.	.J69	Johnson, R. M.
.C89	Crawford, W. H.		Jones, G. W. E 415.9.J6.
.C9	Crittenden, J. J.	.K2	Kaufman, D. S.
	Crockett, David	.K33	Kendall, Amos.
	F 436.C.		Kennedy, J. P.
.D14	Dallas, G. M.		E 415.9.K35.
	Dickinson, D. S.	.K54	King, W. R.
	E 415.9.D5.	.L4	Lawrence, Abbott.
.D7	Dodge, Henry.	.L5	Legaré, H. S.
	Douglas, S. A.		Lincoln, Abraham
	E 415.9.D73.		E 457.
	Duane, W. J. F 153.D.	.L7	Linn, L. F.
.E2	Earle, Thomas.		McArthur, Duncan
	Edwards, Ninian		E 353.1.M15.
	F 545.E.	.M2	McLean, John.
.E8	Everett, Edward.		Marsh, G. P. E 183.7.M.
	Everett's collected	.M4	Menefee, R. H.
	works in E 337.8.E.	.M5	Mercer, C. F.
.E9	Ewing, Thomas.	.M7	Monroe, James (1799–
.F16	Fairfield, John.		1870.)
	Fillmore, Millard E 427.	.M8	Morris, Thomas.
.F86	Frelinghuysen, Theo-		Noah, M. M. E 335.N.
	dore.	.O8	Otis, H. G.
	Gallatin, Albert	.P3	Pearce, J. A.
	E 302.6.G16.	.P54	Phelps, S. S.
	Garrison, W. L.		Pickens, F. W. E 577.P.
	E 449.G.		Pierce, Franklin E 432.
	Giddings, J. R.	.P75	Poindexter, George.
	E 415.9.G4.	.P77	Poinsett, J. R.
.G48	Gilpin, H. D.		Polk, J. K. E 417.
.G6	Gordon, W. F.	.P9	Prentiss, S. S.
.G7	Granger, Francis.		Ripley, E. W.
.G8	Grundy, Felix.		E 353.1.R5.
	Hallock, Gerard	.S18	Saltonstall, Leverett.
	E 415.9.H18.		Sawyer, Lemuel
	Hammond, Charles		E 302.6.S3.
	F 495.H.	.S6	Smith, William.
	Harrison, W. H. E 392.		Tyler, John E 397.
.H4	Hayne, R. Y.		Van Buren, Martin
	Houston, Samuel		E 387.
	F 390.H.		Walker, R. J.
	Hunter, R. M. T.		E 415.9.W2.
	E 415.9.H9.	.W4	Webster, Daniel.
.H9	Huntington, J. W.		Webster's collected
.I48	Ingersoll, C. J.		works in E 337.8.W.
.I5	Ingersoll, J. R.	.W6	White, H. L.
.I55	Ingham, S. D.	.W73	Winthrop, R. C.
.J3	Jarvis, Leonard.	.W79	Wirt, William.
	Jay, William E 449.J.	.W8	Woodbury, Levi.
	Johnson, Andrew		Yancey, Bartlett
	E 667.		F 258.Y.

EARLY NINETEENTH CENTURY—Continued.

341 **Madison's administrations, 1809–1817.**
>> See also E 365–370.
>> Tippecanoe campaign E 83.81.
>> 1st Creek war, 1813–1814 E 83.813.
>> Troubles with England E 357.
>> War of 1812 E 351–364.
>> Seizure of West Florida west of the Perdido. F 301.

342 **Biography of Madison.**
>> Madison's collected works E 302.

349 **Presidential campaign of 1812.**

WAR OF 1812.

351 Periodicals. Societies. Collections.
>> Societies of veterans.
>> .2 National convention of the soldiers of the war of 1812.
>> .23 Pennsylvania association of the defenders of the country.
>> .27 New England association of soldiers of the war of 1812.
>> .28 New York state convention of the soldiers of the war of 1812.
>> Patriotic societies of descendants.
>> .3 Society of the war of 1812.
>> .5 Military society of the war of 1812.
>> .6 National society of United States daughters of 1812.

353 Biography, Collected.
>> Chiefly military and naval leaders.
>> Statesmen and politicians E 302.5–.6 and E 339–340.
>> .1 Individual.

.A19	Adair, John.	.M15	McArthur, Duncan.
	Armstrong, John	.M2	McDonough, Thomas.
	E 302.6.A7.	.M3	Macomb, Alexander.
.B2	Bainbridge, William.	.M37	McRee, William.
.B26	Barney, Joshua.		Madison, James E 342.
	Barron, James E 335.B.		Mercer, C. F. E 340.M5
.B5	Biddle, James.	.M6	Miller, James.
.B8	Brock, Sir Isaac.	.M8	Morris, Charles.
.B9	Brown, Jacob.	.P4	Perry, O. H.
	Cass, Lewis E 340.C3.		Pinckney, Thomas
.C8	Croghan, George.		E 302.6.P57
	Dearborn, Henry		Pike, Z. M. F 592.P.
	E 302.6.D3.	.P7	Porter, David.
.D29	Decatur, Stephen.	.P8	Porter, P. B.
.E4	Elliott, J. D.	.P9	Proctor, H. A.
.G14	Gaines, E. P.	.R3	Reid, S. C.
.H2	Hampton, Wade (1st).	.R5	Ripley, E. W.
	Harrison, W. H. E 392.	.R7	Rodgers, John.
.H8	Hull, Isaac.		Scott, Winfield
.H9	Hull, William.		E 403.1.S4
	Jackson, Andrew E 382.		Shelby, Isaac F 455.S.
	Jesup, T. S. E 83.836.J.		Smith, Samuel
	Johnson, R. M.		E 302.6.S6
	E 340.J69.	.S8	Stewart, Charles.
.J6	Jones, Jacob.		Taylor, Zachary E 422
.L4	Lawrence, James.	.W6	Wilkinson, James.
.L5	Lewis, Morgan.	.W7	Winder, W. H.

354 **Comprehensive works.**
  Manners and customs, and general travels of the period E 165.

355 **Military operations. Campaigns and battles.**
  Indian wars, 1812–1815 E 83.812.
  .1 Regional military history.
  .2 1812. Northwestern campaigns. Hull's advance, and surrender of
       Detroit. Expeditions under Hopkins and Harrison. Van Rens-
       selaer and Smyth at Niagara, Oct.–Nov. Dearborn at Lake Cham-
       plain, Nov.
  .4 1813. Harrison in the Northwest. Proctor. Perry's victory. Ex-
       peditions against Chesapeake Bay and Norfolk. Dearborn and
       Wilkinson on Lake Ontario and the St. Lawrence. Niagara region.
       Hampton on Lake Champlain.
       1st Creek war E 83.813.
  .6 1814–15. Brown in the Niagara region. Capture of Washington and
       attempt on Baltimore. McDonough on Lake Champlain. Expe-
       dition against New Orleans.

356 **(If preferred this number may be used for battles, alphabeti-
    cally, rather than classing in E 355.)**

357 **Political history, including controversy with England since
    1797.**
  Cf. E 314, 336, 336.5.
  .2 Right of search and impressment.
  .3   The "Chesapeake" affair.
  .6 Opposition of the New England Federalists.
  .7   Hartford convention, 1814.
  .9 Effects of the war.

358 **Diplomatic history.**

359 **Armies. Troops.**
  The American army.
  .2 **Regulars.**
  .4 **Pensioners. Bounties.**
       Military pensions, U. S. UB 373.
       Illinois military tract F 547.M6.
  .5 **The states, etc., and their participation (alphabetically).**

.C2	Canada.	.N6	New York.
.G4	Georgia.	.N7	North Carolina.
.K5	Kentucky.	.O2	Ohio.
.M2	Maryland.	.P3	Pennsylvania.
.M3	Massachusetts.	.V3	Virginia.
.N4	New Jersey.		

  .8 **The British army. Canadian troops.**

360 **Naval history. Privateers. Narratives of sailors. Naval
    battles on the ocean.**
  Biography of naval leaders E 353–353.1.
  "Chesapeake" affair E 357.3.
  Naval battles in connection with military operations E 355.

361 **Personal narratives.**
  Sailors' narratives E 360.
  Prisoners' narratives E 362.

362 **Prisons. Lists of prisoners. Hospitals.**

WAR OF 1812—Continued.

363 Celebrations. Anniversaries. Museums.

364 Illustrative matter. Poetry. Drama, etc.

Madison's administrations (continued).
Cf. E 341-349.

365 War with Algeria, 1815.
Relations with the Barbary states in general E 335.
Decatur, Stephen E 353.1.D29.

370 Presidential campaign of 1816.

371 **Monroe's administrations, 1817-1825.**
1st Seminole war, 1817-1818 E 83.817.

372 Biography of Monroe.
Monroe's collected works E 302.

373 Missouri compromise.
Early American slavery and political agitation growing out of it
E 446.
Repeal of the Missouri compromise E 433.
Missouri F 461-475.

374 Foreign relations.
Monroe doctrine JX 1425.
Execution of Arbuthnot and Ambrister, 1818 E 83.817.
Spanish treaty of 1819 and cession of Florida F 314.

375 Presidential campaign of 1824. Charge of a corrupt bargain
between Adams and Clay.

376 **J. Q. Adams' administration, 1825-1829.**
Northeastern boundary dispute E 398.
Panama congress F 1404.
Tariff of 1828 HF 1754.

377 Biography of Adams.
Foreign relations, 1825-1829 E 376.

380 Presidential campaign of 1828.

381 **Jackson's administrations, 1829-1837.**
Bank of the United States 1816-1836 HG 2525-2529.
Northeastern boundary troubles E 398.
Black Hawk war E 83.83.
Tariff of 1833 HF 1754.
2d Seminole war E 83.835.
2d Creek war E 83.836.

382 Biography of Jackson.

383 Presidential campaign of 1832.

384 .3 Nullification.
Tariff controversy HF 1754.
South Carolina politics, 1775-1865 F 273.
Poinsett, J. R. E 340.P77.

.7 Removal of deposits. Vote of censure. Expunging resolutions.
Bank of the U. S. 1816-1836 HG 2525-2529.

.8 Foreign relations.
Mexican protest against advance of U. S. troops F 390.
Texan war of independence, and recognition by U. S. F 390.

385 Presidential campaign of 1836.

WAR WITH MEXICO.

Biography.

403 .1 Individual—Continued.

.Q5 Quitman, J. A.
Santa Anna, A. L. de
F 1232.S.

.S4 Scott, Winfield.
Semmes, Raphael
E 467.1.S47.

.S5 Shields, James.

.S6 Sloat, J. D.
.S7 Smith, P. F.
.S8 Stockton, R. F.
Taylor, Zachary   E 422.
.T9 Twiggs, D. E.
.W8 Wool, J. E.
.W9 Worth, W. J.

404 Comprehensive works.

405 Military operations.   Campaigns.

.1 Taylor's campaign, 1846–1847.
Palo Alto, Resaca de la Palma, Monterey, Buena Vista.

.2 Occupation of New Mexico and California.
Kearney, Doniphan, Sloat, Stockton.
Cf. F 800, F 864.

.4 Chihuahua campaign.
Wool's march from San Antonio to Saltillo.

.6 Scott's campaign, 1847.
Vera Cruz, Cerro Gordo, Contreras, Churubusco, Molino del Rey, Chapultepec, Mexico.

406 (If preferred, this number may be used for battles, alphabetically, rather than classing in E 405.)

407 Political history.   Causes.

Revolt and annexation of Texas   F 390.

408 Diplomatic history.   Treaty of Guadalupe Hidalgo.

Mexican boundary   F 786.
Gadsden purchase, 1853   F 786.

409 Armies.   Troops.

The American army.

.2   Regulars.

.4   Pensioners.   Bounties.

Military pensions, U. S.   UB 373.

.5   The states and their participation (alphabetically).

.D6   District of Columbia.
.I4   Illinois.
.I7   Indiana.
.M2   Maryland.

.N6   New York.
.P3   Pennsylvania.
.S7   South Carolina.

.8   The Mexican army.

410 Naval history.   Narratives of sailors.

Biography of naval leaders   E 403–403.1.
Operations in connection with military campaigns   E 405.

411 Personal narratives.

Sailors' narratives   E 410.
Prisoners' narratives   E 412.

412 Prisons.   Hospitals.

413 Celebrations.   Anniversaries.

Societies of veterans   E 401.

415 Illustrative matter.   Poetry.   Drama, etc.

MIDDLE NINETEENTH CENTURY.

415. 6 Collected writings of statesmen of the period.

Belmont, August.	Phillips, Wendell.
Dana, R. H.	Pierce, Franklin.
Dickinson, D. S.	Seward, W. H.
Field, D. D.	Sumner, Charles.
Foote, H. S.	Tilden, S. J.
Johnson, Andrew.	Toombs, R. A.
Lincoln, Abraham E 457.91.	

415. 7 1845–1870. From outbreak of Mexican war to end of the Civil war. Political aspects of the slavery question from the Mexican war to Emancipation. Extension of slavery to the territories. Squatter sovereignty.

     Wars with the Pacific coast Indians, 1847–1865   E 83.84.
     American party   JK 2341.
     Cuban question   F 1783.

     Biography.

.8   Collected.

     Military leaders of the Mexican war   E 403–403.1.
     Military leaders of the Civil war   E 467–467.1.

415. 9   Individual.

	Anthony, H. B.		Curtis, S. R. E 467.1.C97.
	E 664.A6.	.C96	Cushing, Caleb.
	Baker, E. D.		Dallas, G. M. E 340.D14.
	E 467.1.B16.	.D15	Dana, R. H.
	Banks, N. P.		Dana's collected works
	E 467.1.B23.		in E 415.6.D.
.B4	Bell, John.	.D26	Davis, H. W.
.B45	Belmont, August.		Davis, Jefferson
	Belmont's collected		E 467.1.D26.
	works in E 415.6.B.	.D27	Dayton, W. L.
	Benjamin, J. P.	.D5	Dickinson, D. S.
	E 467.1.B4.		Dickinson's collected
	Blaine, J. G. E 664.B6.		works in E 415.6.D.
.B84	Broderick, D. C.	.D6	Dix, J. A.
.B87	Brown, B. G.	.D68	Dodge, A. C.
.B9	Brownlow, W. G.	.D73	Douglas, S. A.
	Buchanan, James E 437.		Lincoln - Douglas de-
.C18	Cameron, Simon.		bates in E 457.4.
	Chandler, Zachariah	.D9	Dunn, W. M.
	E 664.C4.		English, W. H.
.C4	Chase, S. P.		E 664.E58.
.C6	Clayton, J. M.		Everett, Edward
.C63	Clingman, T. L.		E 340.E3.
.C68	Colfax, Schuyler.		Ewing, Thomas
	Conkling, Roscoe		E 340.E9.
	E 664.C75.	.F4	Fessenden, W. P.
	Cooper, James F 153.C.	.F5	Field, D. D.
	Corwin, Thomas		Field's collected works
	E 340.C76.		in E 415.6.F.
.C96	Curtis, B. R.		Field, R. S. F 138.F.

MIDDLE NINETEENTH CENTURY.

1845–1870. From outbreak of Mexican war to end of the Civil war, etc.

Biography.

415.9   Individual—Continued.

	Fillmore, Millard E 427.	.K7	Körner, G. P.
	Fish, Hamilton		Körner's memoirs in
	E 664.F52.		E 415.7.K.
.F64	Floyd, J. B.		Lane, J. H. F 685.L.
.F7	Foote, H. S.	.L2	Lane, Joseph.
	Foote's collected works	.L38	Lawrence, A. A.
	in E 415.6.F.	.L4	Lawrence, W. B.
.F8	Fremont, J. C.	.L7	Lieber, Francis.
	Garfield, J. A. E 687.		Lincoln, Abraham E 457.
.G2	Garnett, M. R. H.	.M16	Maclay, W. B.
	Garrison, W. L. E 449.G.		Martin, M. L. F 586.M.
.G4	Giddings, J. R.	.M2	Mason, J. M.
.G46	Gilbert, W. A.	.M3	Maury, D. H.
.G7	Graham, W. A.	.M4	Memminger, C. G.
.G8	Greeley, Horace.	.M5	Meredith, W. M.
	Presidential campaign	.M8	Moorhead, J. K.
	of 1872 in E 675.		Morehead, J. M.
.G85	Grimes, J. W.		F 258.M.
.G86	Grinnell, J. B.		Morrill, J. S. E 664.M8.
.H15	Hale, J. P.		Morton, O. P. E 506.M.
.H18	Hallock, Gerard.		Palmer, J. M. E 664.P2.
.H2	Hamlin, Hannibal.		Peckham, R. W. F 124.P.
	Harlan, James E 664.H27.	P4	Pendleton, G. H.
.H28	Harris, B. G.		Phillips, Wendell
	Harris court martial,		E 449.P.
	1865 E 458.8.H.		Pierce, Franklin E 432.
.H3	Harris, Ira.	.P78	Pomeroy, S. C.
	Harris, I. G. E 664.H31.		Quitman, J. A.
.H35	Haskin, J. B.		E 403.1.Q8.
	Hatton, Robert		Rusk, T. J. F 389.R.
	E 467.1.H44.		Scales, A. M. E 664.S23.
	Hendricks, T. A.		Schenck, R. C.
	E 664.H49.		E 467.1.S32.
.H6	Hicks, T. H.		Scott, Winfield
.H65	Hilliard, H. W.		E 403.1.S4.
.H9	Hunter, R. M. T.	.S4	Seward, W. H.
	Ingersoll, J. R. E 340.I5.		Seward's collected works
J5	Jenckes, T. A.		in E 415.6.S.
	Johnson, Andrew E 667.	.S5	Seymour, Horatio.
	Johnson, Joseph F 230.J.		Shields, James
J6	Jones, G. W.		E 403.1.S5.
J7	Jones, J. G.		Stanton, E. M.
J9	Judd, N. B.		E 467.1.S8.
	Kelly, John F 128.47.K.	.S84	Stevens, Thaddeus.
.K35	Kennedy, J. P.		Stockton, R. F.
.K52	King, Horatio.		E 403.1.S8.

1845–1870. From outbreak of Mexican war to end of the Civil war, etc.

Biography.

415.9 Individual—Continued.

.89 Sumner, Charles.
    Brooks' assault in E 434.8.
    Sumner's collected works in E 415.6.S.
.T5 Tilden, S. J.
    Tilden's collected works in E 415.6.T.
.T6 Toombs, R. A.
    Toombs' collected works in E 415.6.T.

    Tyler, John E 397.
.V2 Vallandigham, C. L.
    Van Buren, Martin E 387.
.W16 Wade, B. F.
.W2 Walker, R. J.
.W6 Wilson, Henry.
    Winthrop, R. C. E 340.W73.

416 **Polk's administration, 1845–1849. Slavery question in politics. Wilmot proviso. Slavery in the territories. Government of the newly acquired Spanish possessions in the Southwest.**
Oregon question and Northwestern boundary to 1846 F 880.
Annexation of Texas F 390.

417 **Biography of Polk.**

420 **Presidential campaign of 1848.**

421 **Taylor's administration, 1849–July 9, 1850.**
Admission of California F 864.
Organization of New Mexico and Utah territories F 801, F 826.
Payment to Texas for claim on part of New Mexico F 801.

422 **Biography of Taylor.**

423 **Slavery question, 1849–1853. Clay's Omnibus bill (Compromise of 1850). Southern convention, Nashville, 1850.**
Fugitive slaves and the new law of 1850 E 450.

426 **Fillmore's administration, July 9, 1850–1853.**

427 **Biography of Fillmore.**

429 **Foreign relations, 1849–1853. Intervention. Political refugees from abroad.**
Gadsden purchase F 786.
Clayton-Bulwer treaty, 1850 F 1438.
Cuban question F 1783–1784.

430 **Presidential campaign of 1852.**

431 **Pierce's administration, 1853–1857. Foreign relations. Ostend manifesto, Oct., 1854.**
Cuban question F 1783.
Wars with Pacific coast Indians E 83.84.
3d Seminole war, 1855–1857 E 83.855.
American party JK 2341.
Gadsden purchase, Dec., 1853 F 786.
Bombardment of Greytown, 1854 F 1536.82.
Filibuster war in Nicaragua, 1855–1857 F 1526.

432 **Biography of Pierce.**

431   Pierce's administration, etc.
433   Slavery question, 1853–1857. Repeal of the Missouri com-
        promise. Kansas-Nebraska bill, May, 1854.
            Squatter sovereignty   E 415.7.
            Kansas troubles   F 685.
            Moral and economic aspects of the slavery question   E 449–450.
434. 5   Election of speaker of the House.
   .8   Brooks' assault on Senator Sumner.
            Biography of Sumner   E 415.9.S9.
435   Presidential campaign of 1856.
            Biography of Fremont   E 415.9.F8.
436   Buchanan's administration, 1857–1861.
            Walker's Filibuster wars, 1855–1860   F 1526.
            Spirit Lake massacre, 1857   E 83.857.
            Mill Creek war, 1857–1865   E 83.858.
            Mormon rebellion, 1857–1859   F 826.
            Cuban question   F 1783.
437   Biography of Buchanan.
            Buchanan's collected works   E 337.8.B.
438   Slavery question, 1857–1861.
            Kansas and the Lecompton constitution   F 685.
            Dred Scott decision, 1857   E 450.
            Lincoln-Douglas debates, 1858   E 457.4.
            John Brown raid, 1859   E 451.
440   Presidential campaign of 1860.
   .5   State of the country, Nov., 1860–Mar. 4, 1861. Secession of
        certain states. Attempts at compromise. Peace confer-
        ence at Washington.
            Cf. E 471, 458.1.

SLAVERY IN THE U. S. ANTI-SLAVERY MOVEMENTS.

Cf. E 335 Political history, 1811-1860, also the various aspects of the slavery question
in politics E 301-459, especially 373, 407, 415.7, 416, 423, 433, 438, 440.5.
Slavery in general and the slave trade HT.
General works on the Negroes in the U. S., including Negroes since the civil
war, and the race issue E 185.

441   General works. Histories.

442   The internal slave trade. Slave markets and auctions.

443   Slave life. Duties of slaves and masters. Overseers.

444   Personal narratives of slaves. Biography.
      Cf. Biography of negroes E 185.97.

445   Slavery by states (alphabetically).

.A3	Alabama.	.N5	New England.
	Negroes in Alabama	.N54	New Jersey.
	E 185.93.A3.	.N55	New Mexico.
.C7	Connecticut.	.N56	New York.
.D3	Delaware.		Negroes in New York
.D6	District of Columbia.		E 185.93.N56.
.G3	Georgia.		Negro plot in New York
	Negroes in Georgia		city 1741 F 128.4.
	E 185.93.G4.	.N8	North Carolina.
.I2	Illinois.	.P3	Pennsylvania.
.K5	Kentucky.		Negroes in Pennsylvania
.L3	Louisiana.		E 185.93.P4.
	Negroes in Louisiana	.R4	Rhode Island.
	E 185.93.L6.	.S7	South Carolina.
.M3	Maryland.		Trouble with Mass. over
	Negroes in Maryland		negro citizens of latter
	E 185.93.M2.		state in S. C. F 273.
.M4	Massachusetts.		Negroes in South Caro-
	Negroes in Massachusetts		lina E 185.93.S7.
	E 185.93.M3.	V8	Virginia.
.M6	Mississippi.		Negroes in Virginia
	Negroes in Mississippi		E 185.93.V8.
	E 185.93.M6.		Southampton insurrec-
.M67	Missouri.		tion F 232.S7.
	Negroes in Missouri	.W8	Wisconsin.
	E 185.93.M7.		

446   History to about 1830. Attempts to revive slave trade. Early
anti-slavery movements.
      Ordinance of 1787 E 309.
      Birney, J. G. E 340.B6.
      Missouri compromise E 373.

447   Important events. Slave insurrections. Slave ships (Creole
Amistad, etc.)
      History of a single insurrection in local history, e. g., Southampton
insurrection (Nat Turner) F 232.S7.

SLAVERY IN THE U. S.—Continued.

448 **Colonization. American colonization society and affiliated organizations.**
> Liberia DT 621–637.

449 **History of slavery, 1830–1863. Period of abolition agitation. Biographies: Douglass, Frederick; Garrison, W. L.; Jay, William; Mott, Mrs. Lucretia; Phillips, Wendell; etc.**
> Political aspects of the slavery question E 338–459.
> Morris, Thomas E 340.M8.
> Sumner, Charles E 415.9.S9.
> Brooks' assault E 434.8.
> Adams, J. Q. E 377.
> Holley, Myron F 123.H.
> Alton riot, 1837 F 549.A4.
> Earle, Thomas E 340.E2.
> Hale, J. P. E 415.9.H15.
> Dispute between South Carolina and Massachusetts over negro citizens of the latter state, 1845 F 273.
> Wilmot proviso E 416.
> Compromise of 1850 E 423.
> Giddings, J. R. E 415.9.G4.
> Kansas F 685.
> Lincoln, Abraham E 457.

450 **Fugitive slaves. Anthony Burns case in Boston; Christiana riot (trial of Hanway and others for assault on Gorsuch); etc. Slaves in the free states. Dred Scott case. Underground railroad. Personal liberty laws.**

451 **Harpers Ferry raid. John Brown.**
> John Brown in Kansas F 685.

453 **Slaves and the slavery question in the civil war. "Contrabands." Emancipation. Slavery in the C. S. A.**
> (General matter only; local is classed in E 445 or E 185.93.)
> Negroes in the U. S. in general, and the race question E 185.
> Negro soldiers in the civil war E 540.N3; 585.N3.
> Freedmen. Freedmen's bureau E 185.2.
> Port Royal mission, S. C. E 185.93.S7.
> 13th–15th amendments to the Constitution JK 169.

THE CIVIL WAR, 1861-1865.

456 Lincoln's administrations, 1861–Apr. 15, 1865.
Election and events preceding inauguration E 440–440.5.
Presidential campaign of 1864 E 458.4.
Wars with Dakota Indians, 1862–1863 E 83.86.
Indian wars, 1863–1865 E 83.863.

457 Biography of Lincoln. Comprehensive works (including campaign biographies 1860, 1864). Lincoln as president.
Political history of the country, 1861–1865 E 456, 458–459.

.15 Anecdotes relating to Lincoln. Personal reminiscences of contemporaries (not including formal biographies).

.2 Special. Character, Kindness, Religion, Literary art, etc. Relations with special classes; as Jews, private soldiers, etc. Attitude toward slavery, temperance, etc. Lincoln as a lawyer.
Lincoln as a statesman E 457.

By period:
.3 Early life to 1861.
Campaign biographies E 457.
Lincoln's home in Springfield, Ill. F 549.87.

.32 Antecedents. Family and parents. Life in Kentucky and Indiana. (To 1830).

.35 First years in Illinois. Black Hawk war. Illinois legislature. Professional career. (1830–1846).

.4 In national politics. Congressional service. Lincoln-Douglas debates. In the campaign of 1860. Journey to Washington. (1846–1861).
The slavery question E 449, 415. 7.
Presidential campaign of 1860 E 440.
State of the country, Nov., 1860–Mar., 1861 E 440. 5.

Presidency E 457, 458, 459.
Civil war E 456–655.
Presidential campaign of 1864 E 458.4.

.5 Assassination. The conspirators (Booth, Surratt, etc.) Their trials.

.52 Death of Lincoln. Funeral journey to Springfield. Burial. Memorial services throughout the country and abroad. Guard of honor. Tomb.
Funeral sermons E 457. 8.

.6 Monuments. Statues. Life and death masks. Portraits.
Lincoln tomb, Springfield, Ill. E 457.52.
Local monuments and statues in F; e. g. Lincoln statue in Washington. F 203. 4.L.

.63 Cartoons. Caricatures. Satirical and comic works.

55

Biography of Lincoln, etc.—Continued.

457.65   Lincoln relics.   Museums.

.7   Celebrations.   Anniversaries.   Memorials (since 1865 only; funeral and memorial services in E 457.52); Lincoln day; centennials.

.8   Addresses.   Sermons.   Lectures.   Essays.   (Those delivered since his assassination; those before Apr. 1865 in E 440, 457 or 458.1–.5.)

> Funeral services   E 457.52.
>
> Personal reminiscences   E 457.15.

.9   Poetry.   Drama.   Fiction.

Writings of Lincoln.

457.91   Collected works (By date).

.92   Selected works.   Partial editions (By date).

Separate works.

> Classification by subject is to be preferred; e. g. Lincoln's Cooper institute address in E 438; Emancipation proclamation, E 453; etc.

.94   State papers (By date).

.95   Addresses, lectures, etc. (By date).

> Lincoln-Douglas debates, E 457.4.

.96   Letters.   Single letters and special collections.

.98   Miscellaneous.

.99   Stories, anecdotes, axioms, brief extracts, etc., attributed to Lincoln (alphabetically by editor or title).

458   Contemporary political history.   Including questions at issue between North and South, and also the internal politics of the U. S.

> Treatises, addresses, etc. Collections covering more than a single year. Material published after the close of the war, in E 459; addresses and sermons E 649–650.
>
> Foreign public opinion   E 469.8.

.1   Mar. 4–Dec. 31, 1861.

> Cf. E 440.5: Nov. 1860–Mar. 4, 1861.

.2   1862.

.3   1863.

> Emancipation   E 453.

.4   1864.

> Presidential campaign of 1864, including campaign literature.
>
> Biography of McClellan   E 467.1.M2.

.5   Jan.–May 1865.

.7   Union men in the South.   Refugees.

.8   Confederate sympathizers in the North.   Conspiracies.   Disloyal organizations.   Knights of the golden circle, etc. Suspension of the writ of habeas corpus.   Prisoners of state. Harris court-martial, 1865.   (Cf. E 415.9.H28.)

> Cf. JK 343–355; E 615–616.
>
> Vallandigham, C. L.   E 415.9.V2.

459 Political history of the civil war.

> (Publications since May 1865. Treatises only; addresses, sermons, etc., E 649–650.)

HISTORY OF THE CIVIL WAR.

461 Periodicals.

> Confederate periodicals   E 482.

462 Societies of veterans, etc.

> Confederate societies   E 483.

.1   Grand army of the republic.

.15   Woman's relief corps.

.17   Ladies of the Grand army of the republic.

.2   Military order of the loyal legion of the United States.

.4   Union veteran legion of the United States.

.5   National association of naval veterans.

.9   Sons of veterans of the United States.

.99   Other societies, alphabetically.

> First defenders   E 493.9.
> United States veteran signal corps association   E 608.
> National association of civil war nurses   E 621.

463 Patriotic societies during the war. Loyal publication society.

> Union league clubs   HS 2725.

464 Collections. Collected works. Papers read before Loyal legion, G. A. R., etc.

> Collections of political pamphlets   E 458–459.
> Anecdotes of the civil war   E 655.
> Confederate collections   E 484.

467 Biography, Collected. Union and Confederate.

> Rolls of college men in the war   E 541, 586.
> Nurses   E 621.
> Prisoners of war   E 611–616.

.1   **Biography, Individual.**

> Chiefly for lives of commanders and other officers. Biography of political leaders preferably E 415.9 (except a few like Davis, Stanton, and Benjamin, whose careers culminated in the war). Regimental officers and privates with their regiments E 495–582. Personal narratives of war service E 601–605.

.A2	Adams, C. F.	.B5	Berry, H. G.
.A3	Alexander, A. J.	.B6	Birney, D. B.
.A4	Allen, H. W.	.B7	Boomer, G. B.
.A8	Ashby, Turner.	.B78	Buell, D. C.
.A89	Audenried, J. C.	.B8	Burnside, A. E.
.B16	Baker, E. D.	.B67	Butler, B. F.
.B23	Banks, N. P.	.B9	Butterfield, Daniel.
.B26	Barnes, James.	.C2	Canby, E. R. S.
.B29	Bartlett, W. F.	.C52	Chetlain, A. L.
.B8	Bayard, G. D.		Clingman, T. L.
.B38	Beauregard, P. G. T.		E 415.9.C63.
.B39	Beaver, J. A.		Cooper, James
.B392	Belger, James.		E 340.C72.
.B393	Benedict, Lewis.		Cox, J. D. E 664.C78.
.B4	Benjamin, J. P.	.C97	Curtis, S. R.

HISTORY OF THE CIVIL WAR.

467.1   Biography, Individual—Continued.

.C98	Cushing, W. B.	J15	Jackson, T. J.
.C99	Custer, G. A.	J73	Johnston, A. S.
.D13	Dahlgren, J. A.	J74	Johnston, J. E.
.D18	Daniels, J. M.		Johnston, W. P. LD 5436.
.D24	Davis, C. H.	J86	Jouett, J. E.
.D26	Davis, Jefferson.	.K24	Kearney, Philip.
	De Peyster, J. W.	.L39	Lee, Fitzhugh.
	F 123.D.	.L4	Lee, R. E.
.D4	Devens, Charles.		Lincoln, Abraham
	Dix, J. A. E 415.9.D6.		E 457.
.D6	Dodge, G. M.	.L6	Lowell, C. R.
.D9	DuPont, S. F.	.L9	Lyon, Nathaniel.
.E4	Elliott, Stephen.	.M17	McAllister, Robert.
.E47	Ellsworth, E. E.	.M2	McClellan, G. B.
	Evans, R. D. E 182.E.	.M28	McCulloch, Ben.
.E9	Ewing, Charles.	.M35	Maffitt, J. N.
.F23	Farragut, D. G.		Mason, J. M. E 415.9.M2.
	Fisk, C. B. E 664.F53.		Maury, D. H. E 415.9.M3.
	Floyd, J. B.	.M38	Meade, G. G.
	E 415.9.F64.		Meade, R. W. E 182.M.
.F64	Flusser, C. W.	.M4	Meagher, T. F.
.F68	Foote, A. H.		Memminger, C. G.
.F72	Forrest, N. B.		E 415.9.M4.
.F83	Franklin, W. B.		Miles, N. A. E 83.866.M.
	Fremont, J.C. E 415.9.F8.	.M52	Miller, M. S.
.F87	French, S. G.	.M6	Mitchel, O. M.
.G15	Garesche, J. P.	.M82	Moore, Alexander.
	Garfield, J. A. E 687.		Morgan, J. T. E 664.M7.
.G2	Garland, Samuel, jr.	.O97	Owen, J. T.
.G29	Geary, J. W.		Palmer, J. M. E 664.P2.
	George, J. Z. E 664.G34.	.P26	Parsons, L. B.
.G6	Gooding, O. P.	.P3	Payne, W. H.
.G66	Gordon, J. B.	.P37	Pendleton, W. N.
	Grant, U. S. E 672.	.P4	Perkins, G. H.
.G7	Green, Thomas.	.P5	Pettigrew, J. J.
.H18	Halleck, H. W.		Phelps, C. E. F 186.P.
.H19	Hampton, Wade (3d).	.P57	Pickett, G. E.
.H2	Hancock, W. S.	.P6	Pike, Albert.
	Harney, W. S. E 181.H.		Pillow, G. J. E 403.1.P6.
	Harrison, Benjamin	.P7	Polk, Leonidas.
	E 702.	.P8	Porter, Fitz-John.
.H4	Hartranft, J. F.		Conduct at 2d Bull Run
.H44	Hatton, Robert.		and court martial in
	Hayes, R. B. E 682.		E 473.772.
.H58	Hood, J. B.		Preble, G. H. E 182.P.
.H6	Hooker, Joseph.		Ransom, M. D.
.H7	Hovey, A. P.		E 664.R2.
.H8	Howard, O. O.	.R4	Reynolds, J. F.
.H89	Hunt, H. J.	.R7	Rosecrans, W. S.
.H9	Hunter, David.		Sands, B. F. E 182.S.

467.1 Biography, Individual—Continued.

.S22	Sartori, L. C.	.S76	Smyth, T. A.	
	Scales, A. M. E 664.S23.	.S8	Stanton, E. M.	
.S32	Schenck, R. C.	.S84	Steedman, J. B.	
.S35	Schofield, J. M.	.S85	Stephens, A. H.	
	Schurz, Carl E 664.S39.	.S87	Stone, C. P.	
	Scott, Winfield	.S9	Stuart, J. E. B.	
	E 403.1.S4.	.T4	Thomas, G. H.	
.S4	Sedgwick, John.		Toombs, R. A.	
.S47	Semmes, Raphael.			E 415.9.T6.
	Seward, W. H.		Twiggs, D. E.	
	E 415.9.S4.			E 403.1.T9.
.S54	Sheridan, P. H.	.W13	Wadsworth, J. S.	
.S55	Sherman, W. T.	.W3	Wallace, W. H. L.	
	Shields, James	.W4	Warren, G. K.	
	E 403.1.S5.	.W5	Wheeler, Joseph.	
.S57	Sickles, D. E.	.W61	Whiting, W. H. C.	
.S58	Sigel, Franz.	.W72	Williams, A. S.	
.S63	Slocum, H. W.		Wool, J. E. E 403.1.W8.	

468   Comprehensive works.   General histories.
Causes and principles   E 458–459.
Military operations   E 470–478.
Description and travel of the period   E 167.
The Confederate States of America   E 482–489; F 214.

.3   Chronology.
Chronological lists of battles   E 470.1.

.5   Historiography.   Criticisms of histories and textbooks.   Accuracy and bias of writers.

.7   Photographic works.
(Those important solely or chiefly for the illustrations.)
War museums   E 646.

.9   Miscellaneous.

469   Diplomatic history.   Trent affair.   Gilmore and Jaquess' conference with Davis, 1864.   Hampton Roads conference, 1865.   Construction of Confederate war vessels in England.   (Their subsequent careers   E 596–599).
Washington peace conference, 1860   E 440.5.
Confederate diplomatic history   E 488.
Adams, C. F.   E 467.1.A2.
French intervention in Mexico   F 1233.
Alabama claims   JX 238.A4–.A7.
Confederates in Canada, and St. Albans raid   E 470.95.

469.8   Foreign public opinion.
Contemporary addresses on the war   E 458–458.5.

470   Military operations.   Campaigns.   Military histories of the war.   Narratives of commanders.
Works not restricted to a single region or campaign.
General histories of the war   E 468.
Personal narratives of minor officers and privates   E 601–605.

470.1   Battles.   Lists, chronologic or alphabetic.

HISTORY OF THE CIVIL WAR.

Military operations, etc.—Continued.

Operations by region.

470.2   Eastern border states.

> Virginia, Maryland, District of Columbia, and Pennsylvania. Army of the James, Army of the Potomac, Army of Virginia, Army of northern Virginia (C. S. A.).
>
> N. B.—A personal narrative of service in the Army of the Potomac, if not classed under campaign or regiment, would be classed in E 601 rather than E 470.2.

.3   Shenandoah Valley.

.4   Western border states.

> Ohio Valley and central Mississippi Valley (W. Va., Ky., Tenn., O., Ind., Ill., Mo., Ark.). Army of West Virginia.

.45   Border warfare. Guerrillas.

.5   Cumberland and Tennessee valleys. Chattanooga region.

> Armies of the Cumberland and the Tennessee. Army of Tennessee (C. S. A.)

.6   Lower South.

> (States of N. C., S. C., Ga., and region west.)
> Sherman's march   E 476.69.

.65   South Atlantic coast line.

> Naval operations and blockade running   E 591-600.

.7   Gulf States. (Fla., Ala., Miss., La., Tex.)

> (Society of the army and navy of the Gulf.)
> Naval operations and blockade running   E 591-600.

.8   Mississippi Valley.

.9   Trans-Mississippi region.

> (Tex., Ind. Ter., Kan., N. Mex., etc.)

.95   Northern frontier of U. S. Confederates in Canada. St. Albans raid.

471–478   Special campaigns and battles.

> This classification follows that used in "The war of the rebellion: A compilation of the official records of the Union and Confederate armies," series I, volumes I-LIII (111 parts). The volume number in right-hand margin, in angular brackets, indicates the volume in that work where the corresponding records are found.
>
> The student of a campaign will seek his material not only here in E 471-478, but in
>
> (1) Military operations by region   E 470.2-470.95.
> (2) Biography of leaders   E 467.1.
> (3) History of armies   E 470.2-470.95.
>   History of corps, divisions, and brigades   E 493, 547.
>   History of regiments   E 495-537, 551-582.
> (4) General military histories, and memoirs of commanders   E 470.
> (5) Comprehensive histories of the war   E 468.
> (6) Personal narratives of combatants   E 601, 605.

471–478 Special campaigns and battles—Continued.

A history of a regiment in a particular campaign or battle is
classed in E 471–478, rather than E 495–582. The literature
of the national military parks (Chickamauga and Chattanooga, Gettysburg, Vicksburg, etc.) is regularly classed with
the battle; also descriptive works dealing with the battlefield. Cf. local guide books in F, e. g. Chattanooga F 444.04.
Naval operations in connection with military movements are
classed in E 471–478 rather than E 591.

471   Opening events.   <v. 1>
.1   S. C., Dec. 20, 1860–Apr. 14, 1861.   Charleston
           Harbor (Fort Sumter.)
.5   Other southern states.
               Cf. General political history E 440.5, E 458.1,
               E 551–582.
.51   Ga., Jan. 3–26, 1861.
.52   Ala. and Miss., Jan. 4–20, 1861.
.53   Fla., Jan. 6–Aug. 31, 1861.
.54   N. C., Jan. 9–May 20, 1861.
.55   La., Jan. 10–Feb. 19, 1861.
.56   Tex. and N. Mex., Feb. 1–June 11, 1861.
.57   Ark., Ind. Ter., Mo., Feb. 7–May 9, 1861.
472.1   Md., Pa., Va., and W. Va., Apr. 16–July 31, 1861.
                                                              <v. 2>
.13   Conflict between U. S. troops and mob in Balti-
           more, Apr. 19.
.14   Engagement at Big Bethel, June 10.
.16   Operations in Shenandoah Valley, July 2–25.
.17   Campaign in West Virginia, July 6–17.
.18   Bull Run campaign, July 16–22. (1st Bull Run,
           July 22.)
472.2   Mo., Ark., Kan. and Ind. Ter., May 10–Nov. 19,
           1861.   <v. 3>
.23   Battle of Wilson's Creek, Aug. 10.
.25   Siege of Lexington, Mo., Sept. 13–20.
.28   Engagement at Belmont, Mo. and demonstration
           from Paducah upon Columbus, Ky., Nov. 7.
472.3   Tex., N. Mex. and Ariz., June 11, 1861–Feb. 1,
           1862.   <v. 4>
.32   Skirmish at Mesilla, evacuation of Fort Fillmore
           and surrender of Union forces at San Augustine,
           June 25–27.
472.4   Ky. and Tenn., July 1–Nov. 19, 1861.
472.5   N. C., and southeastern Va., Aug. 1, 1861–Jan. 11,
           1862.
472.6   Md., northern Va. and W. Va., Aug. 1, 1861–Mar. 17,
           1862.   <v. 5>
.63   Operations on the Potomac near Leesburg, Va.,
           including engagement at Ball's Bluff and action
           near Edward's Ferry, Oct. 21–24.
472.7   Coasts of S. C., Ga., and middle and east Fla., Aug.
           21, 1861–Apr. 11, 1862.   <v. 6>
.79   Bombardment and capture of Fort Pulaski, Apr.
           10–11.

HISTORY OF THE CIVIL WAR.

471–478   **Special campaigns and battles.**

         Northern Va., W. Va., and Md.—Continued.

. 76   Battle of Cedar Mountain, Aug. 9.

. 77   Campaign in northern Va., Aug. 16–Sept. 21.   (2d Bull Run, Chantilly.)

. 772   Fitz-John Porter case.

473. 8   Mo., Ark., Kan., Ind. Ter., and the Dept. of the Northwest, Apr. 10–Nov. 20, 1862.   <v. 13>
         Sioux war E 83.86.

473. 9   Coasts of S. C., Ga., and middle and east Fla., Apr. 12, 1862–June 11, 1863.   <v. 14>

. 92   Engagement at Secessionville, S. C., June 16.

. 96   Engagement in Charleston Harbor, Apr. 7.

474. 1   West Fla., southern Ala., southern Miss. and La., May 12, 1862–May 14, 1863.

         Tex., N. Mex. and Ariz., Sept. 20, 1862–May 14, 1863.   <v. 15>

. 11   Operations against Vicksburg, Miss., and Baton Rouge, La., May 18–Aug. 6.

. 17   Operations against and about Port Hudson, Mar. 7–27.

. 18   Operations in west La., Apr. 9–May 14.

474. 3   Ky., middle and east Tenn., north Ala., and southwest Va., June 10–Oct. 31, 1862.   <v. 16>

. 32   Morgan's first Ky. raid, July 4–28.

. 34   Action at and surrender of Murfreesborough, Tenn., July 13.

. 37   Battle of Richmond, Ky., Aug. 30.

. 38   Evacuation of Cumberland Gap., Sept. 17–Oct. 3.

. 39   Battle of Perryville, Ky., Oct. 8.

474. 4   West Tenn. and northern Miss., June 10, 1862–Jan. 20, 1863.   <v. 17>

. 42   Engagement at Iuka, Miss., Sept. 19.

. 44   Battle of Corinth, Miss., and pursuit of the Confederate forces, Oct. 3–12.

. 46   Forrest's expedition into west Tenn., Dec. 15–Jan. 2.

. 47   Operations against Vicksburg, Dec. 20–Jan. 2.

. 48   Expedition against Arkansas Post or Fort Hindman, Ark., and operations in that vicinity, Jan. 4–17.

474. 5   N. C. and southeastern Va., Aug. 20, 1862–June 3, 1863.   <v. 18>

. 52   Expedition from New Berne to Goldsborough, N. C., Dec. 11–20, 1862.

. 55   Siege of Washington, N. C., and pursuit of the Confederate forces, Mar. 30–Apr. 20, 1863.

474. 6   Northern Va., W. Va., Md. and Pa., Sept. 3–Nov. 14, 1862.   <v. 19>

. 61   The Maryland campaign, Sept. 3–20.

. 65   Battle of Antietam. Antietam national cemetery.

. 67   Stuart's expedition into Md. and Pa., Oct. 9–12.

HISTORY OF THE CIVIL WAR.

471-478 Special campaigns and battles—Continued.

471–478 Special campaigns and battles—Continued.

HISTORY OF THE CIVIL WAR.

CONFEDERATE STATES OF AMERICA.

482   Periodicals.

483   Societies.

     .1   United Confederate veterans.
     .2   Confederate veteran association of Kentucky.
     .25   Society of the army and navy of the Confederate States, Md.
     .28   Grand camp Confederate veterans.   Dept. of Va.
     .4   United sons of Confederate veterans.
     .5   United daughters of the confederacy.
     .7   Southern historical society.
     .72   Confederated southern memorial association.
     .75   Confederate memorial literary society.

484   Collections.   Collected works.

Biography.   Collected and individual   E 467–467.1.
Description and travel.   Social conditions, etc.   F 214.

487   General political and civil history of the Confederate States. Memoirs and reminiscences of civil officials and noncombatants.

     General histories of the war.   E 468.
     Military operations.   E 470–478.
     Political history.   Principles involved.   Causes   E 456–459.
     Constitutional history C. S. A.   JK 9801–9803.

488   Diplomatic history.

     Diplomatic history of the U. S.   E 469.
     The foreign-built Confederate cruisers   E 468, 596–599.
     Mason, J. M.   E 415.9.M2.
     Pike, Albert.   E 467.1.P6.
Army.   Troops.   Histories of individual states in the war   E 545–586.
     Separate armies (e. g. Army of northern Virginia)   E 470.2–.9.
Naval history   E 591–599.
Secret service.   Signal corps   E 608.
Flags   E 646.
Military prisons   E 611–612.
Union men in the South   E 458.7.
Hospitals   E 625.
Commemorations, Memorial day   E 645.
     Battle abbey, Richmond   F 234.R5.
Addresses, sermons, etc.   E 650.

489   Miscellaneous.

ARMIES. TROOPS. PARTICIPATION OF THE STATES.

491 The Union army. Administration. Organization. Volunteering. Conscription. Statistics. Numbers and losses. Civil war medals of honor. Sanitary condition. Transportation.

> History of military operations E 470-478.
> The separate armies (e. g. Army of the Potomac) E 470.2-.9.
> Bounties, Military UB 373-374.
> Hospitals, charities, etc. E 621-635.
> Flags E 646.

492 The various arms of the service. Artillery. Cavalry. Infantry.

.3 U. S. regular troops in the civil war.

> General histories of regular army organizations are classed in U.

.4 Infantry.

> e. g., 12th U. S. infantry. E 492.4.12th.

.5 Cavalry.

.6 Artillery.

.7 Miscellaneous: Engineers, Sharpshooters, etc.

> Secret Service. Signal corps. E 608.

.9 Negro regiments. Corps d'Afrique, etc.

> General subject of negroes in the war E 540.N3.
> Various state regiments of negroes E 495-537.

493.1 Corps. Divisions.

> e. g., all histories of the Third corps or its divisions are numbered E 493.1.3d with such further designations as are found necessary. Special corps, cavalry, etc. receive special numbering.

.5 Brigades.

> A brigade consisting entirely of troops from a single state whether infantry or cavalry, may be classed in E 495-537, subdivision .4 under state number (e. g. Crocker's Iowa brigade E 507.4).

.9 First defenders or Minute men of 1861.

> Collected works on the troops which responded to President Lincoln's first call of April 15, 1861.

494 Lists of soldiers or officers covering more than a single state.

> Census or reunion lists of veterans residing in a particular state (but soldiers residing in a county or town, with local biography in F). Pension lists. (Pensions UB 373-374) Rolls of interments in national cemeteries.
> Lists of prisoners E 611-612.

CIVIL WAR—ARMIES. TROOPS.

495–537 Civil war history of the States. State political history, 1861–1865. Quotas in the war. War governors.

Military operations in a state   E 470.2–.9.

Relief associations.   E 629.

Under each State, subdivide as follows:

.1   Official publications on the raising, equipment, and service of the troops in the war.

.2   Adjutant-generals' reports covering period 1861–1865.
> Cf. UA 43 for full series.

.3   Lists of soldiers. Lists of the state's dead.
> A census or list of all ex-soldiers residing in a state at any period since the war E 494.

.4   Histories of the states' troops. Collected biographies or lists of officers. General associations of survivors. The draft. State brigades. State memorials and monuments (a monument on a particular battlefield, E 471–478; a monument or other memorial to soldiers of a locality in local history, F 1–900). The state's battle flags. Lists of citizens serving in organizations of other states.

> Military organizations. (Regimental associations of veterans are classed with regiment. A comprehensive history of a state militia regiment is classed in U even if civil war service is given.)

.5   Infantry.

.6   Cavalry.

.7   Artillery, Heavy.

.8   Artillery, Light.

.9   Other.

> History of a town or county's participation in the Civil war, and local lists of soldiers, are classed in local history (F 1–900). If, however, the town was the seat of military operations, as Chambersburg, Pa., Shiloh, etc., literature is found in E 471–478, or where several sieges or battles are covered, in E 470.2–.9 (e. g., a history of all military operations around Richmond).

> For the seceded states, Alabama, etc., the subdivisions .3–.9 above are used for Union troops; general and political history of the state is classed in E 551–582, unless relating to civil or military government actually recognized by the U. S. as in Louisiana, Tennessee, Virginia.

> For Confederate troops see E 551–582, subdivisions .3–.9 under each.

495 Alabama.
> Confederate history   E 551, 471.52.
> Campaigns and battles   E 470.6–.7, 471–478.

496 Arkansas.
> Confederate history   E 552, 471.57.
> Campaigns and battles   E 470.4, 470.8, 471–478.

497 California.
> The California column, 1862   E 473.46.

498 Colorado.

499 Connecticut. Gov. W. A. Buckingham.

Dakota Territory, *see* South Dakota.

. 495–537   **Civil war history of the States, etc.—Continued.**

500   Delaware.
501   District of Columbia.
         Campaigns and battles   E 470.2, 471–478.
502   Florida.
         Confederate history   E 558, 471.53.
         Campaigns and battles   E 470.6–.7, 471–478.
503   Georgia.
         Confederate history   E 559, 471.51.
         Campaigns and battles   E 470.6, 471–478.
505   Illinois.
         Campaigns and battles   E 470.4, 471–478.
     Indian Territory.
         Special Indian tribes   E 99.
         Preliminaries of the war   E 471.57.
         Campaigns and battles   E 470.9, 471–478.
506   Indiana.   Gov. O. P. Morton.
         Campaigns and battles   E 470.4, 471–478.
507   Iowa.
508   Kansas.
         Campaigns and battles   E 470.9, 471–478.
509   Kentucky.
         Confederate history   E 564.
         Campaigns and battles   E 470.4, 470.5, 470.8, 471–478.
510   Louisiana.   Butler's government.
         Confederate history   E 565, 471.55.
         Campaigns and battles   E 470.7–.8, 471–478.
511   Maine.
512   Maryland.
         Confederate history   E 566.
         Campaigns and battles   E 470.2, 471–478.
         Prisoners of state   E 458.8.
513   Massachusetts.   Gov. J. A. Andrew.
514   Michigan.
515   Minnesota.
         Indian wars   E 83.86, 83.863.
516   Mississippi.
         Confederate history   E 568, 471.52.
         Campaigns and battles   E 470.6–.7, 471–478.
517   Missouri.
         Confederate history   E 569, 471.57.
         Campaigns and battles   E 470.4, 470.8–.9, 471–478.
518   Nebraska.
519   Nevada.
520   New Hampshire.
521   New Jersey.   Gov. Joel Parker.
522   New Mexico.
         Confederate history   E 571.
         Preliminaries of the war   E 471.56.
         Campaigns and battles   E 470.9, 471–478.
523 . New York.
         Draft riots, N. Y. city   F 128.44.
524   North Carolina.
         Confederate history   E 573, 471.54.
         Campaigns and battles   E 470.6, 471–478.

CIVIL WAR—ARMIES. TROOPS.

495–537   Civil war history of the States, etc.—Continued.

        North Dakota, *see* South Dakota.

     525   Ohio.
           Campaigns and battles   E 470.4, 471–478.
        Oklahoma, *see* Indian Territory.

     526   Oregon.
     527   Pennsylvania.
           Campaigns and battles   E 470.2, 471–478.
     528   Rhode Island.
     529   South Carolina.
           Confederate history   E 577, 471.1.
           Campaigns and battles   E 470.6, 471–478.
           Negroes in the Sea Island district   E 185.93.S7.
     530   [South Dakota] Dakota Territory.
           Indian wars   E 83.86, 83.863.
     531   Tennessee.
           Confederate history   E 579.
           Campaigns and battles   E 470.4–.5, 470.8, 471–478.
           Johnson, Andrew   E 667.
     532   Texas.
           Confederate history   E 580, 471.56.
           Campaigns and battles   E 470.7, 470.9, 471–478.
     533   Vermont.
           St. Albans raid   E 470.95.
     534   Virginia.   Gov. F. H. Peirpoint.
           Confederate history   E 581.
           Campaigns and battles   E 470.2–.3, 471–478.
     535   Washington (State).
     536   West Virginia.
           Confederate history   E 582.
           Campaigns and battles   E 470.3, 470.4,.471–478.
     537   Wisconsin.

540   Special classes.

     .F8   Friends, Society of.
     .G3   Germans.
     .H6   Hungarians.
     .I3   Indians.
           Indian wars, 1861–1865   E 83.86, E 83.863.
     .I6   Irish.
           Special Irish regiments or other organizations   E 492–537.
     .M5   Methodists.
     .N3   Negroes.
           U. S. negro regiments   E 492.9.
           State negro regiments   E 495–537.
           Slavery as affected by the war   E 453.

541   Colleges and schools (alphabetically).

     .A5   Amherst college.
     .B7   Bowdoin college.
     .B8   Brown university.
     .E13   East Maine conference seminary, Bucksport.
     .H2   Harvard university.
     .M3   Marietta college.
     .N2   Nazareth hall, Nazareth, Pa.
     .N5   New York. College of the city of New York.
     .O2   Oberlin college.
     .P9   Princeton university.
     .W7   Williams college.
     .Y2   Yale university.

CONFEDERATE STATES ARMY.

545   Administration. Organization. Volunteering. Conscription. Statistics.

> History of military operations and the military memoirs of Confederate leaders   E 470–470.9.
>
> The separate armies (e. g. Army of northern Virginia)   E 470.2–.9.
>
> Flags   E 646.
>
> Amnesty   E 668.

546   The various arms of the service. Artillery. Cavalry. Infantry.

> Secret service. Signal corps   E 606.

547. 1   Corps. Divisions.

> Cf.   E 493.

     .5   Brigades.

> Brigades consisting entirely of troops from one state may be classified in E 551–582, subdivision .4 under state number (e. g. Texas brigade, E 580.4).

548   Lists of soldiers or officers covering more than a single state, etc. (cf. E 494).

> Lists of prisoners   E 615–616.

551–582   Civil war history of the individual Confederate States (and border states with troops in the Confederate army).

> For subdivisions and explanations see note at head of E 495–537.
>
> Under the border states (Kentucky, Maryland, Missouri, and West Virginia, and territory of New Mexico) the subdivisions .3–.9 are used for Confederate troops, all general and political history of the state being classed in E 509, 512, 517, 536, and 522.
>
> Union troops from the seceded states (Alabama, etc.) are classed in E 495, etc., subdivisions .3–.9 under each.
>
> > Military operations in a state   E 470.2–.9.
> >
> > Southern relief agencies   E 639.
>
> **551**   Alabama.
>
> > Preliminaries of the war   E 471.52.
> >
> > Union history   E 495.
> >
> > Campaigns and battles   E 470.6–.7, 471–478.
>
> **553**   Arkansas.
>
> > Preliminaries of the war   E 471.57.
> >
> > Union history   E 496.
> >
> > Campaigns and battles   E 470.4, 470.8, 471–478.
>
> **558**   Florida.
>
> > Preliminaries of the war   E 471.53.
> >
> > Union history   E 502.
> >
> > Campaigns and battles   E 470.65–.7, 471–478.
>
> **559**   Georgia.
>
> > Preliminaries of the war   E 471.51.
> >
> > Union history   E 503.
> >
> > Campaigns and battles   E 470.6, 471–478.
>
> Indian Territory.
>
> > Preliminaries of the war   E 471.57.
> >
> > Campaigns and battles   E 470.9, 471–478.
> >
> > Special Indian tribes   E 99.

CONFEDERATE STATES ARMY.

551–582   Civil war history of the individual Confederate States,
etc.—Continued.

    564   Kentucky.
        Union history   E 509.
        Campaigns and battles   E 470.4, 470.5, 470.8, 471–478.
    565   Louisiana.
        Preliminaries of the war   E 471.55.
        Union history   E 510.
        Campaigns and battles   E 470.7, 470.8, 471–478.
    566   Maryland.
        Union history   E 512.
        Campaigns and battles   E 470.2, 471–478.
    568   Mississippi.
        Preliminaries of the war   E 471.52.
        Union history   E 516.
        Campaigns and battles   E 470.6, 470.7, 470.8, 471–478.
    569   Missouri.
        Preliminaries of the war   E 471.57.
        Union history   E 517.
        Campaigns and battles   E 470.4, 470.8, 470.9, 471–478.
    571   New Mexico.
        Preliminaries of the war   E 471.56.
        Union history   E 522.
        Campaigns and battles   E 470.9, 471–478.
    573   North Carolina.
        Preliminaries of the war   E 471.54.
        Union history   E 524.
        Campaigns and battles   E 470.6, 471–478.
        Oklahoma, see Indian Territory.
    577   South Carolina.   Gov. F. W. Pickens.
        Preliminaries of the war   E 471.1.
        Union history   E 529.
        Campaigns and btatles   E 470.6, 471–478.
    579   Tennessee.
        Union history   E 531.
        Campaigns and battles   E 470.4, 470.5, 471–478.
    580   Texas.
        Preliminaries of the war   E 471.56.
        Union history   E 532.
        Campaigns and battles   E 470.7, 470.9, 471–478.
    581   Virginia.
        Union history   E 534.
        Campaigns and battles   E 470.2, 470.3, 471–478.
    582   West Virginia.
        Union history   E 536.
        Campaigns and battles   E 470.3, 470.4, 471–478.

585   Special classes (alphabetically).
    .N3   Negroes.

586 Colleges and schools (alphabetically).

.N8 North Carolina. University.

.S7 South Carolina. University.

.V5 Virginia military institute, Lexington.

.V6 Virginia. University.

NAVAL HISTORY.

591 General. Union navy. Operations. Registers. Naval reminiscences. Special fleets or squadrons. Cruisers.

Naval operations in combination with military campaigns E 470–478.
Monitor-Merrimac battle E 473.2.
National association of naval veterans E 462.5.
Lives of naval commanders E 467–467.1.
Naval contracts E 480.

595 Special ships (alphabetically).

596 Confederate navy. Registers. Privateers and cruisers. Naval reminiscences.

Construction of Confederate cruisers abroad E 469.

599 Special ships (alphabetically).

600 Blockade and blockade running.

PERSONAL NARRATIVES. DIARIES.

The narratives of general or staff officers are usually classed in E 470, unless relating to special armies or campaigns, in which case they are placed in E 470.2–.9 or E 471–478. (Cf. E 467.1, Biography of commanding officers.)

The following numbers are used for narratives of regimental officers and privates; if they contain rolls or are otherwise valuable for regimental histories E 495–537 or 551–582 are to be preferred, as the case may be; while those of value for military history of special campaigns should be placed in E 471–478.

Narratives of non-combatants are not to be classed here; if relating to military operations, class in E 470–478; otherwise E 456, 468, 491, 545, F 214, or under state E 495–582.

Collections of narratives E 464, E 484.
Prisoners' narratives E 611–616.
Sailors' narratives E 591–600.
Collections of anecdotes E 655.
Women's narratives, Nurses E 621–628.

601 Union narratives.

Refugees from the South E 458.7.

605 Confederate narratives.

Travel and social life F 214.

607 Army life. The private soldier.

608 Secret service. Signal corps. United States veteran signal corps association. Telegraph service. U. S. military telegraph corps. Spies.

Both northern and southern.

PRISONERS OF WAR. PRISON LIFE. MILITARY PRISONS.

611   Confederate prisons. General lists of prisoners. Exchanges.

612   Special prisons (alphabetically).

.A5 Andersonville, Ga. Military prison.	.L6 Libby prison, Richmond.
	.L7 Liggon's tobacco warehouse prison, Richmond.
.B3 Belle Isle prison, Richmond.	
.C2 Cahaba, Ala. Military prison.	.M1 Macon, Ga. Military prison.
.D2 Danville, Va. Military prison.	.S15 Salisbury, N. C. Military prison.

615   Union prisons.

> Treason and traitors in the North, prisoners of state, and suspension of writ of habeas corpus. E 458.8. Cf. JK 343–355.

616   Special prisons.

.A4 Alton, Ill. Military prison.	.J7 Johnson's Island, Lake Erie.
.C4 Camp Chase, Columbus, O.	.L8 Point Lookout, Md.
.D3 Fort Delaware.	.M8 Camp Morton, Indianapolis, Ind.
.D4 Camp Dennison, O.	
.D7 Camp Douglas, Chicago, Ill.	.R6 Rock Island, Ill. Military prison.
.E4 Elmira, N. Y. Military prison.	

HOSPITALS, CHARITIES, ETC.

621   Hospitals. Nurses. Ambulance service. Transportation of wounded. Mortality and health statistics.

625   Southern hospitals. Nurses.

628   Women's work.

629   Agencies for the relief and aid of soldiers. Refreshment saloons. Relief associations.

631   United States sanitary commission and its branches.

632   Sanitary fairs.

635   Religion in the army. United States Christian commission.

CELEBRATIONS, ILLUSTRATIVE MATERIAL, ETC.

641   Celebrations. Anniversaries. General works on cemeteries and monuments.

> (Cf. note under E 495–537.)
> National cemeteries in connection with battlefields E 471–478.
> Other national cemeteries in local history, e. g. Arlington F 234.A7.
> Registers of dead (general) E 494, 548.
> Registers of deceased prisoners of war E 611–616.
> Reunion of veterans of a single state or group of states E 494, 548.

642   Memorial day services and addresses.

645   Celebrations, etc., Confederate. Confederate memorial day.

> Cf. note under E 641.

646   War museums. Trophies. Flags. Exhibitions. Illustrative material.

647   Poetry. Drama. Cartoons.

648   Fiction.

649   Addresses. Sermons.

       Those delivered since the war.
         Contemporary addresses, etc.   E 458–458.5.
         Lincoln memorial addresses   E 457.8.
         Memorial day addresses   E 642.

650   Southern addresses and sermons.

       Confederate memorial day addresses   E 645.

655   Anecdotes.

PERIOD SINCE THE CIVIL WAR.

660   Collected works of statesmen of the period.

       Garfield, J. A.   McKinley, William.
       Harrison, Benjamin.   Roosevelt, Theodore.

661   General histories of the U. S. since 1865. History from the civil war to the Spanish war, 1865–1898.

       Indian wars, 1866–1895   E 83.866.
       Negroes. The race question   E 185.
       Reconstruction   E 668.
       History since 1898   E 712.

661. 7   Foreign relations.

      Biography.

663   Collected.

664   Individual.

.A5	Angell, J. B.	.C8	Cox, S. S.
.A6	Anthony, H. B.	.D18	Daniel, J. W.
	Arthur, C. A. E 692.	.D58	Dingley, Nelson, jr.
.B2	Bailey, J. W.		Dodge, G. M. E 467.1.D6.
	Banks, N. P. E 467.1.B23.	.E58	English, W. H.
.B23	Barbour, J. S.	.E88	Evarts, W. M.
.B3	Bayard, T. F.	.F16	Fairbanks, C. W.
.B6	Blaine, J. G.		Field, D. D. E 415.9.F5.
.B64	Bland, R. P.	.F46	Field, S. J.
.B7	Boutwell, G. S.	.F52	Fish, Hamilton.
.B87	Bryan, W. J.	.F53	Fisk, C. B.
	Buckingham, W. A.	.F69	Foraker, J. B.
	E 499.B.	.F9	Frye, W. P.
	Burnside, A. E.		Garfield, J. A. E 687.
	E 467.1.B8.	.G34	George, J. Z.
	Butler, B. F. E 467.1.B87.		Gordon, J. B. E 467.1.G66.
.C29	Carpenter, M. H.	.G6	Gorman, A. P.
.C4	Chandler, Zachariah.	.G73	Grady, H. W.
.C49	Clark, Champ.		Grant, U. S. E 672.
	Cleveland, Grover E 697.		Greeley, Horace
.C75	Conkling, Roscoe.		E 415.9.G8.
.C78	Cox, J. D.		

PERIOD SINCE THE CIVIL WAR.

Biography.

664   Individual—Continued.

	Hampton, Wade (3d)	.O3	O'Connor, M. P.
	E 467.1.H19.	.O37	O'Conor, Charles.
	Hancock, W. S.	.O42	O'Ferrall, C. T.
	E 467.1.H2.	.P2	Palmer, J. M.
.H24	Hanna, M. A.	.P34	Payne, H. C.
.H27	Harlan, James.		Pendleton, G. H.
.H31	Harris, I. G.		E 415.9.P4.
	Harrison, Benjamin		Phelps, C. E. F 186.P.
	E 702.	.P53	Phelps, W. W.
.H41	Hay, John.	.P7	Platt, O. H.
	Hayes, R. B. E 682.	.P96	Proctor, Redfield.
.H48	Henderson, D. B.	.Q2	Quay, M. S.
.H49	Hendricks, T. A.	.R2	Ransom, M. D.
.H53	Hill, B. H.	.R3	Reed, T. B.
.H54	Hill, D. B.		Roosevelt, Theodore
.H65	Hoar, G. F.		E 757.
.H73	Hobart, G. A.		Rosecrans, W. S.
	Hovey, A. P. E 467.1.H7.		E 467.1.R7.
.I4	Ingalls, J. J.		Sands, B. F. E 182.S.
	Johnston, T. D. F 259.J.	.S23	Scales, A. M.
.K2	Kelley, W. D.	.S39	Schurz, Carl.
.K35	Kernan, Francis.		Seymour, Horatio
.K4	Kerr, M. C.		E 415.9.S5.
.L2	Lamar, L. Q. C.		Slocum, H. W.
	Langston, J. M.		E 467.1.S63.
	E 185.97.L2.	.S66	Smoot, Reed.
	Leavenworth, E. W.		Sumner, Charles
	F 123.L.		E 415.9.S9.
	Lee, Fitzhugh		Taft, W. H. E 762.
	E 467.1.L39.		Tilden, S. J. E 415.9.T5.
.L7	Lodge, H. C.		Wheeler, Joseph
	McKinley, William		E 467.1.W5.
	E 711.6.		Williams, A. S.
.M25	Mallory, S. R., jr.		E 467.1.W72.
.M7	Morgan, J. T.		Wilson, Woodrow E 767.
.M8	Morrill, J. S.	.W8	Wolcott, E. O.

666   Johnson's administration, April 15, 1865–1869.   Impeachment of President.

Fenian invasion of Canada, 1866   F 1032.

Beecher Island fight   E 83.868.

13th amendment to Constitution 1865   JK 169.

14th amendment to Constitution 1868   JK 169.

667   Biography of Johnson.

Johnson's collected works   E 415.6.J.

PERIOD SINCE THE CIVIL WAR—Continued.

691 Arthur's administration, Sept. 19, 1881–1885.
   Apache war, 1883–1886 E 83.88.
692   Biography of Arthur.
695   Presidential campaign of 1884.
   Blaine, J. G. E 664.B6.
696 Cleveland's 1st administration, 1885–1889.
   Apache war, 1883–1886 E 83.88.
697   Biography of Cleveland.
700   Presidential campaign of 1888.
701 Harrison's administration, 1889–1893.
   Dakota Indian war, 1890–91 E 83.89.
   International American conference, 1889–90 F 1405.
   McKinley tariff, 1890 HF 1755.
702   Biography of Harrison.
705   Presidential campaign of 1892.
706 Cleveland's 2d administration, 1893–1897.
   Hawaiian revolution 1893–1898 DU 627.19–.2.
   Currency question HG 529–534.
   Venezuela-British Guiana boundary controversy F 2331.B7
   Wilson tariff HF 1755.
710   Presidential campaign of 1896.
   Bryan, W. J. E 664.B87.
711 McKinley's 1st administration, 1897–1901.
   Annexation of Hawaii DU 627.3–.5.
   Territorial expansion E 713.
   Dingley tariff HF 1755–1756.
   See also E 750.
 .6 Biography of McKinley.
   McKinley's collected works. E 660.M.
 .9   Assassination. Czolgosz.

THE UNITED STATES SINCE 1898.

712 General works.
   U. S. since the civil war E 661.
713 Territorial expansion. Imperialism. Anti-imperialism.
   Historical geography of U. S. E 179.5.
   Insular acquisitions F 970.
   Annexation of Hawaii DU 627.3–.5.
   Annexation of Porto Rico F 1971.
   Annexation of Philippine Islands DS 679–685.
   Question of Cuban annexation F 1785.

SPANISH-AMERICAN WAR.

714 Periodicals. Collections.
714.3 Societies.
 Biography.
714. 5 Collected.
 .6 Individual.

.C5	Clark, C. E.		Miles, N. A. E 83.866.M.
.D51	Dewey, George.		Roosevelt, Theodore E 757.
.D55	Dickinson, W. M.	.S3	Schley, W. S.
	Evans, R. D. E 182.E.		Wheeler, Joseph E 467.1.W5.

715 Comprehensive works.
717 Military operations. Campaigns and battles.
 .1 Cuban campaign.
 Cuban revolution, 1895–1899 F 1786.
 Naval battle off Santiago E 727.
 .3 Porto Rican campaign.
 .7 Philippine campaign. Battle of Manila Day.
 Philippine insurrection, 1898 DS 679–684.
719 (Battles may be placed here, if it is preferred not to class in E 717.)
721 Political history. Question of intervention after destruction of the "Maine."
 Cuban question before February 1898 F 1783–1786.
 Cuban insurrection 1895–1899 F 1786.
 .6 Destruction of the "Maine," Feb. 15, 1898.
723 Diplomatic history.
725 Armies. Troops.
 .3 U. S. army. Corps. Brigades.
 .4 Regulars. U. S. volunteers.
 .5 Special classes: Irish, Negroes, etc.
 Negro regiments E 725.4, 726.
 .6 Colleges.
 .8 Registers.
 .9 Spanish army.
726 War history of the states. Regimental histories.

.A3 Alabama.
.C1 California.
.C7 Connecticut.
.I2 Illinois.
.I3 Indiana.
.I4 Iowa.
.K2 Kansas.
.M4 Massachusetts.
.M6 Michigan.
.M7 Minnesota.
.M8 Missouri.
.N4 New Jersey.
.N5 New York.

SPANISH-AMERICAN WAR.

726   War history of the states.   Regimental histories—Continued.
     .N8   North Carolina.
     .O3   Ohio.
     .P4   Pennsylvania.
     .R4   Rhode Island.

727   Naval history.   U. S. Navy.   Destruction of Cervera's fleet.
     Destruction of the Maine   E 721.6.
     Battle of Manila Bay.   E 717.7.

.8   Spanish navy.

729   Personal narratives.
     Sailors' narratives   E 727.

731   Prisons.   Hospitals.   Camps.   Red Cross.

733   Celebrations.

735   Miscellaneous.   Addresses.   Poetry.   Cartoons, etc.

TWENTIETH CENTURY.

McKinley's 1st administration (continued).
     Boxer insurrection in China, 1900   DS 771.

750   Presidential campaign of 1900.

751   **McKinley's 2d administration, Mar. 4–Sept. 14, 1901.**
     Biography of McKinley, and assassination   E 711.6–.9.

756   **Roosevelt's administrations, Sept. 14, 1901–1909.**

757   Biography of Roosevelt.

758   Presidential campaign of 1904.

760   Presidential campaign of 1908.
     Bryan, W. J.   E 664.B87.

761   **Taft's administration, 1909–1913.**
     Regulation of the trusts   HD 2771–2795.
     Payne-Aldrich tariff   HF 1756.
     Reciprocity with Canada   HF 1732.C2.

762   Biography of Taft.

765   Presidential campaign of 1912.

766   **Wilson's administration, 1913–.**

767   Biography of Wilson.

UNITED STATES LOCAL HISTORY

83

The letter (a), (b), (c), or (d) after name of each state in the schedules indicates the form used.

(a)

1   Periodicals. Societies. Collections.

> Includes besides historical and genealogical societies, social organizations and clubs which by virtue of aims or limitation of membership may be regarded as patriotic societies. (Local societies in subdivision 12 or 14.) Purely social clubs not limited in membership to citizens or descendants of citizens and (former) residents of particular sections or states of the United States are classified in HS 2301—. Note that state societies and local chapters of national organisations are classed with the general body; e. g. Society of Mayflower descendants in the state of Illinois in F 68.8, *not* F 536; Cincinnati chapter D. A. R. in E 202.5.O, *not* F 449.C5.

> Collections include: the publications of societies, collections of archive material, and essays or collected works of individual authors. Collections of documents, etc., if confined to a period, are to be classified preferably in subdivision 7–11.

2   Gazetteers. Dictionaries. Lists of Indian and other local names.

2.5   Directories, General.

> directory of a special element in the population, in subdivision 15 below; e. g. A directory of French Canadians in Maine, F 30.F8.

.6   Elite.

.7   Business.

3   Biography and genealogy, Collected.[1]

> The biography of an individual if prominent in state affairs is placed in his period (7–11, below). History of a single family in CS 71. Genealogical periodicals in subdivision 1 above.

4.   General works. Histories. Compends.

5   Miscellaneous. Historic buildings. Collections of illustrative material, stories, etc. Cf. source material in 1, above.

---

[1] BIOGRAPHY.—It is the practice of the Library of Congress to classify both collected and individual biography with the subject. Usually a number is provided for collected biography, but in F this number is intended for *comprehensive* general works. Collected biography confined to a period brought out in the scheme should be classed with period; e. g. collected biography of colonial Virginia in F 229 not F 225.

The rule is to class the biography of an individual with the epoch, historical event or locality with which we consider his life especially identified. Thus lives of presidents are classed with their administrations, those of generals under the wars in which they were most prominent, statesmen under the period to which they belong (preferring E to F where they were distinguished in both national and state affairs), and local celebrities under county, city, or town.

Having settled where a man belongs, references are made from other places in the classification where he might be looked for; e. g. A. S. Johnston's number is k 467.LJ73, with references from F 390 and F 826.

While it is intended that all general biographies of an individual shall be classed together (e. g. all lives of U. S. Grant in E 672, even if they are almost exclusively military biographies), yet a work on some period or event in a man's career should be classed under subject; e. g. a criticism of Gov. Tompkins' administration in New York in F 123.T (general biography E 302.6.T8), Tryon's raid in Connecticut E 235 (general biography F 257.T).

The life of a member of the family of a noted person is classed with his own biography, unless of special significance elsewhere; e. g. Dolly Madison E 342.

6   Antiquities.

> Mounds and moundbuilders in the state E 74, (e. g. Mounds in Ohio
> E 74.O3); Indians in the state E 78, (e. g. Indians of Connecticut
> E 78.C7, but special tribe in E 99 as Pequots E 99.P53).

7–11   By period. (Including in each case general works on the whole period
and such special events falling within it as are not provided for elsewhere.)
e.g. 7 (Early) to 1775. Colonial life.

> For earliest explorations and description see E 101–135.
> Boundary disputes (12, below) usually contain material
> on earliest period.

         8 (Later) 1775–1865.

         9 (Recent) 1865–

Variations in the use of these period numbers are specified in the schedules.

12   Regional. Counties. Parishes covering more than a single village or city.
Rivers. Mountains. Lakes. Boundaries.

> In general it is preferred to take the county as the unit, and classify
> with the county such mountains, lakes, caves, rivers, etc., as lie
> wholly within its limits (unless wholly within some town). If
> these natural features extend over several counties, they take
> their own number in 12. By exception, certain well-known
> islands, with considerable literature of their own, have special
> number even when forming part of a county. And national
> parks, other than battlefield cemeteries, are to take separate num-
> ber, though situated within the limits of a county.
>
> See note under "q" in General order of subdivisions on p. 9.

13   Metropolis. Chief city.

> This number has been used for Boston, New York, Philadelphia,
> and Chicago, only.

14   Other places. Towns and cities.

> Including historical and descriptive matter on the town or city and
> subdivisions, local biography, genealogy, vital records, directo-
> ries, histories of the colonial churches reaching back to the settle-
> ment, local societies of a historical character, centennial, and other
> local celebrations, old home week, views, historic buildings, etc.
> Also estates not within the limits of any town or city, as Mount
> Vernon, F 234.M9.

15   Topics not elsewhere provided for.

> E. g. Foreign elements in the population; (nationalities which were
> prominent in settlement, as Dutch in New York, Germans in
> Pennsylvania are not usually considered as foreign elements).

(b)

Identical with "a" except that 7–11 are not used, historical and descriptive material
for any period being placed in 4.

(c)

1   Periodicals.
2   Societies. Historical, genealogical, etc.
3   Collections.
4   Gazetteers. Dictionaries. Lists of Indian and other local names.
.5   Directories, General.
.6   Elite.
.7   Business.

5   Biography and genealogy, Collected.
          See 3 under "a".
6   General works.   Histories.
7   Miscellaneous.
8   Antiquities.
          See 6 under "a".
9-11   By period.
          See 7-11 under "a".
12   Regional.
          See 12 under "a".
13   Metropolis.
14   Other places.
          See 14 under "a".
15   Topics.
          See 15 under "a".

(d)

Identical with "c" except that 9-11 are not used, historical and descriptive material for any period being placed in 6.

SUBDIVISIONS UNDER METROPOLIS.

.1   Periodicals.   Societies.   Collections.
.2   Directories.
.22   Elite.
.24   Business.
.25   Biography and genealogy, Collected.   Vital records.   Epitaphs.
.3   Comprehensive works.   General history.
.37   Miscellaneous.
.39   Antiquities.
.4   By period (Early) e. g. to 1775.
.44   (Later) e. g. 1775-1865.
.5   (Recent) e. g. 1865-
.6   Sections.   Localities.   Districts, etc.
.61   Cemeteries.
          Collections of epitaphs in .25.
.62   Churches.
          Church history in [BN] save that original colonial churches are classed here.
          Parish registers of baptisms, etc. in .25.
.   Harbor.
.   Monuments.   Statues.
.   Parks.   Squares.   Circles.
.63   Streets.   Bridges.   Railroads.
.68   Suburbs.   Sections of the city.   Rivers, etc.
          A particular suburb unless an actual part of the city goes with towns (subdiv. 14 under states); as also a section of the city annexed within recent years, which has a considerable literature of its own.
.69   Wards.
.7   Buildings.   Collectively, e. g. Theaters; Churches; Public buildings.
.8   Buildings, Individual.
          A church building in .62.
.9   Topics: Foreigners, etc.

1–15 **New England** (a).

7   Before 1775. The Plymouth company 1606. Voyagers after 1607: Smith, Gosnold, Pring, Waymouth. Council for New England 1620. Puritans. United Colonies of New England.

> Norsemen; Vinland   E 105.
> Early voyages before 1607   E 121–135.
> Popham colony   F 22.
> Pequot war, 1636–1638   E 83.63.
> King Philip's war, 1675–1676   E 83.67.
> Witchcraft   BF 1575–1576.
> King William's war, 1689–1697   E 196.
> Queen Anne's war, 1702–1713   E 197.
> War with eastern Indians, 1722–1726   E 83.72.
> King George's war, 1744–1748   E 198.
> Pepperrell, Sir William   E 198.P.
> French and Indian war, 1755–1763   E 199.

7.5   Consolidated province of New England (English colonies north of Pennsylvania) and Gov. Andros, 1688. Revolution of 1689.

8   1775–1865.
> Attitude toward war of 1812   E 357.6–.7.

9   1865–

12   Regions.

Berkshire Hills F 72.B5.	Isles of Shoals F 42.I8.
.C7 Connecticut River and Valley.	Merrimac River and Valley F 72.M6.
Cf. F 42.C65, F 57.C7, F 72.C7, F 102.C7.	White Mountains F 41.

15   Topics.

.C2 Catholics.	Negro slavery E 445.N5.
.F8 French Canadians.	.S4 Scotch-Irish.
.J5 Jews.	

16–30 **Maine** (a).

> Various grants, sometimes conflicting, were made in this region by the Plymouth company, and the Council for New England. The eastern portion was usually considered part of Acadia. The territory between the Kennebec and the St. Croix was granted by the Council in 1635–1638 to Sir William Alexander, sold to the Duke of York in 1663 and included in his province of New York 1664–1686 as Cornwall County. In the latter year it was set off to Massachusetts. Grants were made to Gorges and others covering the region west of the Kennebec, and settlement begun at several points. In the 17th century the whole of the English settlements were absorbed by Massachusetts, formally annexed by the province charter of 1691 and thenceforth known as the District of Maine. State 1820.

Table of subdivisions (a), (b), (c), or (d) under each state may be found on pages 85–87.

16–30   **Maine**—Continued.

22   Attempts at colonization before 1620. Popham colony. Sabino.

23   Colonial period to 1775. Biographies: Godfrey, Edward; Cleve, George; Pepperrell, William, sr.; etc.

       Acadia   F 1036–1039.
       Ancient boundary between French and English possessions   F 1039.B7.
       War with eastern Indians, 1722–1726; Rasles   E 83.72.
       Pepperrell, Sir William   E 198.P.
       Kennebec patent   F 27.K3.
       Pejepscot company (Brunswick proprietors)   F 29.B9.
       Muscongus patent   F 27.M95.

24   1775–1865. Separation from Massachusetts 1820. Biographies: King, William; Merrick, John; etc.

       Revolutionary war   E 263.M4.
         Military operations   E 230.5–239.
       Tucker, Samuel   E 207.T8.
       Knox, Henry   E 207.K74.
       Jarvis, Leonard   E 340.J3.
       Cilley, Jonathan   E 340.C5.
       Fairfield, John   E 340.F16.
       Fessenden, W. P.   E 415.9.F4.
       Hamlin, Hannibal   E 415.9.H2.
       International boundary troubles and Aroostook war   E 398.
       Civil war   E 511.

25   1865–   Biographies: King, M. F.; etc.

       Hamlin, Hannibal   E 415.9.H2.
       Blaine, J. G.   E 664.B6.
       Frye, W. P.   E 664.F9.
       Reed, T. B.   E 664.R3.
       Dingley, Nelson, jr.   E 664.D58.

27   Regions. Counties. Boundaries.

.A5	Androscoggin Co.	.H3	Hancock Co.
.A53	Androscoggin River and Valley.		Cf. F 27.M9.
			Isles of Shoals F 42.I8.
.A7	Aroostook Co. Aroostook River and Valley. Cf. F 1044.A7.	.K2	Kennebec Co.
		.K3	Kennebec purchase. Plymouth company (1749–1816).
.B7	Boundaries.		
	International boundary E 398.	.K32	Kennebec River and Valley.
	Ancient Acadian boundary F 1039.B7.	.L7	Lincoln Co. Cf. F 27.M7.
	New Hampshire boundary F 42.B7.	.M7	Monhegan Island.
		.M8	Moosehead Lake region.
.C9	Cumberland Co. Casco Bay. (Saco Bay and River F 27.Y6.)	.M9	Mount Desert Island. Jesuit station, 1609 F 1038.
.D2	Dead River and Valley.		

Table of subdivisions (a), (b), (c), or (d) under each state may be found on pages 85–87.

16–30 Maine.

27 Regions. Counties. Boundaries—Continued.

.M95 Muscongus lands. The Waldo patent (including greater part of Waldo and Knox and a portion of Lincoln counties).

.O9 Oxford Co. Parmachene Lake.

.P3 Passamaquoddy Bay.
   Cf. F 1044.P3.
   Pejepscot patent (Brunswick) F 29.B9.

.P37 Penobscot Bay region.
.P38 Penobscot Co.
.P4 Penobscot River and Valley.

.P48 Piscataqua River and Valley, Me.
   Cf. F 42.P4.

.P5 Piscataquis Co. Debsconeag Lake region.

.R2 Rangeley Lakes.

.S2 St. Croix River and Valley.
   Cf. F 1044.S17.

.S3 St. John River and Valley, Me.
   Cf. F 1044.S2.

.W3 Washington Co. Narraguagus Valley. St. Croix (Dochet) Island.

.Y6 York Co. Saco Bay. Saco River and Valley.

31–45 New Hampshire (a).

Mason's province, between Piscataqua and Merrimac rivers, 1629. United with Massachusetts about 1641. A royal province 1680.

37 Before 1775. Mason's grant.

Bachiler, Stephen F 67.B.
Wars with eastern Indians, 1722–1726; Pigwacket fight E 83.72.
Pepperrell, Sir William E 198.P.
New Hampshire Grants F 52.
French and Indian war, 1755–1763 E 199.

38 1775–1865. Biographies: Hill, Isaac, etc.

Revolutionary war E 263.N4.
Bartlett, Josiah E 302.6.B2.
Sullivan, John E 207.S9.
Plumer, William E 302.6.P73.
Webster, Daniel E 340.W4.
Woodbury, Levi E 340.W8.
Pierce, Franklin E 432.
Hale, J. P. E 415.9.H15.
Civil war E 520.

39 1865– Biographies: Harriman, Walter; Doe, Charles; Hale, S. W.; etc.

41 White Mountains.

.1 Periodicals.
.2 Gazetteers. Dictionaries.
.37 Miscellaneous.
.44 Before 1865.
.5 1865–
.6 Regions. Localities. (Political divisions of White Mountain region F 42–44.)

Table of subdivisions (a), (b), (c), or (d) under each state may be found on pages 85–87.

31–45   New Hampshire—Continued.

42   Other regions.   Counties.   Boundaries.

.B4   Belknap Co.

.B7   Boundaries.

.C3   Carroll Co. Kearsarge Mountain; Ossipee Mountain.

.C5   Cheshire Co.

.C65   Connecticut River and Valley, N. H. Cf. F 12.C7.

.C7   Coos (Coös) Co. Indian Stream.

.G7   Grafton Co. Newfound (Pasquaney) Lake.

.H6   Hillsborough Co.

.I8   Isles of Shoals.

.M4   Merrimac River and Valley, N. H. Cf. F 72.M6.

.M5   Merrimack Co. Kearsarge Mountain.

.P4   Piscataqua River and Valley. Cf. F 27.P48.

.R7   Rockingham Co. Lake Massabesic. Cf. F 42.I8.

.S8   Strafford Co.

.S87   Sullivan Co.

.S9   Sunapee Lake. White Mountain region F 41.

.W7   Lake Winnepesaukee.

45   Topics.

.S9   Swedes.

46–60   Vermont (a).

This region was practically unsettled down to the middle of the 18th century and the question of its ownership scarcely thought of. In 1749 the dispute began between the governments of New Hampshire and New York. During the next few years the former state disposed of a large part of the area by means of township grants (whence the name "New Hampshire Grants" by which it was commonly known). In 1765 the King of England adjudged the Connecticut River to be New York's eastern boundary, north of Massachusetts. At first the whole "New Hampshire Grants" were annexed to Albany County; later (1768) Cumberland County was erected in the southeast, Gloucester in the northeast (1770), and the northwestern half of the "Grants" in 1772 formed the eastern part of Charlotte County (the remainder lying west and south of Lake Champlain). New York insisted on annulling the land grants of New Hampshire; the settlers resisted and from 1777 to 1791 formed an independent state, but were denied representation in Congress. In 1791 the state was admitted to the union.

52   Before 1791.   New Hampshire Grants.   Green Mountain boys.   Biographies: Allen, Ira; Chittenden, Thomas; etc.

Lyon, Matthew   E 302.6.L9.

New York colonial history   F 122.

New Hampshire colonial history   F 37.

Albany Co.,   N. Y.   F 127.A3.

Charlotte (now Washington) Co., N. Y.   F 127.W3.

Allen, Ethan   E 207.A4.

Revolutionary war   E 263.V5.

Military operations   E 230.5–239.

Table of subdivisions (a), (b), (c), or (d) under each state may be found on pages 85–87.

46–60 Vermont—Continued.

53   **1791–1865. Biographies: Collamer, Jacob; etc.**

    Chittenden, Thomas   F 52.C.

    Lyon, Matthew   E 302.6.L9.

    War of 1812; military operations   E 355.

    Marsh, G. P.   E 183.7.M.

    Phelps, S. S.   E 340.P54.

    Civil war   E 533.

      St. Alban's raid   E 470.95.

54   **1865–**

    Proctor, Redfield   E 664.P96.

57   **Regions.   Counties.   Boundaries.**

.A2	Addison Co. Lake Dunmore.	.E7	Essex Co.
		.F8	Franklin Co. Missisquoi River and Valley.
.B4	Bennington Co. Hoosic River and Valley, Vt.		Cf. F 1054.B8.
	Cf. F 127.H73.	.G7	Grand Isle Co.
.B7	Boundaries.	.G8	Green Mountains.
	Massachusetts boundary F 72.B7.	.L2	Lamoille Co.
		.M3	Mt. Mansfield.
	New Hampshire boundary F 42.B7.	.M5	Lake Memphremagog region.
	New York boundary F 127.B7.		Cf. F 1054.M5.
.C2	Caledonia Co.	.O7	Orleans Co.
.C4	Lake Champlain region, Vt.	.R9	Rutland Co. Lake Bomoseen.
	Cf. F 127.C6; F 57.G7.	.W3	Washington Co.
.C5	Chittenden Co.	.W7	Windsor Co.
.C7	Connecticut River and Valley, Vt.		
	Cf. F 12.C7.		

61–75 Massachusetts (a).

    Part of the grant to the Plymouth Company 1606 and later to the Council for New England. Settlements were chiefly made under latter's grants. (Pilgrims at Plymouth 1620. Wessagusset or Weymouth 1622. Cape Ann 1624. Wollaston or Quincy 1625. Massachusetts Bay company 1628–1630.) The province charter 1691 united all the separate settlements within the present state limits, as well as the District of Maine. Western lands claimed under early charters were ceded to U. S., 1785 except those in western N. Y. which were surrendered to that state in 1786. (Cf. note under F 127.G19.)

    Table of subdivisions (a), (b), (c), or (d) under each state may be found on pages 85–87.

61-75 Massachusetts—Continued.
67   Before 1775. Puritans. Dorchester company. Massachu-
        setts Bay company. Persecution of Quakers. Province
        of Massachusetts. Biographies: Conant, Roger; Ende-
        cott, John; Higginson, Francis; Cradock, Mathew; Win-
        throp, John; Dudley, Thomas; Humfrey, John; Bachiler,
        Stephen; Hutchinson, Mrs. Anne; Dyer, Mrs. Mary; Har-
        vard, John; Denison, Daniel; Pike, Robert; Mather,
        Increase; Dudley, Joseph; Randolph, Edward; Sewall,
        Samuel; Mather, Cotton; Lynde, Benjamin; Tailer,
        William; Quincy, Edmund; Shute, Samuel; Dummer,
        William; Quincy, John; Hutchinson, Thomas; Kilby,
        Christopher; Frankland, Charles H.; Pownall, Thomas;
        Oliver, Peter; Bernard, Sir Francis; etc.
            King Philip's war, 1675–1676 E 83.67.
            Andros and his province of New England, 1688–1689 F 7.5.
            King William's war, 1689–1697 E 196.
            Bellamont, Richard Coote, earl of F 122.B.
            Queen Anne's war, 1702–1713 E 197.
            War with eastern Indians, 1722–1726 E 83.72.
            Shirley, William E 195.S.
            King George's war, 1744–1748 E 198.
            Pepperrell, Sir William E 198.P.
            Adams, Samuel E 302.6.A2.
            Quincy, Josiah (2d) E 263.M4Q.
            French and Indian war, 1755–1763 E 199.
            Hancock, John E 302.6.H23.
            Otis, James E 302.6.O8.
            Foster, Jedediah E 263.M4F.
68   New Plymouth Colony. Pilgrims. Annexed to Massa-
        chusetts 1691 (forming counties of Plymouth, Bristol
        and Barnstable). Biographies: Brewster, William;
        Standish, Myles; Allerton, Isaac; Fuller, Samuel; etc.
            Plymouth. F 74.P8.
69   1775–1865. Shays' rebellion 1786–1787. Biographies:
        Bowdoin, James; Revere, Paul; Cobb, David; Thomas,
        Isaiah; Strong, Caleb; Parsons, Theophilus; Higginson,
        Stephen; Minot, G. R.; Russell, Benjamin; Brooks,
        John; Gore, Christopher; Lawrence, Amos; Howe,
        Samuel; Perkins, T. H.; Willard, Joseph; Henshaw,
        David; King, D. P.; Gordon, G. W., etc.
            Ward, Artemas E 207.W2.
            Adams, Samuel E 302.6.A2.
            Hancock, John E 302.6.H23.

Table of subdivisions (a), (b), (c), or (d) under each state may be found on pages 86–87.

61–75   **Massachusetts.**

  69   1775–1865—Continued.

         Revolutionary war   E 263.M4.
           Preliminaries   E 211–216.
           Military operations   E 230.5–239.
         Pickering, Timothy   E 302.6.P5.
         Cabot, George   E 302.6.C11.
         Lincoln, Benjamin   E 207.L6.
         Knox, Henry   E 207.K74.
         Paterson, John   E 207.P3.
         Cession of western lands   E 309; F 483.
         King, Rufus   E 302.6.K5.
         Dearborn, Henry   E 302.6.D3.
         Ames, Fisher   E 302.6.A5.
         Otis, H. G.   E 340.O8.
         Lands in western N. Y.   F 127.G19, .H7, .T6.
         Quincy, Josiah (3d).   E 302.6.Q7.
         Ripley, E. W.   E 353.1.R5.
         War of 1812   E 359.5.M3.
         Webster, Daniel   E 340.W4.
         Everett, Edward   E 340.E8.
         Cushing, Caleb   E 415.9.C98.
         Choate, Rufus   E 340.C4.
         Lawrence, Abbott   E 340.L4.
         Adams, C. F.   E 467.1.A2.
         Winthrop, R. C.   E 340.W73.
         Sumner, Charles   E 415.9.S9.
         Saltonstall, Leverett   E 340.S18.
         Boutwell, G. S.   E 664.B7.
         Curtis, B. R.   E 415.9.C96.
         Trouble with S. C. over negro citizens, 1845   F 273.
         Banks, N. P.   E 467.1.B23.
         Lawrence, A. A.   E 415.9.L38.
         Hoar, G. F.   E 664.H65.
         Butler, B. F.   E 467.1.B87.
         Civil war   E 513.
         Andrew, J. A.   E 513.A.

  70   1865–   Biographies: Pierce, H. L.; Porter, E. G.; Mason, Albert; etc.

         Winthrop, R. C.   E 340.W73.
         Curtis, B. R.   E 415.9.C96.
         Butler, B. F.   E 467.1.B87.
         Dana, R. H.   E 415.9.D15.
         Hoar, G. F.   E 664.H65.
         Lodge, H. C.   E 664.L7.
         War with Spain   E 726.M4.

Table of subdivisions (a), (b), (c), or (d) under each state may be found on pages 86–87.

61–75   Massachusetts—Continued.

72   Regions.   Counties.   Boundaries.

       Barnstable Co.   F 72.C3.

.B5   Berkshire Co.   Berkshire Hills.   Mount Everett. Greylock Mountain. Hoosic River and Valley, Mass.   Cf. F 127.H73. Paterson, John E 207.P3.

.B7   Boundaries.

       New Hampshire boundary   F 42.B7.

       Ancient boundary of Acadia   F 1039.B7.

.B8   Bristol Co.

.B9   Buzzards Bay region.

.C3   Cape Cod.   Barnstable Co. Cape Cod Bay.

.C7   Connecticut River and Valley, Mass. Cf. F 12.C7. Duke's Co.   F 72.M5.

.E7   Essex Co. Cape Ann. North shore. Saugus River.

.F8   Franklin Co.   Deerfield River. Pocumtuck Valley.

.H2   Hampden Co.

.H3   Hampshire Co. Mill River Mt. Holyoke. Mt. Tom.

.M5   Martha's Vineyard. Duke's Co.

.M6   Merrimac River and Valley. Cf. F 42.M4.

.M7   Middlesex Co.   Concord River.

.N2   Nantucket Co. Island of Nantucket.

.N8   Norfolk Co.

.P7   Plymouth Co. North River. South shore.

.S9   Suffolk Co. Cf. Boston, F 73.

.W9   Worcester Co. Wachusett Mountain.

73   Boston.   (Metropolis subdivisions.)

.4   Before 1775.

     Mather, Cotton   F 67.M.

     Events just prior to revolution   E 215.4–.8.

.44   1775–1865.

     Fugitive slave riots   E 450.

.5   1865–   Fire of 1872.

.68   Suburbs.   Sections of the city.

       Brighton   F 74.B73.

.C3   Castle Island.

       Charlestown   F 74.C4.

       Dorchester   F 74.D5.

.E2   East Boston.

.R2   Rainsford Island. Roxbury   F 74.R9.

.S7   South Boston. West Roxbury   F 74.W486.

9.   Topics.

.I7   Irish.

.I8   Italians.

.R9   Russians.

75   Topics.

.I6   Irish.

     Negroes   E 185.93.M3.

     Slavery   E 445.M4.

Table of subdivisions (a), (b), (c), or (d) under each state may be found on pages 85–87.

76–90 Rhode Island (a).

82   Before 1775. Settlements at Providence, Portsmouth, Newport, and Warwick 1636–1643 form a union. First R. I. charter 1663. The Narragansett country. Biographies: Williams, Roger; etc.

        Dyer, Mrs. Mary F 67.D.
        King Philip's war, 1675–1676 E 83.67.

83   1775–1865.

        Revolutionary war E 263.R4.
          Gaspee affair E 215.6.
          Military operations E 230.5–239.
        Ellery, William E 302.6.E3.
        Burges, Tristam E 340.B9.
        Jenckes, T. A. E 415.9.J5.
        Anthony, H. B. E 664.A6.
        Lawrence, W. B. E 415.9.L4.
        Civil war E 528.

83.4   Dorr rebellion, 1842. Dorr, T. W.

84   1865–

        Jenckes, T. A. E 415.9.J5.
        Anthony, H. B. E 664.A6.
        Burnside, A. E. E 467.1.B8.
        War of 1898 E 726.R4.

87   Regions. Counties. Boundaries.

.B6	Block Island.	.N2	Narragansett Bay region.
.B7	Boundaries.	.N5	Newport Co. Island of Rhode Island.
	Connecticut boundary F 102.B7.		Cf. F 87.B6.
	Massachusetts boundary F 72.B7.	.P3	Pawtuxet River and Valley.
	Mass. claims to Narragansett country F 82.	.P9	Providence Co.
.K3	Kent Co.	.W3	Washington Co.

90   Topics.

    .G3 Germans.
    .I6 Irish.
        Negro slavery E 445.R4.

91–105 Connecticut (a).

    The whole region was claimed by the Council for New England and grants made under its authority. Connecticut River and region west was also claimed by the Dutch of New Netherland, and trading posts established. The English settlements at Windsor, Saybrook, Wethersfield and Hartford (1633–1636) organized a government as Connecticut in 1639. New Haven, settled 1638, maintained a separate existence till 1662 when a royal charter united it to Connecticut. Connecticut had some pretensions to jurisdiction over eastern Long Island till the latter was confirmed to N. Y. 1674–5. Claims to western lands were surrendered to U. S. in 1786, the state retaining only the right to sell to settlers

Table of subdivisions (a), (b), (c), or (d) under each state may be found on pages 85–87.

91-105   **Connecticut—Continued.**

         the tract known as the Western Reserve. Connecticut's claim to a strip of territory south of Pennsylvania's northern boundary was the cause of an extended controversy with the latter state. Cf F 157.W9.

97   Before 1775. Early grants by the Council for New England. Dutch posts.

         Pequot war, 1636–1638   E 83.63.
         King Philip's war, 1675–1676   E 83.67.
         Government of Andros, 1688–1689   F 7.5.
         French and Indian war, 1755–1763   E 199.
         Susquehanna claims in Penn.; Wyoming Valley   F 157.W9.
         Parsons, S. H.   E 207.P2.

98   New Haven colony.

         New Haven   F 104.N6.
         New Haven Co.   F 102.N5.

99   1775–1865.

         Sherman, Roger   E 302.6.S5.
         Johnson, W. S.   E 302.6.J7.
         Revolutionary war   E 263.C5.
            Military operations   E 230.5–239.
         Ellsworth, Oliver   E 302.6.E4.
         Cession of western lands   E 309; F 483; F 497.W5.
         Susquehanna claims   F 157.W9.
         Hartford convention, 1814   E 357.7.
         Huntington, J. W.   E 340.H9.
         Buckingham, W. A.   E 499.B.
         Civil war   E 499.

100   1865–

         Platt, O. H.   E 664.P7.
         War of 1898   E 726.C7.

102   Regions. Counties. Boundaries.

   .B7 Boundaries.
         Massachusetts boundary F 72.B7.
         New York boundary F 127.B7.
         Connecticut Gore, Susquehanna claim F 157.W9.
   .C7 Connecticut River and Valley, Conn. Cf. F 12.C7.
   .F2 Fairfield Co.
   .H3 Hartford Co.
   .L6 Litchfield Co., Litchfield Hills.

      Long Island F 127.L8.
   .M6 Middlesex Co.
   .N2 Naugatuck River and Valley.
   .N5 New Haven Co. Cf. F 98.
   .N7 New London Co.
   .T6 Tolland Co.
      Western Reserve F 497.W5.
      Westmoreland Co. (Pa.). F 157.W9.
   .W7 Windham Co.

105   Topics.

         Negroes   E 185.93.C7.
         Slavery   E 445.C7.

Table of subdivisions (a), (b), (c), or (d) under each state may be found on pages 85–87.

106   **Atlantic Coast of North America.   Middle Atlantic states. Delaware River and Valley.   Delaware Bay.**
> (For later literature only; descriptive and historic works on the Atlantic states before 1825, in E 162–165, and E 186–375.)
>> Susquehanna River   F 157.S8.
>> Potomac River   F 187.P8.
>> Chesapeake Bay   F 187.C5.
>> Atlantic coast of Canada   F 1035.8.

116–130   **New York (a).**
> Settled by the Dutch. New Netherland in its broadest extent included the Hudson Valley and eastward to the Connecticut, the lower Mohawk, Long Island and the Dutch and Swedish settlements on the Delaware River (Del., N. J.; and southeastern Pa.) It was conquered by the English in 1664 and reduced in limits, though the claim still extended to the Connecticut River, while N. J. was for many years attached to N. Y. under the same governor; also Martha's Vineyard and Nantucket, and modern Maine east of the Kennebec, for a time. Claims to the west bank of the Connecticut River were surrendered to Conn. and Mass. in colonial times, and later to Vt. During the early colonial period, what is now the western part of the state was Indian country with a few missionaries, and having relations quite as much with New France (F 1030) as with New York. After the revolution, Massachusetts enforced territorial claims to western New York, under her charters, but never exercised governmental rights.   cf. F 127.G19.

122   **Before 1775.   English province 1664–1774.   Dutch reconquest 1673–1674.   Biographies: Bayard, Nicholas; Dongan, Thomas; Leisler, Jacob; Bellamont, Richard Coote, earl of; Atwood, William; Falckner, Justus; Colden, Cadwallader; De Lancey, James, etc.**
> Early voyages   E 101–135.
>> Champlain, Samuel de   F 1030.1.
>> Hudson, Henry   E 129.H8.
> French explorations, invasions and missionaries in western N. Y.   F 1030–1030.8.
> Andros and his government, 1688–1689   F 7.5.
> King William's war, 1689–1697   E 196.
> Palatine immigration   F 130.P2.
> Johnson, Sir William   E 195.J.
> French and Indian war, 1755–1763   E 199.
> Livingston, Philip   E 302.6.L7.
> Tryon, William   F 257.T.

122. 1   **New Netherland.   Dutch colony 1610–1664.   Biographies: Michaelius, Jonas; Curler, Arent van; Donck, Adriaen van der; Stuyvesant, Peter; etc.**
> Rensselaerswyck   F 127.R4.
> Subjugation of the Swedes on the Delaware, 1655   F 167.
> Indian uprising of 1655   E 83.655.
> Esopus Indian war, 1663–1664   E 83.663.

Table of subdivisions (a), (b), (c), or (d) under each state may be found on pages 86–87.

116–130 New York—Continued.

123 1775–1865. Biographies: Kent, James; Wells, John; Johnson, Jeremiah; Holley, Myron; Jay, P. A.; De Peyster, J. W.; King, J. A.; Leavenworth, E. W.; Kent, William; etc.

Schuyler, Philip J. E 207.S3.
Duane, James E 302.6.D8.
Clinton, George E 302.6.C6.
Livingston, R. R. E 302.6.L72.
Revolutionary war E 263.N6.
 Military operations E 230.5–239.
Morris, Gouverneur E 302.6.M7.
Jay, John E 302.6.J4.
Hamilton, Alexander E 302.6.H2.
Lewis, Morgan E 353.1.L5.
Clinton, James E 207.C62.
Paterson, John E 207.P3.
King, Rufus E 302.6.K5.
Clinton, DeWitt E 340.C65.
Burr, Aaron E 302.6.B9.
Noah, M. M. E 335.N.
Van Buren, Martin E 387.
Porter, P. B. E 353.1.P8.
Tompkins, D. D. E 302.6.T8.
War of 1812 E 359.5.N6.
 Military operations E 355.
Granger, Francis E 340.G7.
Erie canal TC 625.E6.
Jay, William E 449.J.
Fillmore, Millard E 427.
Anti-masonic movement HS 525–527.
Dix, J. A. E 415.9.D6.
Monroe, James (1799–1870) E 340.M7.
Fish, Hamilton E 664.F52.
Seymour, Horatio E 415.9.S5.
Dickinson, D. S. E 415.9.D5.
Burning of the Caroline; McLeod F 1032.
Greeley, Horace E 415.9.G8.
Anti-rent troubles, 1839–1846 HD 199.
Tilden, S. J. E 415.9.T5.
Belmont, August E 415.9.B45.
Harris, Ira E 415.9.H3.
Field, D. D. E 415.9.F5.
War with Mexico E 409.5.N6.
Evarts, W. M. E 664.E88.
Maclay, W. B. E 415.9.M16.
Haskin, J. B. E 415.9.H35.
Peckham, R. W. F 124.P.
Gilbert, W. A. E 415.9.G46.
Wadsworth, J. S. E 467.1.W13.

Table of subdivisions (a), (b), (c), or (d) under each state may be found on pages 25–27.

116–130 **New York**—Continued.

124   1865– Biographies: Drew, Daniel; Peckham, R. W.;
          Husted, J. W.; King, J. A., jr.; McMahon, M. T.;
          O'Brien, M. J.; O'Gorman, J. A.; McCarren, P. H.;
          Higgins, F. W.; Dix, J. A.; etc.

> Tilden, S. J.   E 415.9.T5.
> O'Conor, Charles   E 664.O37.
> Conkling, Roscoe   E 664.C75.
> Sigel, Franz   E 467.1.S58.
> Slocum, H. W.   E 467.1.S63.
> Kernan, Francis   E 664.K35.
> Hill, D. B.   E 664.H54.
> Roosevelt, Theodore   E 757.
> Cleveland, Grover   E 697.
> War of 1898   E 726.N5.
> Lake Champlain tercentenary, 1909   F 127.C6.

127   Regions.   Counties.   Boundaries.

.A2   Adirondack Mountains.
      Blue Mountain Lake.
      Fulton Chain. Keene
      Valley.   Long Lake.
      Lake Placid.   Ra-
      quette Lake. Saranac
      Lake. Mt. Seward.

.A3   Albany Co.
      Cf. F 52, F 127.R4.

.A4   Allegany Co.

.A45 Allegheny River and Val-
      ley, N. Y.
      Cf. F 157.A5.

.B7   Boundaries.
      Massachusetts bound-
      ary F 72.B7.
      New Jersey boundary
      F 142.B7.

.B8   Broome Co.
      Cf. F 127.G19, .T6.

.C3   Catskill Mountains.

.C4   Cattaraugus Co.

.C5   Cayuga Co.

.C52 Cayuga Lake.

.C6   Lake Champlain region.
      Cf. F 57.C4; F 57.G7.
      Lake Champlain tercen-
      tenary, 1909.
      Charlotte Co.   F 127.W3.

.C7   Chautauqua Co.   Lake
      Chautauqua.

.C72 Chemung Co.

.C73 Chemung River and Val-
      ley.
      Cf. F 157.C37.

.C76 Chenango Co.

.C77 Clinton Co.

.C8   Columbia Co.   Livingston
      Manor.
      Cornwall Co.   (Maine)
      F 23.

.C85 Cortland Co.
      Cumberland Co.   (Vt.)
      F 52.

.D3   Delaware Co.

.D4   Delaware River and Val-
      ley, N. Y.
      Cf. F 106.

.D8   Dutchess Co.   Little or
      Upper Nine Partners'
      patent.   Oblong tract.

.E6   Erie Co.

.E65 Lake Erie region, N. Y.
      Cf. F 555.

.E8   Essex Co.   Au Sable Riv-
      er and Valley.   Au Sable
      chasm.
      Fisher's Island (Southold)
      F 129.S74.

.F8   Franklin Co.

.F9   Fulton Co.
      Gardiner's Island (East
      Hampton) F 129.E13.

Table of subdivisions (a), (b), (c), or (d) under each state may be found on pages 85–87.

116–130   New York.

127   Regions.   Counties.   Boundaries—Continued.

.G19   Genesee region. Phelps and Gorham's purchase.[1]

.G3   Lake George.

     Gloucester Co. (Vt.) F 52.

     Grand Island F 129.G.

.G7   Greene Co.

.H5   Herkimer Co.

.H7   Holland purchase.[2]

.H73   Hoosic River and Valley. Cf. F 57.B4; F 72.B5.

.H8   Hudson River and Valley. Palisades. Hudson-Fulton celebration. Cf. F 142.H83; F 142.B4.

.J4   Jefferson Co.

.K4   Keuka Lake.

.K5   Kings Co. Cf. F 129.B7 (Borough of Brooklyn).

.L6   Lewis Co.

.L7   Livingston Co.

.L8   Long Island.

.M2   Madison Co.

.M55   Mohawk River and Valley.

.M6   Monroe Co.

.M7   Montgomery Co. (Tryon Co. 1772–1784).

.N2   Nassau Co. Cf. F 127.Q3. New York Co. F 128.

.N5   Niagara Co.

.N6   Niagara River region. Cf. F 1059.N5.

.N8   Niagara Falls. State reservation. Cf. F 1059.Q3.

.O5   Oneida Co.

.O6   Onondaga Co. Onondaga Lake.

.O7   Ontario Co. (erected 1789, to include all of the state west of the Mass. pre-emption line. Cf. F 127.G19 and .H7.)

.O72   Lake Ontario region, N. Y. Cf. F 556.

.O8   Orange Co. Minisink region. Newburgh Bay.

.O9   Orleans Co.

.O91   Oswego Co.

.O93   Otsego Co.

.P9   Putnam Co.

.Q3   Queens Co. Cf. F 128.68.Q4; F 127.N2.

.R3   Rensselaer Co.

.R4   Rensselaerswyck. The manor of the Van Rensselaers. Cf. Anti-rent movement HD 199.

     Richmond Co. F 127.S7.

---

[1] Among the numerous claims of the seaboard colonies to western territory was that of Massachusetts to the Indian lands west of the settled region of New York State. In December, 1786, an agreement was reached that sovereignty should rest with New York, while Massachusetts received the preemption right to the entire region north of Pennsylvania and west of a line through Seneca Lake. New York reserved to herself a strip 1 mile wide along Niagara River, but granted to Massachusetts an additional tract of 200,000 acres in Montgomery County (now Tioga and Broome), known as the "Massachusetts (or Boston) Ten Townships." This agreement gave to Massachusetts the exclusive right to purchase six or seven million acres from the Indians. The claim in Montgomery County was at once disposed of to Samuel Brown and associates; and in 1788 the state sold all her preemption rights west of the Seneca Lake, or "preemption" line, to O. Phelps and N. Gorham. The new proprietors proceeded to extinguish the Indian title to the eastern third of their tract as far west as the junction of Genesee River and Canaseraga Creek; but becoming financially embarrassed they then induced the State of Massachusetts to cancel the sale of the balance and receive back the portion west of the Genesee.

After disposing of a part of their holdings, Phelps and Gorham sold the balance in 1790 to Robert Morris, who resold to an Englishman, Sir William Pulteney. Cf. F 127.H7, .O7, .T6.

[2] In 1791 Massachusetts sold the preemption right to the part of modern New York west of the Genesee River (the tract contracted for by Phelps and Gorham, but not actually purchased by them) to Robert Morris. Morris bought from the Indians all the land they were willing to sell, and after reserving several large tracts for himself, sold the balance to some Amsterdam merchants, who organized the Holland Land Company. Cf. F 127.G19, .O7.

Table of subdivisions (a), (b), (c), or (d) under each state may be found on pages 85–87.

116–130   **New York.**

127   Regions. Counties. Boundaries.—Continued.

.R6   Rockland Co.
.S2   St. Lawrence Co.
.S23   St. Lawrence River and Valley, N. Y.
     Cf. F 1050; F 127.T5.
.S26   Saratoga Co. Mt. Mc-Gregor.
.S27   Schenectady Co.
.S3   Schoharie Co.
.S34   Schuyler Co. Watkins Glen. State reservation.
.S4   Seneca Co.
.S7   Staten Island. Richmond Co. Richmond borough, N. Y. city.
.S8   Steuben Co.
.S9   Suffolk Co. Fire Island. State park.
.S91   Sullivan Co.
.S96   Susquehanna River and Valley, N. Y.
     Cf. F 157.S8.
.T5   Thousand Islands.

.T6   Tioga Co. "Massachusetts (or Boston) Ten Townships."
     Cf. F 127.G19.
     Paterson, John
     E 207.P3.
.T7   Tompkins Co.
     Tryon Co. F 127.M7.
.U4   Ulster Co. Mount Meenahga. Lake Minnewaska. Lake Mohonk. Shawangunk Mountains.
.W2   Warren Co. Luzerne Lake.
.W3   Washington Co. (Charlotte Co. 1772.) Cf. F 52.
.W4   Wayne Co.
.W5   Westchester Co. Philipse Manor. Van Cortlandt Manor.
     Cf. F128.68.B8.
.W9   Wyoming Co.
.Y3   Yates Co.

128   **New York (City). (Metropolis subdivisions.) New York Co.**

.4   Before 1775. New Amsterdam. Negro plot, 1741.
     Cf. F 122, 122.1.
.44   1775–1865. Draft riot, 1863.
     Revolutionary war, military operations E 230.5–239.
.47   1865–1897. Biographies: Kelly, John; etc.
.5   1898–. Greater New York.
     Cf. F 127.Q3; F 127.S7; F 129.B7.
.68   Suburbs. Sections of the city.

.B6   Bloomingdale.
.B8   Borough of the Bronx.
     Cf. F 127.W5.
     Borough of Brooklyn F129.B7.
     Coney Island F 129.C75.

     Long Island City F 129.L78.
.Q4   Borough of Queens.
     Cf. F 127.Q3.
     Borough of Richmond. Staten Island F127.S7.
     Rockaway Beach F 129.R8.

.G7   Governor's Island.
.G8   Greenwich.
.H3   Harlem.

.S9   Stuyvesant Village.

.–   Topics.

.C2   Canadians.
.C3   Catholics.
.C5   Chinese.
.G3   Germans.

.I6   Irish.
.J2   Japanese.
.J5   Jews.
.S9   Syrians.

Table of subdivisions (a), (b), (c), or (d) under each state may be found on pages 86–87.

116–130   New York—Continued.
130   Topics. [New York (State)]

.G4	Germans.		Negroes E 185.93.N56
	Weiser, Conrad F 152.W.		Slavery E 445.N56.
.H8	Huguenots.	.P2	Palatines.
.I6	Irish.	.S2	Scandinavians.
.J4	Jews.	.S4	Scotch.

131–145   New Jersey (a).

This region was claimed by the Dutch of New Netherland as part of their dominion, and such Swedes as had obtained a footing in the southern part were subjugated in 1655. The English crown, however, never relinquished its claim to the whole Atlantic coast of North America, and the claim was made by the Plowden family and heirs that a royal grant was made in 1634 to Sir Edmund Plowden, of "New Albion" covering Long Island and the whole region between New York and Virginia. Explorations were made but no settlement. In 1664 the Duke of York conquered New Netherland, granting New Jersey to Berkeley and Carteret. The former in 1674 sold his undivided half to Fenwick and Byllinge of the Society of Friends, by whom in turn it was transferred to trustees. In 1676 was executed the "Quintipartite deed" whereby the eastern part was given to Carteret under name of East Jersey, and the western part to the Trustees, as West Jersey. Carteret's portion was sold in 1682 to a board of proprietors, also Friends. The two provinces maintained separate governments till 1702 when Queen Anne united them as the province of New Jersey.

137   Before 1775. Plowden's New Albion grant. East and West Jersey 1676–1702. Biographies: Carteret, Sir George; Fenwick, John; Franklin, William; etc.

New Sweden F 167.
Colonial wars E 196–199.
Fenwick's colony F 142.S2.

138   1775–1865. Biographies: Houston, W. C.; Kirkpatrick, Andrew; Field, R. S.; etc.

Revolutionary war E 263.N5.
   Military operations E 230.5–239.
Paterson, William E 302.6.P3.
Bayard, John E 263.P4B.
Witherspoon, John E 302.6.W7.
War of 1812 E 359.5.N4.
Frelinghuysen, Theodore E 340.F86.
Dayton, W. L. E 415.9.D27.
Parker, Joel E 521.P.
Phelps, W. W. E 664.P53.
Civil war E 521.

Table of subdivisions (a), (b), (c), or (d) under each state may be found on pages 85–87.

131–145 **New Jersey**—Continued.
139 1865– Biographies: Jackson, J. P., jr.; McGill, A. T.;
Pitney, H. C.; etc.

> Field, R. S. F 138.F.
> Parker, Joel E 521.P.
> Phelps, W. W. E 664.P53.
> Hobart, G. A. E 664.H73.
> Fisk, C. B. E 664.F53.
> McClellan, G. B. E 467.1.M2.
> Wilson, Woodrow E 767.
> War of 1898 E 726.N4.

142 Regions. Counties. Boundaries.

.A8	Atlantic Co.	.H9	Hunterdon Co.
.B4	Bergen Co. The N. J. palisades. Cf. F 127.H8.	.M5	Mercer Co.
		.M7	Monmouth Co.
.B7	Boundaries.	.M8	Morris Co. Cedar Lake. Schooley's Mountain.
.B9	Burlington Co.		
.C16	Camden Co.	.O2	Ocean Co.
.C2	Cape May Co.		Palisades of the Hudson.
.C9	Cumberland Co.		Palisades interstate
.D3	Delaware Bay region, N.J. Cf. F 106; F 172.D3.		park F 127.H8.
		.P2	Passaic Co.
.D4	Delaware River and Valley, N. J. Cf. F 106.	.P3	Passaic River and Valley.
		.R2	Raritan River and Valley.
		.S2	Salem Co. Fenwick's colony.
.E8	Essex Co.		
.G5	Gloucester Co.	.S6	Somerset Co.
.H7	Lake Hopatcong.	.S9	Sussex Co.
.H8	Hudson Co.	.U5	Union Co.
.H83	Hudson River and Valley, N. J. Cf. F 127.H8; F 142.B4.	.W2	Warren Co. Delaware Water Gap, N. J. Cf. F 157.D5.

145 Topics.

> .G3 Germans.
> Negro slavery E 445.N54.

146–160 **Pennsylvania** (a).

> The southeast part was colonized by Swedes and was portion of the colony of New Sweden (cf. F 167); in 1655 it was conquered by the Dutch of New Netherland and formed a part of that colony. In 1664 the Duke of York's conquest of New Netherland transferred it to his control. 1680–82 William Penn received his royal grant of Pennsylvania, extending west from the Delaware River, the Duke of York releasing his claim there, and selling at the same time the region covered by modern Delaware (which was also claimed by Lord Baltimore as forming part of Maryland). The southern boundary was in dispute with Maryland for many years. Connecticut claimed a strip along the northern border (Connecticut Gore or Susquehanna claim F 157.W9) and Virginia considered the Forks of the Ohio [Pittsburgh] and region south and east as included in her territory, and organized county governments. (Cf. Westmoreland County F 157.W5.)

Table of subdivisions (a), (b), (c), or (d) under each state may be found on pages 85–87.

146–160   **Pennsylvania**—Continued.

152   Before 1775. Grant to Penn, 1681. The Paxton boys. Biographies: Pannebecker, Hendrick; Pastorius, F. D.; Logan, James; Keith, Sir William; Antès, Henry; Weiser, Conrad; Kinsey, John; Schlatter, Michael; etc.

> Swedish and Dutch settlements before 1680 F 167.
> Penn, William F 152.2.
> Intercolonial wars, 1689–1763 E 196–199.
>   French and Indian war; Fort Duquesne E 199.
> Franklin, Benjamin E 302.6.F8.
> Franklin, William F 137.F.
> Zeisberger, David E 98.M6Z.
> Pontiac's conspiracy, 1763–1765 E 83.76.
> Connecticut claims in northeastern Pa. F 157.W9.
> Virginia claims in southwestern Pa. F 157.W5.

152.2   The proprietors: William Penn and family.

153   1775–1865. Buckshot war, 1838. Biographies: Hiester, Joseph; Biddle, Charles; Gibson, J. B.; Duane, W. J.; Lewis, Ellis; Woodward, G. W.; Price, E. K.; etc.

> Armstrong, John E 302.6.A7.
> Dickinson, John E 302.6.D5.
> Maclay, William E 302.6.M14.
> Morris, Robert E 302.6.M8.
> Bayard, John E 263.P4B.
> Reed, Joseph E 302.6.R3.
> St. Clair, Arthur F 483.S.
> Mifflin, Thomas E 207.M6.
> Revolutionary war E 263.P4.
>   Military operations E 230.5–239.
> Connecticut settlers in Wyoming Valley; Susquehanna claim F 157.W9.
> McKean, Thomas E 302.6.M13.
> Ingersoll, Jared E 302.6.I6.
> FitzSimons, Thomas E 302.6.F56.
> Muhlenberg, J. P. G. E 207.M96.
> Gallatin, Albert E 302.6.G16.
> Ross, James E 302.6.R8.
> Dallas, A. J. E 302.6.D14.
> Maclay, Samuel E 302.6.M138.
> Whisky insurrection, 1794 E 315.
> Boudinot, Elias E 302.6.B7.
> Fries' rebellion, 1798–1799 E 326.
> Ingersoll, C. J. E 340.I48.
> Ingham, S. D. E 340.I55.
> Buchanan, James E 437.
> War of 1812 E 359.5.P3.
> Dallas, G. M. E 340.D14.
> Meredith, W. M. E 415.9.M5.

Table of subdivisions (a), (b), (c), or (d) under each state may be found on pages 85–87.

146–160   **Pennsylvania.**
153   **1775–1865—Continued.**

Stevens, Thaddeus   E 415.9.S8.
Cameron, Simon   E 415.9.C18.
Ingersoll, J. R.   E 340.I5.
Gilpin, H. D.   E 340.G48.
Cooper, James   E 340.C72.
Moorhead, J. K.   E 415.9.M8.
Jones, J. G.   E 415.9.J7.
War with Mexico   E 409.5.P3.
Kelley, W. D.   E 664.K2.
Civil war   E 527.
Military operations   E 470.2; 471–478.

154   **1865–   Biographies: Jackson, G. D.; Lemon, J. A.; Kemerer, J. B.; Lemon, M. B.; Hackett, H. B.; Harrison, J. T.; Rowland, G. F.; Patton, A. E.; Matson, Myron; etc.**

Price, E. K.   F 153.P.
Hartranft, J. F.   E 467.1.H4.
Geary, J. W.   E 467.1.G29,
Beaver, J. A.   E 467.1.B39.
Molly Maguires   HV 6452.P4.
Quay, M. S.   E 664.Q2.
War of 1898   E 726.P4.

157   **Regions.   Counties.   Boundaries.**

.A2   Adams Co.
    Cf. F 157.C75.
.A4   Allegheny Co. Sewickley Valley.
.A5   Allegheny River and Valley.
    Cf. F 127.A45.
.A7   Armstrong Co.
.B2   Beaver Co.   Ohio River and Valley, Pa.
    Cf. F 516–520.
.B23   Beaver River and Valley.
.B3   Berks Co.
.B5   Blair Co.
.B7   Boundaries.   Mason and Dixon's line.
    New York boundary F 127.B7.
    Ohio boundary F 497.B7.
    Connecticut boundary dispute (Susquehanna company, Connecticut Gore) F 157.W9.

.B7   Boundaries—Continued.
    Virginia boundary (latter's claim to land south and east of Ohio River) F 157.W5.
.B76   Bradford Co.
.B8   Bucks Co.
    Cf. F 157.M7.
.B83   Butler Co.
.C16   Cambria Co.
.C18   Cameron Co.
.C2   Carbon Co.
.C3   Centre Co.
.C37   Chemung River and Valley, Pa.
    Cf. F 127. C73.
.C4   Chester Co. Brandywine Creek, Pa.
.C5   Clarion Co.
.C53   Clearfield Co.
.C6   Clinton Co.
.C7   Columbia Co.
.C73   Conemaugh River and Valley.

Table of subdivisions (a), (b), (c), or (d) under each state may be found on pages 86–87.

146–160 **Pennsylvania.**
157   Regions. Counties. Boundaries—Continued.

.C75	Conewago Creek and Valley.	.L8	Luzerne Co.
		.L9	Lycoming Co.
.C77	Crawford Co. Conneaut Lake.	.M2	McKean Co.
		.M3	Mahoning River and Valley, Pa.
.C8	Cumberland Co.		Cf. F 497.M2.
.C85	Cumberland road. National road. Cf. HE 356. C8.	.M5	Mercer Co.
		.M55	Mifflin Co.
.C9	Cumberland (or Kittochtinny) Valley. (in Cumberland and Franklin cos.)	.M58	Monongahela River and Valley. Cf. F 247. M6.
		.M6	Monroe Co. Pocono Mountain.
.D2	Dauphin Co.		Cf. F 157.D5.
.D3	Delaware Co.	.M7	Montgomery Co. Perkiomen River and Valley (in Montgomery and Bucks cos.)
.D4	Delaware River and Valley, Pa. Cf. F 106.		
.D5	Delaware Water Gap. Cf. F 142.W2.	.M8	Montour Co.
		.N7	Northampton Co.
.E4	Elk Co.	.N8	Northumberland Co.
.E6	Erie Co. Lake Erie region, Pa. Cf. F 555.		Ohio River and Valley, Pa. F 157.B2.
		.O3	Oil regions.
.F2	Fayette Co.	.P5	Perry Co.
.F7	Forest Co.	.P56	Philadelphia Co. (County merged into city 1854. Cf. F 158.)
.F8	Franklin Co. The part of Cumberland or Kittochtinny Valley in Franklin Co. Conococheague Creek and Valley. Cf. F 157.C9; F 187.W3.	.P6	Pike Co.
		.P8	Potter Co.
		.S3	Schuylkill Co.
		.S5	Snyder Co.
		.S6	Somerset Co.
.G8	Greene Co	.S67	Sullivan Co.
.H9	Huntingdon Co.	.S7	Susquehanna Co.
.I3	Indiana Co.	.S8	Susquehanna River and Valley. Cf. F 127.S96; F 187.S8.
.J4	Jefferson Co.		
.J7	Juniata River and Valley.		
.L15	Lackawanna Co.	.S9	West branch of the Susquehanna.
.L17	Lackawanna River and Valley.		
		.T5	Tioga Co.
.L2	Lancaster Co. Pequea Creek.	.V4	Venango Co.
		.W2	Warren Co.
.L3	Lawrence Co.	.W3	Washington Co. (Organized 1781.) Cf. F 157.W5.
.L4	Lebanon Co.		
.L5	Lehigh Co.		
.L6	Lehigh River and Valley.	.W35	Wayne Co.

Table of subdivisions (a), (b), (c), or (d) under each state may be found on pages 85–87.

146-160   **Pennsylvania.**
     157   Regions.   Counties.   Boundaries—Continued.

.W5	Westmoreland Co.	.W8	Wyoming Co.
	Old Westmoreland Co.	.W9	Wyoming Valley. Con-
	organized 1773 (in-		necticut claims. Sus-
	cluding present West-		quehanna company.
	moreland, Washing-		"Connecticut Gore."
	ton, Fayette and		Connecticut town and
	Greene cos.). Bound-		county of Westmore-
	ary disputes with		land.
	Va. down to 1784 and	.Y6	York Co.
	her organization of		Cf. F 157.O75.
	the region (district of		
	West Augusta, coun-		
	ties of Monongalia,		
	Yohogania and Ohio).		

     158   Philadelphia.   (Metropolis subdivisions.)
         .4   To 1775.
         .44   1775-1854 Riots of 1844, etc. Consolidation act, merging the
              county of Philadelphia in the city.
         .5   1854–
              Centennial exposition, 1876 T.
         .68   Suburbs. Sections of the city.

.E4	Elmwood.	.N78	North Penn.
.F2	Falls of Schuylkill.	.N8	Northern Liberties.
	Germantown F 159.G3.	.O8	Oxford Township.
.L4	League Island.	.W7	Windmill Island.

     160   Topics.

.D9	Dutch.	.I5	Irish.
.F8	French.		Negroes E 185.93. P4.
.G3	Germans.		Slavery E 445. P3.
.H8	Huguenots.	.S4	Scotch-Irish.
		.W4	Welsh.

161-175   **Delaware (a).**
         The first settlements in the region were made by the Dutch about
         1629. 1638 the Swedes colonized the region about the lower Dela-
         ware River and Bay, in Del., southeastern Pa. and N. J., calling
         their colony New Sweden. In 1655 the Dutch of New Nether-
         land conquered and held it till 1664 when it was included in the
         English conquest. Claimed by both Lord Baltimore and William
         Penn, and adjudged to the latter. Known as the "Lower Counties
         on the Delaware." A separate province 1703.

     167   Before 1775. Swedish settlements on the Delaware
         River; New Sweden. Dutch conquest 1655. Eng-
         lish conquest 1664. Part of Penn's grant 1681.
         The "Lower Counties on the Delaware."
             Penn, William   F 152.2.
             Rodney, Caesar   E 302.6.R6.
             McKean, Thomas   E 302.6.M13.
             Read, George   E 302.6.R27.

Table of subdivisions (a), (b), (c), or (d) under each state may be found on pages 85-87.

161–175   **Delaware**—Continued.
    168   1775–1865.   Biographies: Pusey, Pennock; etc.
          Rodney, Caesar   E 302.6.R6.
          Read, George   E 302.6.R27.
          Revolutionary war   E 263.D3.
          Bayard, J. A.   E 302.6.B3.
          Clayton, J. M.   E 415.9.C6.
          Civil war   E 500.
          Gilpin, E. W.   F 169.G.

    169   1865–   Biographies: Gilpin, E. W.; Addicks, J. E.; etc.
    172   Regions.   Counties.   Boundaries.

.B7	Boundaries.	.D4	Delaware River and Valley,
	Pennsylvania boundary;		Del.
	Mason and Dixon's		Cf. F 106.
	line F 157.B7.	.K3	Kent Co.
	Maryland boundary	.N5	New Castle Co.
	F 187.B7.		Bohemia Manor F 187.C3.
.D3	Delaware Bay region, Del.	.S8	Sussex Co.
	Cf. F 106, F 142.D3.		

    175   Topics.
          Negro slavery   E 445.D3.

176–190   **Maryland** (c).
          Territory included in Virginia by early charters.   Granted 1632 to
            Lord Baltimore under whom the colony was settled.   Boundary dis-
            putes with Pa. and Va. formed an important part of the early history.
    184   Before 1775.   The Calverts, proprietors of Maryland.
          Baltimore, George Calvert, 1st baron of.   Baltimore,
          Cecilius Calvert, 2d baron of.   Kent Island and
          Claiborne.   Toleration in Md.
          Mason and Dixon's line   F 157.B7.
          French and Indian war, 1755–1763   E 199.
          Eden, Sir Robert   E 263.M3E.

    185   1775–1865. Biographies: McMahon, J.V.; Lowe, E.L.; etc.
          Carroll, Charles   E 302.6.C3.
          Revolutionary war   E 263.M3.
            Military operations   E 230.5–239.
          Henry, John   E 302.6.H4.
          McHenry, James   E 302.6.M12.
          Pinkney, William   E 302.6.P6.
          War of 1812   E 359.5.M2.
            Baltimore riot, 1812   F 189.B1.
            Military operations   E 355.
          Pearce, J. A.   E 340.P3.
          Kennedy, J. P.   E 415.9.K35.
          War with Mexico   E 409.5.M2.
          Hicks, T. H.   E 415.9.H6.
          Harris, B. G.   E 415.9.H23.
          Davis, H. W.   E 415.9.D26.
          Civil war   E 512.
            Confederate   E 566.
            Military operations   E 470.2, 471–478.

Table of subdivisions (a), (b), (c), or (d) under each state may be found on pages 85–87.

176–190 **Maryland**—Continued.
 186   1865–   Biographies: Knott, A. L.;   Phelps, C. E.;   etc.
      Gorman, A. P.   E 664.G6.
 187   Regions.   Counties.   Boundaries.

.A4	Allegany Co.		.H2	Harford Co. Deer Creek.
.A6	Anne Arundel Co. St.		.H8	Howard Co.
	Ann's Parish.		.K3	Kent Co. St. Paul's Par-
.B2	Baltimore Co.			ish.
.B7	Boundaries.		.M7	Montgomery Co. Prince
	Pennsylvania boundary			George's Parish.
	F 157.B7.		.P8	Potomac River and Val-
	Mason and Dixon's line			ley.
	F 157.B7.			Cf. F 202.P8; F 232.P8;
	District of Columbia			F 247.P8.
	boundary F 202.B7.		.P9	Prince Georges Co.
.C15	Calvert Co.		.S2	St. Marys Co.
.C2	Caroline Co.		.S8	Susquehanna River and
.C3	Cecil Co. Bohemia Manor.			Valley, Md.
.C5	Chesapeake Bay region.			Cf. F 157.S8.
	Cf. F 187.E2; F 232.C43;		.T2	Talbot Co.
	F 232.E2.		.W3	Washington Co. Antie-
.D6	Dorchester Co.			tam Creek. Blue Moun-
.E2	Eastern shore of Maryland.			tain. Conococheague
.F8	Frederick Co.			Creek and Valley, Md.
.G2	Garrett Co.			Cf. F 157.F8.

 190   Topics.
   .F8   Friends, Society of.
   .G3   Germans.
   J5   Jews.
     Negroes   E 185.93.M2.
     Slavery   E 445.M3.

191–205   **District of Columbia. Washington (a).**
    Cessions authorized by Maryland and Virginia 1788–89. District
    located under acts of Congress 1790–1791, and established by proc-
    lamation in latter year. In 1801 it was divided into two counties.
    Washington and Alexandria, separated by the Potomac River,
    1846 Alexandria County was retroceded to Virginia. Before 1871
    there was no general government for the District. Georgetown
    was already a city when ceded by Maryland, and Washington
    received a municipal charter in 1802. The rural portions of the
    District were under county governments at the head of which
    were Levy courts. In 1871 the city charters were revoked and
    the county government abolished, and the entire District consoli-
    dated under a governor and Legislative assembly. In 1874 three
    temporary commissioners were substituted, and 1878 came the
    reorganization in present form, with two civilian and one engineer
    commissioner.

 Table of subdivisions (a), (b), (c), or (d) under each state may be found on pages 85–87.

191–205   **District of Columbia. Washington—Continued.**
195   Miscellaneous. Location of national capital. L'Enfant and his plan. Retrocession. Question of the removal of capital.
        Alexandria Co., Va. F 232.A4.
197   Before 1815.
198   1815–1878.
        Kendall, Amos   E 340.K33.
        Explosion on frigate Princeton, 1844   E 396.
        Mexican war   E 409.5.D6.
        Retrocession of Alexandria Co., 1846   F 195.
        Civil war   E 501.
          Military operations   E 470.2, 471–478.
        Paschal, G. W.   F 391.P.
199   1878–
202   Regions. Suburbs. Boundaries.

.A5	Anacostia River and Valley.	.L4	Le Droit Park.
		.M9	Mount Pleasant.
.B7	Boundaries.	.P8	Potomac River and Valley,
.B8	Brightwood.		D. C.
.C6	Columbia Heights.		Cf. F 187.P8, F 203.3.
.G3	Georgetown.	.W5	West Brookland.

203   Localities, etc. Special.

.1	Cemeteries.	.5	Parks.	
	Arlington national cemetery	.7	Streets. Bridges. Railroads.	
	F 234.A7.			
.2	Churches.	.9	Wards.	
.3	Harbor.			
.4	Monuments. Statues.			
	Cf. F 204.C2 (The Capitol;			
	Hall of statuary).			

204   Buildings, Collective and individual.
205   Topics.
        Negro slavery   E 445.D6.

206–220   **The South (a). South Atlantic States.** Region south of Mason and Dixon's line and Ohio River.
        Slavery in the U. S.   E 441–453.
210   Miscellaneous. Mountain whites of the South.
212   Before 1775.
        Early grants of Virginia, Raleigh's colonies, etc.   F 229.
·213   1775–1865.
        Campaigns of the revolutionary war   E 230.5–239.
        Slavery   E 441–453.
        Southern convention, Nashville 1850   E 423.S.
214   Civil war period (Travel and description).
        History of the war   E 468.
        Confederate States of America   E 482–489.

Table of subdivisions (a), (b), (c), or (d) under each state may be found on pages 85–87.

206–220 **The South**—Continued.

215   1865–

216   Reconstruction period, 1865–1877.   Northern societies formed to ameliorate conditions at the South.

> Histories of reconstruction   E 668.

217   Regions.

.A3   Alleghany Mountains.
      Atlantic coast   F 106.
.B6   Blue Ridge Mountains.
      Chesapeake Bay region
      F 187.C5.
      Gulf coast   F 296.
      Ohio River and Valley
      F 516–520.

Old Southwest; Lower Mississippi Valley   F 396.
Potomac River and Valley
F 187.P8.
.T3   Tennessee River and Valley.
      Cf. F 332.T2;   F 443.T3;
      F 457.T3.

221–235 **Virginia** (c).

> Name first applied in the reign of Queen Elizabeth to the region extending indefinitely northward from Florida.   First attempted settlement was that of Raleigh under his patent of 1584.   Virginia was defined under King James' 1st, 2d and 3d charters 1606–1612. The later Pa., Md., and Carolina charters took off large sections of land already given to Virginia.   The Quebec act of 1774 cut off her western territory north of the Ohio River until it was won back by G. R. Clark during the revolution.   At the close of that war Great Britain abandoned her claim to that region.   Others of the states had conflicting charter rights, all of which were eventually given up to the U. S.   Virginia surrendered the territory northwest of the Ohio 1784, and that south of the same river in 1789 (in addition to relinquishing in 1789 claims to land in southwest Pa.).   While the civil war was in progress, a Union government with capital at Alexandria was recognized by the U. S. and that part of the state held by United States troops.   West Virginia was lost to Va. during the war, that section of the state declaring against secession.

229   Before 1775.   Raleigh's explorations and colonies, 1584–1590.   Virginia company of London.   Jamestown settlement.   John Smith.   Indian massacres.   Bacon's rebellion, 1676.   The parsons' cause.

> Washington, George   E 312.
> French and Indian war, 1755–1763   E 199.
> Lee, R. H.   E 302.6.L4.
> Mason, George   E 302.6.M45.
> Cherokee war, 1759–1761   E 83.759.
> Pontiac's conspiracy, 1763–1765   E 83.76.
> Dunmore's war, 1774; Battle of Point Pleasant   E 83.77.
> Explorations in Ohio Valley   F 517.

Table of subdivisions (a), (b), (c), or (d) under each state may be found on pages 86–87.

221–235   **Virginia—Continued.**
  230   1775–1865.   Biographies: Johnson, Joseph; Martin, Joseph; Peyton, W. M.; Peyton, J. H.; etc.
         Bailey, Mrs. Ann   F 241.B.
         Lee, R. H   E 302.6.I4.
         Mason, George   E 302.6.M45.
         Henry, Patrick   E 302.6.H5.
         Jefferson, Thomas   E 332.
         Revolutionary war   E 263.V8.
           Military operations   E 230.5–239.
           Clark's conquest of the Northwest   E 234.
         Madison, James   E 342.
         Randolph, Edmund   E 302.6.R18.
         Monroe, James   E 372.
         Marshall, John   E 302.6.M4.
         Cession of territory north of Ohio River, 1784   E 309; F 483.
         Relinquishment of claims in southwestern Pa.   F 157.W5.
         Lee, Henry   E 207.L5.
         Washington, Bushrod   E 302.6.W15.
         Final withdrawal of claims to Ky.   F 454.
         Wirt, William   E 340.W79.
         Randolph, John   E 302.6.R2.
         Mercer, C. F.   E 340.M5.
         Virginia resolutions, 1798   E 328.
         Mason, A. T.   E 302.6.M43.
         Tyler, John   E 397.
         War of 1812   E 359.5.V3.
           Military operations   E 355.
         Gordon, W. F.   E 340.G6.
         Mason, J. M.   E 415.9.M2.
         Nat. Turner's insurrection, 1831   F 232.S7.
         Hunter, R. M. T.   E 415.9.H9.
         Floyd, J. B.   E 415.9.F64.
         Garnett, M. R. H.   E 415.9.G2.
         John Brown at Harper's Ferry   E 451.
         Civil war   E 581.
           Union.   Gov. Peirpoint   E 534.
           Separation of West Virginia   F 241.
           Military operations   E 470.2–.3, 471–478.
  231   1865–   Reconstruction.
         Controversies with West Virginia   F 241
         Barbour, J. S.   E 664.B23.
         Daniel, J. W.   E 664.D18.
         O'Ferrall, C. T.   E 664.O42.
         Lee, Fitzhugh   E 467.1.L39.

Table of subdivisions (a), (b), (c), or (d) under each state may be found on pages 85–87.

221–235   **Virginia—Continued.**
    232   **Regions. Counties. Parishes. Boundaries.**

.A15	Accomac Co. Cf. F 232.E2.	.K4	King and Queen Co.
.A3	Albemarle Co.	.K5	King William Co.
.A4	Alexandria Co.	.L8	Loudoun Co.
	Cf. F 191–205.	.M4	Mecklenburg Co.
.A9	Augusta Co. Weyer's cave.	.M6	Middlesex Co.
.B3	Bath Co.	.M7	Montgomery Co.
.B4	Bedford Co.	.N2	Nansemond Co.
.B7	Boundaries.	.N3	New Kent Co.
	Old Va.-Pa. boundary		Cf. F 232.82.
	including Virginia's	.N5	New River and Valley,
	claims in southwest		Va. Cf. F 247.N5.
	Pa. F 157.W5.	.N8	Norfolk Co.
	D. C. boundary F 202.B7.	.O6	Orange Co.
	Md. boundary F 187.B7.	.O9	Overwharton Parish.
.B8	Bristol Parish.	.P2	Page Co. Luray cave.
.B9	Brunswick Co.	.P8	Potomac River and Val-
.B92	Bruton Parish.		ley, Va. Cf. F 187.P8.
.B94	Buchanan Co.	.P9	Pulaski Co.
.C2	Caroline Co.	.R6	Roanoke Co.
.C3	Charles City Co.	.R63	Roanoke River and Val-
.C4	Charlotte Co.		ley, Va. Cf. F 262.R5.
.C43	Chesapeake Bay region,	.S15	St. George's Parish.
	Va. Cf. F 187.C5.	.S2	St. Mark's Parish.
.C5	Clarke Co.	.S25	St. Peter's Parish.
.C9	Culpeper Co.	.S47	Shenandoah Co.
.D7	Dismal swamp. Lake Drum-	.S5	Shenandoah River and
	mond. Cf. F 262.D7.		Valley. Cf. F 247.S5.
.E2	Eastern shore of Va.	.S7	Southampton Co. Nat
.E7	Essex Co.		Turner's insurrection.
.F2	Fairfax Co.	.S8	Spottsylvania Co.
.G4	Giles Co. Mountain Lake.		Cf. F 232.S15.
.G6	Gloucester Co.	.T15	Tangier Island.
.H17	Halifax Co.	.T2	Tazewell Co.
.H2	Hamilton Parish.	.T8	Truro Parish.
.H23	Hampton Roads.	.V2	Valley of Virginia.
	Cf. F 232.J2.		Cf. F 232.S5.
.H4	Henrico Co.	.W3	Washington Co.
.H5	Henrico Parish.		West Augusta District
.I8	Isle of Wight Co.		(Pa.) F 157.W5.
.J2	James River and Valley.	.W8	Wise Co.
	Cf. F 232.H23.	.Y6	York Co.

   235   **Topics.**

.F8	French. Huguenots.	Negroes E 185.93.V8.
.G3	Germans.	Slavery E 445.V8.
.J5	Jews.	

Table of subdivisions (a), (b), (c), or (d) under each state may be found on pages 85–87.

236–250   **West Virginia (d).**

> Those counties of Virginia which refused to secede in 1861. Admitted as a state June 19, 1863.

241   General works. Periods. Controversies between Va. and W. Va. growing out of the separation. Biography: Bailey, Mrs. Ann; etc.

> Johnson, Joseph   F 230.J.
> Civil war history and organization of the state E 536.
> > Union government of Va. Gov. Peirpoint E 534.
> > Confederate E 582.
> > Military operations E 470.2–.4, 471–478.

247   Regions. Counties. Boundaries.

.B2	Barbour Co.	.N5	New River and Valley.
.B5	Berkeley Co.		Cf. F 232.N5.
.B7	Boundaries.	.O3	Ohio Co.
	Md. boundary and old	.P3	Pendleton Co.
	Md.-Va. boundary	.P7	Pocahontas Co.
	F 187.B7.	.P8	Potomac River and Valley,
.G7	Greenbrier Co.		W. Va. Cf. F 187.P8.
.H2	Hampshire Co.	.P9	Preston Co.
.H3	Harrison Co.	.R2	Randolph Co.
J2	Jackson Co.	.R6	Ritchie Co.
.K2	Kanawha Co.	.S5	Shenandoah River and Valley, W. Va.
.K3	Kanawha Valley.		
.M5	Mercer Co.		Cf. F 232.S5.
.M6	Monongahela River and Valley, W. Va.	.S9	Summers Co.
		.T8	Tucker Co.
	Cf. F 157.M58.	.W8	Wood Co.
.M7	Monongalia Co.		

251–265   **North Carolina (a).**

> Within the limits of the present N. C. was planted the first English colony in America, Raleigh's, in 1585 (F 229). The territory comprising the modern Carolinas was all known as Virginia, and formed part of the grant to the Virginia company of London 1606. Not being occupied by the Jamestown settlers, the region was granted in 1629 to Sir Robert Heath under the name of "Carolana." No colony was established and the tract between Virginia and the Spanish colony of Florida was re-granted in 1663 as Carolina to a company of proprietors. Settlement was made at once at Albemarle and Clarendon (the Cape Fear region) in N. C., and a few years later at Charleston in S. C. These settlements were so remote from each other that during most of the proprietary period, their governments were separate in fact, though the colony was not divided till about 1712. 1729 the proprietors released their claims to the crown. The western portion of the state was ceded to the U. S. in 1790 and became the state of Tennessee.

Table of subdivisions (a), (b), (c), or (d) under each state may be found on pages 85–87.

251–265   **North Carolina—Continued.**

257   Before 1775. Grant of Carolina to 8 proprietors 1663. Albemarle and Clarendon settlements. Royal province. War of the regulators, 1766–1771. Biographies: Burrington, George; Everhard, Sir Richard; Waddell, Hugh; Tryon, William; Hunter, James; etc.

          Raleigh's Roanoke colonies, 1584–1590 F 229.

          The original grant of Carolina, before the division F 272.

          Intercolonial wars, 1689–1763 E 196–199.

          Tuscarora war, 1711–1713 E 83.71.

          War with Spaniards of Florida, 1740 F 314.

          Cherokee war, 1759–1761 E 83.759.

258   1775–1865. Biographies: Lane, Joel; Smith, Benjamin; Moore, Alfred; Manly, Charles; Yancey, Bartlett; Davis, George; Morehead, J. M.; etc.

          Hooper, William E 302.6.H7.

          Transylvania colony (Ky.) F 454.

          Revolutionary war E 263.N8.

            Mecklenburg resolutions E 215.9.

            Military operations E 230.5–239.

          Tennessee settlers: Cessions of 1784 and 1790; Watauga, Franklin, etc. F 436.

          Iredell, James E 302.6.I7.

          Macon, Nathaniel E 302.6.M17.

          Davie, W. R. E 302.6.D2.

          Harper, R. G. E 302.6.H29.

          Sawyer, Lemuel E 302.6.S3.

          King, W. R. E 340.K54.

          War of 1812 E 359.5.N7.

          Worth, Jonathan F 259. W.

          Graham, W. A. E 415.9.G7.

          Clingman, T. L. E 415.9.C63.

          Holden, W. W. F 259.H.

          Scales, A. M. E 664.S23.

          Civil war E 573.

            Union E 524.

            Military operations E 470.6, 471–478.

259   1865– Reconstruction. Biographies: Worth, Jonathan; Holden, W. W.; Johnston, T. D.; Aycock, C. B.; etc.

          Davis, George F 258.D.

          Scales, A. M. E 664.S23.

          Ransom, M. D. E 664.R2.

          War of 1898 E 726.N8.

Table of subdivisions (a), (b), (c), or (d) under each state may be found on pages 35–57.

251–265   **North Carolina—Continued.**

    262   Regions. Counties. Boundaries.

.A3	Alamance Co.	.G9	Guilford Co.
.B6	Blue Ridge in N. C.	.H3	Harnett Co.
	Cf. F 217.B6.	.H5	Hertford Co.
.B7	Boundaries.	.M2	Macon Co.
	Georgia boundary	.M4	Mecklenburg Co.
	F 292.B7.	.N5	New Hanover Co.
	Virginia boundary	.P6	Pitt Co.
	F 232.B7.	.R2	Randolph Co.
.B9	Brunswick Co.	.R5	Roanoke River and Valley.
.C2	Cape Fear River.		Cf. F 232.R63.
.C3	Catawba River and Valley,	.R6	Robeson Co.
	N. C. Cf. F 277.C3.	.R8	Rowan Co.
.C4	Chatham Co.	.T7	Transylvania Co.
.D7	Dismal swamp, N. C.		Wachovia F 262.F7.
	Cf. F 232.D7.	.W6	Wilkes Co.
.E2	Edgecombe Co.	.Y2	Yadkin River.
.F7	Forsyth Co. Wachovia.		(Great Pedee River in
.G2	Gaston Co.		S. C. F 277.P3.)

    265   Topics.

.G3	Germans.		Negro slavery E 445.N8.
.J3	Jews.	.S4	Scotch.
.M8	Moravians.		
	Cf. F 262.F7.		

266–280   **South Carolina** (a).

         Like North Carolina, South Carolina was included within the original grants of Virginia. The whole province of Carolina was granted in 1663 to 8 proprietors. The settlements were so remote from each other that necessarily the governments were separate during most of the proprietary period. About 1712 the province was divided, and 1729 the 8 proprietors sold their claims to the crown. Georgia and the territory extending west from it, were taken from South Carolina. Western lands still claimed by the state, consisting of a narrow strip south of Tenn., were granted to the U. S. 1787.

    272   Before 1775. The "Carolana" grant 1629. The original province of Carolina as a whole (1663–1712) Charleston settlement. Locke's Fundamental constitutions. Spanish attack from Florida 1680. Separation of the two Carolinas.

         Huguenot colony at Port Royal, 1562   F 314.
         Carteret, Sir George   F 137.C.
         Northern Carolina settlements   F 257.
         Intercolonial wars, 1689–1763   E 196–199.
         Bohun, Edmund   DA 447.B7.
         Montgomery's Azilia patent   F 289.
         Georgia settlement   F 289.
         St. Augustine expedition, 1740   F 314.
         Cherokee war, 1759–1761   E 83.759.

Table of subdivisions (a), (b), (c), or (d) under each state may be found on pages 55–57.

266–280 **South Carolina—Continued.**
273   1775–1865. Dispute with Massachusetts over latter's negro citizens 1845. Biographies: Lee, Thomas; Hamilton, James; Petigru, J. L.; etc.

Marion, Francis E 207.M3.
Gadsden, Christopher E 207.G2.
Rutledge, John E 302.6.R9.
Pinckney, C. C. E 302.6.P55.
Revolutionary war E 263.S7.
  Military operations E 230.5–239.
Moultrie, William E 207.M85.
Pinckney, Thomas E 302.6.P57.
Sumter, Thomas E 207.S95.
S. C.'s cession of 1787 F 292.B7.
Hampton, Wade (1st) E 353.1.H2.
Smith, William E 340.S6.
Calhoun, J. C. E 340.C15.
Hayne, R. Y. E 340.H4.
Legaré, H. S. E 340.L5.
Tariff of 1828 HF 1754.
Poinsett, J. R. E 340.P77.
Memminger, C. G. E 415.9.M4.
Nullification E 384.3.
Pickens, F. W. E 577.P.
War with Mexico E 409.5.S7.
O'Connor, M. P. E 664.O3.
Pettigrew, J. J. E 467.1.P5.
Perry, B. F. F 274.P.
Civil war E 577.
  Union E 529.
  Military operations E 470.6, 471–478.
  Port Royal mission; Sea Island district E 185.93.S7.

274   1865– Reconstruction. Biographies: Chamberlain, D. H.; Perry, B. F.; Sawyer, F. A.; etc.
Hampton, Wade (3d) E 467.1.H19.
O'Connor, M. P. E 664.O3.

277   Regions. Counties. Boundaries.

.B3 Beaufort Co. Sea Islands. Cf. E 185.93.S7.
.B5 Berkeley Co. Cooper River. St. Stephen's Parish.
.B7 Boundaries. S. C. cession, south of Tenn. F 292.B7.
.C3 Catawba River and Valley. Cf. F 262.C3.
.D2 Darlington Co.
.E2 Edgefield Co.
.M2 Marion Co.
.M3 Marlboro Co.
.N5 Newberry Co. Newberry District.
.O6 Orangeburg Co.
.P3 Peedee region. Great Peedee. Little Peedee.
.S3 Savannah River and Valley, S. C. Cf. F 292.S3.
.S7 Spartanburg Co.
.U5 Union Co.
.W7 Williamsburg Co.

Table of subdivisions (a), (b), (c), or (d) under each state may be found on pages 86–87.

266–280   South Carolina—Continued.
280   Topics.

.H8   Huguenots.   Negroes   E 185.93.S7.
.J5   Jews.   Slavery   E 445.S7.
                           .S4   Scotch-Irish.

281–295   Georgia (c).

A part of the Carolina grant (1663–1665), but not colonized. 1717 Sir Robert Montgomery obtained from the Proprietors of Carolina a grant between the Savannah and the Altamaha, which was forfeited 3 years later as no settlement was made. In 1732 the tract between the Savannah and Altamaha Rivers was granted by the Crown for 21 years to Trustees. At the expiration of the trust it became a royal province. In 1763 the land between the Altamaha and St. Mary's River and region west to the Mississippi was added to Georgia. In 1802 the state assumed its present form by ceding its western lands to the U. S. and receiving so much of the S. C. cession of 1787 as lay north of its reduced limits.

289   Before 1775. Montgomery's Azilia. The Trustees for establishing the colony of Georgia. J. E. Oglethorpe. Royal province.

Intercolonial wars, 1689–1763   E 196–199.
Salzburger immigration   F 295.S1.
St. Augustine expedition, 1740   F 314.

290   1775–1865. Biographies: Clayton, A. S.; etc.

Revolutionary war   E 263.G3.
   Military operations   E 230.5–239.
Elbert, Samuel   E 207.E3.
Jackson, James   E 302.6.J2.
Western lands, ceded to U. S.   F 296, 321–350.
   Yazoo land companies   F 341.
Cherokee troubles   E 99.C5.
Crawford, W. H.   E 340.C89.
War of 1812   E 359.5.G4.
1st Creek war, 1813–1814   E 83.813.
1st Seminole war, 1817–1818   E 83.817.
2d Creek war, 1836   E 83.836.
Toombs, R. A.   E 415.9.T6.
Hill, B. H.   E 664.H53.
Civil war   E 559.
   Union   E 503.
   Military operations E 470.6, 471–478.

291   1865– Reconstruction. Biographies: Jenkins, C. J.; Harden, E. J.; Bullock, R. B.; etc.

Toombs, R. A.   E 415.9.T6.
Hill, B. H.   E 664.H53.
Gordon, J. B.   E 467.1.G66.
Grady, H. W.   E 664.G73.

Table of subdivisions (a), (b), (c), or (d) under each state may be found on pages 85–87.

281–295 Georgia—Continued.

292   Regions. Counties. Boundaries.

.B7	Boundaries. S. C. cession south of Tenn.	.F6	Floyd Co.
		.L6	Liberty Co.
	S.C. boundary F 277.B7.	.M2	Madison Co.
	Fla. boundary F 317.B7.	.P61	Pierce Co.
	Tenn. boundary F 443 .B7.	.S2	St. Mary's River and Valley, Ga. Cf. F 317.S3.
.C4	Chattahoochee River and Valley. Cf. F 317.A6; F 317. J2; F 332.C4.	.S3	Savannah River and Valley. Cf. F 277.S3.
.C6	Cobb Co.	.W2	Ware Co.
		.W7	Wilkes Co.

295   Topics.

.G3	Germans. Cf. F 295.S1.		Negroes E 185.93.G4.
.J5	Jews.		Slavery E 445.G3.
.M8	Moravians.	.S1	Salzburgers.

296   **Gulf states. Gulf coast.**

        South Atlantic states F 206–220.
        Lower Mississippi Valley F 396.
        West Florida F 301.
        Mississippi Territory (1798) F 336–350.

301   **West Florida.**

        The portion of the Louisiana coast east of the Mississippi; settled by French about 1700. Ceded to Great Britain 1763, with the other French possessions east of the Mississippi. Great Britain also received Spanish Florida from Spain in 1763, and soon after divided her possessions on the Gulf coast into the two colonies of East and West Florida, the Chattahoochee-Apalachicola River forming the boundary between them. The northern limit of West Florida was at first 31°; after 1764, 32°, 30′. The 31° was agreed upon as boundary in the American-British treaty of 1783, but both Floridas were ceded to Spain by Great Britain the same year and the former country claimed the 32°, 30′ line as the northern boundary. (The territory in dispute, sometimes known as the Natchez district of West Florida, was surrendered by Spain to the U. S. in 1798 and organized as the Territory of Mississippi; and enlarged 1804 by the addition of Georgia's western lands, and that part of the S. C. cession of 1787 north of it, thus including all modern Ala. and Miss. north of 31°). West Florida, consisting of the Gulf coast south of 31° between the Chattahoochee and the Mississippi, continued a Spanish colony. The inhabitants revolted in 1810, and a presidential proclamation declared West Florida under the jurisdiction of the U. S. The part west of the Pearl River (Baton Rouge district) was added to Louisiana on the latter's admission as a state 1812; the remainder as far east as the Perdido River (Mobile district), annexed to Mississippi Territory the same year. The small remnant east of the Perdido (the Pensacola district, which continued to be known as West Florida) was conquered by Jackson in the 1st Seminole war 1818, returned to Spain next year, and formed part of the Florida purchase of 1819.

        Louisiana boundary F 377.B7.
        Baton Rouge district; Florida parishes of La. F 377.F6.
        Natchez district F 341.
        Pensacola district F 317.W5.
        Mobile F 334. M6.

Table of subdivisions (a), (b), (c), or (d) under each state may be found on pages 85–87.

306–320   Florida (c).

Early claims to this region were made by Spain, France and England. Colonized by the two former nations, but soon recognized as a Spanish possession. Boundaries not defined, but limited by the English on the north and the French on the west. Ceded to Great Britain 1763, who reorganized it as East Florida, bounded west by the Chattahoochee-Apalachicola River and north by 31° and St. Mary's River. Returned to Spain 1783, and after a generation of border troubles with northern neighbors, sold to U. S. 1819 with the part of West Florida still in Spanish hands. A territory 1822. Admitted as a state 1845.

314   Before 1819. French Huguenot colonies, 1562–1565. Menéndez. Gourgues. St. Augustine colony. St. Augustine expedition, 1740. East Florida. Independent "Republic of Florida" between St. John's and St. Mary's rivers 1812–1816. McGregor at Amelia Island, 1817. Treaty of 1819. Spanish Florida claims (in general).

General works on the Spaniards in North America   F 1410.
Ponce de Leon, Juan   E 125.P7.
Narváez, Pánfilo de   E 125.N3.
Soto, Hernando de   E 125.S7.
St. Augustine   F 319.S2.
West Florida   F 301.
Jackson, Andrew   E 382.
1st Creek war, 1813–1814   E 83.813.
1st Seminole war, 1817–1818   E 83.817.
Execution of Arbuthnot and Ambrister   E 83.817.

315   1819–1865. Jackson's administration as governor.

Jackson, Andrew   E 382.
2d Seminole war, 1835–1842   E 83.835.
Brockenbrough, W. H.   E 340.B8.
Civil war   E 558.
    Union   E 502.
    Military operations   E 470.7, 471–478.

316   1865–   Reconstruction.

317   Regions. Counties. Boundaries.

.A4   Alachua Co.
.A6   Apalachicola River and Valley. Cf. F 332.C4.
.B7   Boundaries.
.B8   Brevard Co. Indian River. Chattahoochee River and Valley, Fla. F 317.J2.
.D2   Dade Co. Biscayne Bay. Lake Worth. Cf. F 317.E9.
.E7   Escambia Co. Cf. F 317.P4.

.E9   Everglades.
.H5   Hernando Co.
.H6   Hillsborough Co.
.J2   Jackson Co. Chattahoochee River and Valley, Fla. Cf. F 292.C4; F 317.A6; F 332.C4.
.L3   Lee Co. Cf. F 317.E9.
.L5   Leon Co.
.M2   Manatee Co. Manatee River.

Table of subdivisions (a), (b), (c), or (d) under each state may be found on pages 55–57.

306-320 Florida.

   317   Regions. Counties. Boundaries—Continued.

.M3 Marion Co. Lake Weir.	.S2 St. John's River and Valley.
.N3 Nassau Co. Amelia Island. Cf. F 314.	.S3 St. Mary's River and Valley. Cf. F 292.S2.
.O6 Orange Co.	.W24 Walton Co.
.P4 Perdido River and Valley, Fla. Cf. F 332.P4.	.W5 West Florida region. The Pensacola district after 1819.
.P7 Polk Co.	

321-335 Alabama (d).

> The territory included in the present state of Alabama was, all but the southern extremity, embraced in the Carolina grants 1663-1665; and again under the original Georgia charter of 1732 or the extension thereof, in 1763, (all except a narrow strip along the northern border which belonged to S. C. till ceded to the national government in 1787.) The portion between 31° and 32° 30′ extending west to the Mississippi was detached to form part of the English province of West Florida 1764-1783, and in 1798 was organized as Mississippi Territory. 1804 the remainder, up to 35°, including that part surrendered by Ga. 1802, and S. C. cession, was added. 1812, the Gulf coast from the Perdido to the Pearl River (the Mobile district of West Florida) became part of the Territory. Cf. note under F 336-350. 1817, on the admission of Mississippi as a state, Alabama was organized as a territory with its present limits. State 1819.

   326   General works. Periods. Biographies: Crenshaw, Anderson; Chilton, W. P.; Samford, W. F.; Samford, W. J.; Price, T. W.; etc.

> Early French settlements on the coast (Louisiana) F 372.
> West Florida F 301.
> S. C. cession south of Tenn. F 292.B7.
> Mississippi Territory F 341.
> Cherokee Indians E 99.C5.
> 1st Creek war, 1813-1814 E 83.813.
> Birney, J. G. E 340.B6.
> King, W. R. E 340.K54.
> Smith, William E 340.S6.
> 2d Creek war, 1836 E 83.836.
> Hilliard, H. W. E 415.9.H65.
> Civil war E 551.
>   Union E 495.
>   Military operations E 470.6-.7, 471-478.
> Wheeler, Joseph E 467.1.W5.
> Morgan, J. T. E 664.M7.
> War of 1898 E 726.A3.

Table of subdivisions (a), (b), (c), or (d) under each state may be found on pages 85-87.

321–335   **Alabama—Continued.**

332   **Regions. Counties. Boundaries.**

.B6	Blount Co. Garfield colony.	.J4	Jefferson Co.
		.M3	Marshall Co.
.B7	Boundaries.	.M5	Mobile Bay.
	Tennessee boundary F 443.B7.	.M6	Mobile Co. Dauphin Island.
.B9	Butler Co.	.P4	Perdido River and Valley. Cf. F 317.P4
.C4	Chattahoochee River and Valley, Ala. Cf. F 292 .C4.	.P5	Pickens Co.
		.T2	Tennessee River and Valley, Ala. Cf. F 217.T3.
.C6	Clarke Co.		
.C7	Conecuh Co.	.T6	Tombigbee River and Valley. Cf. F 347.T6.
.C9	Cullman Co.		
.G9	Gulf coast of Alabama. Cf. F 296; F 332.M5.	.T9	Tuscaloosa Co.

335   **Topics.**

         Negroes   E 185.93.A3.
         Slavery   E 445.A3.

336–350   **Mississippi (d).**

Like Alabama, the state of Mississippi, with the exception of its southern extremity, was embraced in the Carolina grants of 1663–1665, and again under the original Georgia charter of 1732 and its extension in 1763; (a narrow strip along the northern border belonging to S. C. till ceded to the U. S. in 1787.) This region was first occupied by the French, and claimed by them as part of Louisiana till ceded to Great Britain in 1763. The territory south of 32° 30′ and west of Georgia formed the English province of West Florida 1764–1783. The area bounded by 31°, 32° 30′ and the Mississippi and Chattahoochee rivers was organized as Mississippi Territory 1798. In 1804 the Ga. cession of 1802, and the part of the S. C. cession of 1787 north of it, was added. In 1812, Spanish West Florida between the Pearl River and the Perdido was joined to it. Admitted as a state, 1817, with present limits, the eastern part being set off as Alabama Territory.

341   **General works. Periods. Natchez district. Yazoo land companies. Biographies: Sargent, Winthrop; etc.**

         West Florida; Mobile district before 1812   F 301.
         S. C. cession south of Tenn.   F 292.B7.
         Poindexter, George   E 340.P75.
         1st Creek war, 1813–1814   E 83.813.
         Quitman, J. A.   E 403.1.Q8.
         Walker, R. J.   E 415.9.W2.
         Foote, H. S.   E 415.9.F7.
         Prentiss, S. S.   E 340.P9.
         Davis, Jefferson   E 467.1.D26.
         Lamar, L. Q. C.   E 664.L2.
         George, J. Z.   E 664.G34.
         French, S. G.   E 467.1.F87.
         Civil war   E 568.
           Union   E 516.
           Military operations   E 470.6–.7, 471–478.

Table of subdivisions (a), (b), (c), or (d) under each state may be found on pages 55–57.

336–350   **Mississippi—Continued.**

   347   Regions.   Counties.   Boundaries.

.B7	Boundaries.		.M3	Marshall Co.
	Louisiana boundary		.M6	Mississippi Valley, Miss.
	F 377.B7.			Cf. F 396, 351–354.
	Tenn. boundary		.P3	Pearl River Cf. F 377.P3.
	F 443.B7.		.P6	Pike Co.
.G9	Gulf coast of Miss.		.T6	Tombigbee River and Val-
	Cf. F 296.			ley, Miss. Cf. F 332.T6.
.H2	Hancock Co.		.W29	Warren Co.
.K3	Kemper Co.			

   350   Topics.

                 Negroes   E 185.93.M6.

                 Slavery   E 445.M6.

351–354   **Mississippi River and Valley.**

   351   General works.   History.

                 Louisiana   F 366–380.

                 Upper Mississippi River and Valley   F 597.

                 Ohio River and Valley   F.516–520.

                 Missouri River and Valley   F 598.

                 Lower Mississippi River and Valley   F 396.

                 Mississippi-Arkansas boundary   F 347.B7.

                 Mississippi-Louisiana boundary   F 377.B7.

   352   Before 1803.   Discoverers and early explorers: Marquette; La Salle; etc.

                 Soto's explorations   E 125.S7.

                 New France   F 1030.

                 Marquette (General works)   F 1030.2.

                 Joliet (General works)   F 1030.3.

                 Hennepin (General works)   F 1030.4.

                 La Salle (General works)   F 1030.5.

                 Louisiana (French and Spanish)   F 372–373.

                 Le Moyne d'Iberville, Pierre   F 372.L.

                 Law's Mississippi scheme   HG 6007.

                 Carver's explorations   F 597.C.

                 Clark's campaign, 1778–1779   E 234.

                 Purchase by U. S.   E 333.

   353   1803–1865.

                 Lewis and Clark expedition, 1804–1806   F 592.

                 Pike's expedition, 1805–1807   F 592.

                 Burr's conspiracy, 1805–1807   E 334.

                 Dodge, Henry   E 340.D7.

                 Black Hawk war, 1832   E 83.83.

                 Civil war; history and campaigns   E 470.8, 471–478.

   354   1865–

                 Jetties of the Mississippi   TC 425.

Table of subdivisions (a), (b), (c), or (d) under each state may be found on pages 85–87.

366–380 Louisiana (a).

> Region lying between Florida and New Spain, claimed by both France and Spain on right of discovery. Settled by Le Moyne d'Iberville 1698; detached from New France as a separate province in 1712, to include the region between the Allegheny and Rocky Mountains, New France and New Spain. The earliest capitals and centres of population were Biloxi and Mobile. Portion east of the Mississippi ceded to Great Britain 1763 (becoming known as West Florida. Cf. F 301); that west of the Mississippi to Spain, the previous year. The latter region was secretly re-ceded to France in 1800 and by that power sold to U. S. 1803. 1804 the province was divided on the line of 33° into the territory of Orleans and the district of Louisiana. The territory of Orleans with the addition of the Baton Rouge district of West Florida was admitted as the state of Louisiana in 1812, the district of Louisiana becoming the territory of Missouri the same year.

372 Before 1803. French Louisiana. Settlement 1698. Crozat's monopoly 1712. Cession to Spain 1763. Biographies: Le Moyne d'Iberville, Pierre; Le Moyne de Bienville, J. B.; etc.

> La Salle F 1030.5; F 352.L.
> Mississippi Valley F 352.
> Mobile F 334.M6.
> Law's Mississippi scheme, 1717–1720 HG 6007.
> Chickasaw war, 1739–1740 E 83.739.

373 1764–1803. Spanish Louisiana. Right of navigation of the Mississippi. Retrocession to France, 1800–01.

> General works on Spaniards in North America F 1410.
> Purchase of La. by the U. S. 1803 E 333.

374 1803–1865. Province of Louisiana 1803–1804. Territory of Orleans 1804–1812. Boundary disputes with Spain. State, 1812. Biographies: Mathews, George; etc.

> West Florida F 301.
> Lewis and Clark expedition F 592.L.
> Spanish treaty of 1819 F 314.
> The "Indian country" F 697.
> Wilkinson, James E 353.1.W6.
> Burr's conspiracy, 1805–1807 E 334.
> War of 1812; military operations E 355.
> Jackson, Andrew E 382.
> Ripley, E. W. E 353.1.R5.
> Benjamin, J. P. E 467.1.B4.
> Allen, H. W. E 467.1.A4.
> Civil war E 565.
>   Union E 510.
>   Military operations E 470.7–.8, 471–478.

375 1865– Reconstruction.

> Hancock, W. S. E 467.1.H2.

Table of subdivisions (a), (b), (c), or (d) under each state may be found on pages 85–87.

366–380   Louisiana—Continued.
   377   Regions. Parishes. Boundaries.

.B5 Bienville Parish.	.O7 Orleans Parish.
.B7 Boundaries.	.O8 Ouachita River and Valley. Cf. F 417.O8.
.C2 Calcasieu Parish.	
.C5 Claiborne Parish.	.P3 Pearl River, La. Cf. F 347.P3.
.C7 Concordia Parish.	
.E2 East Carroll Parish.	.R3 Red River and Valley.
.E3 East Feliciana Parish.	Cf. F 417.R3, F 392.R3,
.F6 Florida parishes. (Baton Rouge district of West Florida since 1812.) Part of state between Pearl and Mississippi rivers.	F 702.R3.
	.S11 Sabine River and Valley. Cf. F 392.S12.
	.S12 St. Bernard Parish.
	.S13 St. Helena Parish.
.G9 Gulf coast of La. Cf. F 296.	.S14 St. Landry Parish.
.M6 Mississippi River and Valley, La. Cf. F 351–354. 396.	.V5 Vermilion Parish.

   380   Topics.

.C9 Creoles.	.G3 Germans.
.F8 French. Acadians.	Negroes E 185.93.L6.
	Slavery E 445.L8.

381–395   Texas (c).

Considered by the Spaniards as part of New Spain, but not colonized. The site of La Salle's French colony 1685–1687. Under Spanish Louisiana but few colonists came in. The region was claimed by the U. S. as part of the Louisiana purchase 1803, but in the treaty of 1819 by which Florida was acquired, these claims were abandoned and the Sabine River recognised as the boundary. 1821–1834 the country was parcelled out by the Mexican government into colonies under proprietors called "impresarios"; the immigrants coming chiefly from the U. S. It was organized as the province of Texas 1821 and joined to Coahuila as the "Department of Coahuila and Texas" 1824. By the revolution of 1835–1836 Texas won her independence. At once the movement for annexation to the U. S. began. Admitted as a state 1845. In 1850 it sold to the national government nearly a third of its area, consisting of the northwestern part (now forming the eastern half of New Mexico and portions of Okl., Kan., Col. and Wy.)

   389   Before 1846. Impresarios. Austin's colony.
                 La Salle's colony 1685–1687 F 1030.5.

   390   1835–1845. War of independence. Republic of Texas. Santa Fe expedition, 1841. Mier expedition, 1842. Annexation to U. S. 1845. Biographies: Houston, Samuel; etc.
                 McCulloch, Ben   E 467.1.M28.
                 Crockett, David   F 436.C.
                 Johnston. A. S.   E 467.1.J73.
                 Kaufman, D. S.   E 340.K2.
                 Santa Anna, A. L. de   F 1232.S.

Table of subdivisions (a), (b), (c), or (d) under each state may be found on pages 35–37.

381–395   **Texas—Continued.**

391   1846–   Reconstruction. Frontier troubles with Mexico.
               Biographies: Paschal, G. W.; MacLeary, J. H.; etc.

Mexican frontier troubles (General) F 1232–1234.
McCulloch, Ben E 467.1.M28.
War with Mexico E 401–415.
Sale of claim to northwest lands, 1850 F 801.
Green, Thomas E 467.1.G7.
Hamilton, James F 273.H.
Civil war E 580.
    Union E 532.
        Military operations E 470.7, 470.9, 471–478.
Bailey, J. W. E 664.B2.

392   Regions. Counties. Boundaries.

.A9	Austin Co.	J6	Johnson Co.
.B6	Bosque Co.	.M2	McLennan Co.
.B7	Boundaries.	.P2	Parker Co.
	International boundary	.P3	Pecos River and Valley.
	F 786.		Cf. F 802.P3.
.C6	Colorado River, Tex.	.R3	Red River and Valley,
.C7	Comal Co.		Tex. Cf. F 377.R3.
.C8	Coryell Co.	.R5	Rio Grande River and
.E16	Eastland Co.		Valley.
.E4	Ellis Co.		Cf. F 802.R5, F 1334.
.F2	Fayette Co.	.S12	Sabine River and Valley,
.F6	Floyd Co.		Tex.
.F7	Fort Bend Co.		Cf. F 377.S11.
.G9	Gulf coast, Tex.	.W8	Wise Co.
	Cf. F 296.		

395   Topics.
        .F8 French.
        .G3 Germans.

396   **The Old Southwest. Lower Mississippi Valley.**

Gulf coast F 296.
Mississippi River and Valley F 351–354.
Red River of La. F 377.R3.
Louisiana F 366–380.
Burr's conspiracy E 334.
U. S.—Mexican boundary F 786.
Wilkinson, James E 353.1.W6.
U. S.—Texas boundary F 392.B7.
Polk, Leonidas E 467.1.P7.

406–420 **Arkansas (d).**

Part of the province of Louisiana under France and Spain. On the
division of Louisiana in 1804 it belonged to the northern portion,
or District of Louisiana which became the Territory of Missouri
in 1812. In 1819 the Territory of Arkansas was set off from Missouri, containing all Louisiana between 33° and 36° 30′, west to
the Spanish possessions. 1824–1828 the territory gave up its western portion as Indian country, and in 1836 was admitted as a state
with substantially its present limits.

Table of subdivisions (a), (b), (c), or (d) under each state may be found on pages 85–87.

406–420   **Arkansas—Continued.**
411   General works. Periods.
       Miller, James   E 353.1.M6.
       Paschal, G. W.   F 391.P.
       Pike, Albert   E 467.1.P6.
       Civil war   E 553.
         Union   E 496.
         Military operations   E 470.4, 471–478.

417   Regions. Counties. Boundaries.

.A7	Arkansas River and Valley. Cf. F 687.A7; F 702.A7; F 782.A7.	.M6	Mississippi Valley, Ark. Cf. F 351–354, 396.
.B6	Boone Co.	.O8	Ouachita River and Valley, Ark. Cf. F 377.O8.
.B7	Boundaries. Mississippi boundary F 347.B7.	.P7	Polk Co.
		.R3	Red River and Valley, Ark. Cf. F 377.R3.
.C4	Carroll Co.		
.C5	Clamorgan land grant (Ark. and Mo.)	.S2	St. Francis River and Valley. Cf. F 472.S25.
.G8	Greene Co.	.W5	White River and Valley. Cf. F 472.W5.
.L4	Lawrence Co.		

420   Topics.
       Negroes   E 185.93.A8.

431–445   **Tennessee (d).**
       Part of North Carolina under her early grants. Settled first, 1769–72, in the neighborhood of the Watauga River in eastern extremity. A local government called the Watauga association was organized in 1772, but soon absorbed by N. C. 1784 that state ceded her western territory to the U. S.; and the Watauga colony formed an independent state (Frankland or Franklin) and applied for admission to the union. N. C. thereupon withdrew her cession, and reestablished her jurisdiction west of the mountains. In 1790, it was again ceded to the U. S. and organized as the "Territory South of the Ohio." Admitted as a state 1796.

436   General works. Periods. Biographies: Robertson, James; Crockett, David; etc.
       Blount, William   E 302.6.B6.
       Jackson, Andrew   E 382.
       White, H. L.   E 340.W6.
       Grundy, Felix   E 340.G8.
       1st Creek war, 1813–1814   E 83.813.
       Bell, John   E 415.9.B4.
       Polk, J. K.   E 417.
       Brownlow, W. G.   E 415.9.B9.
       Johnson, Andrew   E 667.
       Pillow, G. J.   E 403.1.P6.
       Harris, I. G.   E 664.H31.
       Civil war   E 579.
         Union   E 531.
         Military operations   E 470.4–.5, 471–478.

Table of subdivisions (a), (b), (c), or (d) under each state may be found on pages 85–87.

431-445   Tennessee—Continued.

442.1   East Tennessee.
> Mountain whites of the South   F 210.

442.2   Middle Tennessee.   Cumberland Valley, Tenn.
> Cf. F 457.C9.

442.3   West Tennessee.
> Mississippi River and Valley, Tenn.   F 443.M6.

443   Other regions.   Counties.   Boundaries.

.B7	Boundaries.	.M6	Mississippi Valley, Tenn.
	Ky. boundary F 457.B7.		Cf. F 351–354, 396, 442.3.
	S. C. cession, south of	.M8	Montgomery Co.
	Tenn. F 292.B7.	.O9	Overton Co.
.B8	Bradley Co.	.P7	Polk Co.
	Cumberland River and	.S5	Shelby Co.
	Valley F 442.2.	.S8	Sullivan Co.
.D2	Davidson Co.	.S9	Sumner Co.
.H5	Henry Co.	.T3	Tennessee River and Val-
.H6	Hickman Co.		ley, Tenn.
.M15	McNairy Co.		Cf. F 217.T3.
.M4	Maury Co.		

446-460   Kentucky (c).
> Included in the original limits of Virginia. Small settlements were made by pioneers from N. C. and Va. 1766–1775. The Transylvania colony in 1775 tried to secure recognition from the Continental Congress. Va. organized the region as the county of Kentucky 1776 and later as the district of Kentucky including several counties. 1789 Virginia gave her consent for the formation of a new state, and 1792 Kentucky was admitted.

454   Before 1792.   Transylvania.   County and District of Kentucky.   Biographies: Boone, Daniel; etc.
> Bedinger, G. M.   F 455.B.
> Shelby, Isaac   F 455.S.
> Early explorations on Ohio River   F 517.
> Wilkinson, James   E 353.1.W6.
> Wars with northwestern Indians, 1790–1795   E 83.79.

455   1792–1865.   Biographies: Bedinger, G. M.; Shelby, Isaac; Powell, L. W.; etc.
> Mountain whites of the South   F 210.
> Adair, John   E 353.1.A19.
> Edwards, Ninian   F 545.E.
> Clay, Henry   E 340.C6.
> Kentucky and Virginia resolutions, 1798   E 328.
> Lyon, Matthew   E 302.6.L9.
> Burr's conspiracy   E 334.
> Johnson, R. M.   E 340.J69.
> War of 1812   E 359.5.K5.

Table of subdivisions (a), (b), (c), or (d) under each state may be found on pages 56–57.

446–460 Kentucky.

    455   1792–1865—Continued.

        Birney, J. G. E 340.B6.

        Crittenden, J. J. E 340.C9.

        Kendall, Amos E 340.K33.

        Butler, W. O. E 403.1.B9.

        Chambers, John F 621.C.

        Menefee, R. H. E 340.M4.

        Civil war E 509.

            Confederate E 564.

            Military operations E 470.4–.5, 471–478.

    456   1865–

        Palmer, J. M. E 664.P2.

    457   Regions. Counties. Boundaries.

.B5	Big Sandy River and Valley.	.G2	Garrard Co.
		.G8	Green River and Valley.
.B6	Blue grass region.	.H5	Henderson Co.
.B7	Boundaries.	.H6	Henry Co.
.B8	Bourbon Co.	J4	Jefferson Co.
.B83	Boyle Co.	.L7	Livingston Co.
.B9	Breckinridge Co.	.L8	Logan Co.
.C2	Campbell Co.	.M2	Mammoth cave.
.C8	Cumberland Mountains. Cf. F 210 (Mountain whites).	.M6	Mississippi River and Valley, Ky. Cf. F 351–354.
.C9	Cumberland River and Valley, Ky. Cf. F 442.2.	.O3	Ohio River and Valley, Ky. Cf. F 516–520.
.D3	Daviess Co.		
.E2	Edmonson Co. Cf. F 457.M2.	.P6	Pike Co.
.E7	Estill Co.	.T3	Tennessee River and Valley, Ky. Cf. F 217.T3.
.F2	Fayette Co.		
.F8	Franklin Co.	.U5	Union Co.

461–475 Missouri (d).

        Part of the province of Louisiana. In 1804 all that portion above 33° was separated from the lower Louisiana (then called the territory of Orleans) and styled the District of Louisiana, comprising all the possessions of the U. S. west of the Mississippi, above the present state of Louisiana. It became the territory of Louisiana 1805, and territory of Missouri, 1812. 1819 the southern part was detached as the territory of Arkansas, and 1821 Missouri was admitted as a state with nearly its present limits, the irregular northwest corner of the state being added in 1836. The portion of the old province of Louisiana to the north and west, remained unorganized; sometimes designated as "Missouri Territory" but more often as "The Indian country." Cf. notes under F 616, 661, 676, 691.

Table of subdivisions (a), (b), (c), or (d) under each state may be found on pages 86–87.

461-475 **Missouri—Continued.**
  466   General works. Periods.
                Benton, T. H. E 340.B4.
                Missouri compromise, 1820 E 373.
                Linn, L. F. E 340.L7.
                Doniphan, A. W. E 403.1.D6.
                Brown, B. G. E 415.9.B87.
                Kansas troubles, 1854–1859 F 685.
                Civil war E 517.
                  Confederate E 569.
                  Military operations E 470.4, 470.8, 471–478.
                Clark, Champ E 664.C49.
                War of 1898 E 726.M8.

  472   Regions. Counties. Boundaries.

.A5	Andrew Co.		.L2	Lafayette Co.
.A8	Atchison Co.		.L7	Lincoln Co.
.A9	Audrain Co.		.L8	Linn Co.
.B4	Benton Co.		.M2	Macon Co.
.B6	Boone Co.		.M3	Marion Co.
.B7	Boundaries.		.M6	Mississippi River and Valley, Mo.
.B9	Buchanan Co.			
.C2	Caldwell Co.			Cf. F 351–354.
.C3	Callaway Co.		.M7	Missouri River and Valley, Mo.
	Clamorgan land grant F 417.C5.			Cf. F 596.
.C7	Cooper Co.		.N7	Nodaway Co.
.D3	DeKalb Co.		.P7	Platte Co.
.D4	Des Moines River and Valley, Mo.		.R2	Ray Co.
			.S2	St. Charles Co.
	Cf. F 627.D43.		.S25	St. Francis River and Valley, Mo.
.D9	Dunklin Co.			
.G8	Greene Co.			Cf. F 417.S2.
.H7	Holt Co.		.S28	St. Francois Co.
.H8	Howard Co.		.S3	St. Louis Co.
.H9	Howell Co.		.S5	Shelby Co.
.I7	Iron Co.		.W2	Washington Co.
.J2	Jackson Co.		.W3	Wayne Co.
.J3	Jasper Co.		.W5	White River and Valley, Mo. Cf. F 417.W5.
.J6	Johnson Co.			

  475   Topics.
       .B6 Bohemians.
           Negroes E 185.93.M7.
             Slavery E 445.M67.
       .N5 New Englanders.

Table of subdivisions (a), (b), (c), or (d) under each state may be found on pages 86–87.

476–485   **The Old Northwest.   Region between the Ohio and Mississippi rivers and the Great Lakes.**

First explored by the French from New France in the latter part of the 17th century, and various trading posts established. On the formation of the province of Louisiana, the entire Mississippi Valley with the Illinois country was incorporated in it, the northern and eastern portions of the Old Northwest (the Great Lake region and Ohio Valley above modern Louisville) continuing under New France. Certain of the English colonies, notably Virginia, had charter claims to this region, and the dispute over jurisdiction helped to bring on the French and Indian war, one result of which was to transfer all territory east of the Mississippi River to England. But the claims of the individual colonies were ignored by the mother country, and the region west of the Alleghanies as far south as the Ohio was annexed to the province of Quebec in 1774. Then came the Revolution, with Clark's conquest of the Northwest, which led to the abandonment of the British claim in the peace of 1783. New York, Virginia, Massachusetts and Connecticut all ceded their claims to the general government, 1781–1786; and 1787 there was passed an ordinance organizing the "Territory of the United States Northwest of the Ohio". The British posts, however, were not surrendered till 1796. In 1800 the Territory was divided by a line drawn north from the mouth of the Kentucky River, the eastern portion retaining the old name, and including all of Ohio, eastern Michigan and a strip along the eastern edge of Indiana; the western part received the name of Indiana Territory. 1803 Ohio was admitted as a state with substantially its present limits, the remainder of the Northwest Territory being annexed to Indiana Territory.

Upper Mississippi Valley   F 597.
Louisiana   F 366–380.
Ohio Valley   F 516–520.

476   Periodicals.   Societies.   Collections.
477   Gazetteers.   Dictionaries.
478   Biography.   Genealogy.
479   General works.
480   Miscellaneous.
481   Antiquities.
482   To 1763.

New France   F 1030.
Mackinac region; Michilimackinac   F 572.M16.
Detroit, 1701   F 574.D4.
Illinois country   F 544.
Ohio company, 1749   F 517.
French and Indian war, 1755–1763   E 199.

Table of subdivisions (a), (b), (c), or (d) under each state may be found on pages 85–87.

476–485 The Old Northwest—Continued.

483   1763–1803. Cessions by Virginia and other states. Settlement. Virginia military lands (Chillicothe); The Seven ranges. Ohio company (Marietta); Scioto companies, American and French (Gallipolis); Miami purchase or Symmes tract, (Cincinnati); etc. Old Northwest centennial, 1888. Biographies: St. Clair, Arthur; Putnam, Rufus; Massie, Nathaniel; etc.

      Province of Quebec (Canada); Quebec act F 1082.

      Virginia F 229–230.

      Vincennes F 534.V7.

      Kaskaskia F 549.$\bar{K}$3.

      Pontiac's conspiracy, 1763–1765 E 83.76.

      Zeisberger, David E 98.M6Z.

      Revolutionary war E 263.N84.

        Indian wars, 1775–1783 E 83.775.

        Clark's campaigns E 234, 237.

      Clark, G. R. E 207.C5.

      Ordinance of 1787 E 309.

      Parsons, S. H. E 207.P2.

      Indian wars, 1790–1795 E 83.79.

        Wayne's campaign, 1793–1795 E 83.794.

      Harrison, W. H. E 392.

      Western Reserve of Connecticut F 497.W5.

484.3   1803–1865.

      Harrison, W. H. E 392.

      Tippecanoe campaign, 1811 E 83.81.

      War of 1812; military operations E 355.

484.5   1865–

485   Topics.

486–500 Ohio (c).

      Part of the "Territory of the United States Northwest of the Ohio." (Cf. note under F 476.)

495   Before 1865. Biographies: Hammond, Charles; Perkins, J. H.; etc.

      History before 1803 (Old Northwest) F 482–483.

      Massie, Nathaniel F 483.M.

      McArthur, Duncan E 353.1.M15.

      Morris, Thomas E 340.M8.

      McLean, John E 340.M2.

      Tippecanoe campaign, 1811 E 83.81.

      War of 1812 E 359.5.O2.

        Military operations E 355.

      Lucas, Robert F 621.L.

      Ewing, Thomas, sr. E 340.E9.

      Corwin, Thomas E 340.C76.

      Giddings, J. R. E 415.9.G4.

      Chase, S. P. E 415.9.C4.

Table of subdivisions (a), (b), (c), or (d) under each state may be found on pages 86–87.

486–500   **Ohio.**
    495   **Before 1865—Continued.**

                Toledo war, 1836   F 497.B7.
                Wade, B. F.   E 415.9.W16.
                Schenck, R. C.   E 467.1.S32.
                Cox, S. S.   E 664.C8.
                Vallandigham, C. L.   E 415.9.V2.
                Pendleton, G. H.   E 415.9.P4.
                Cox, J. D.   E 664.C78.
                Civil war   E 525.
                  Military operations   E 470.4, 471–478.

    496   **1865–**

                Schenck, R. C.   E 467.1.S32.
                Steedman, J. B.   E 467.1.S84.
                Cox, S. S.   E 664.C8.
                Pendleton, G. H.   E 415.9.P4.
                Cox, J. D.   E 664.C78.
                Garfield, J. A.   E 687.
                Hayes, R. B.   E 682.
                Old Northwest centennial, 1888   F 483.
                McKinley, William   E 711.6.
                Foraker, J. B.   E 664.F69.
                War of 1898   E 726.O3.

    497   **Regions.   Counties.   Boundaries.**

.A2	Adams Co.		.F15	Fairfield Co.
.A4	Allen Co.			Cf. F 497.B86.
.A7	Ashland Co.		.F2	Fayette Co.
.A73	Ashtabula Co.			Firelands F 597.W5.
.A8	Athens Co.		.F8	Franklin Co.
.A9	Auglaize Co.		.F9	Fulton Co.
.B3	Bean Creek and Valley.		.G2	Geauga Co.
	Cf. F 572.B36.		.G7	Greene Co.
.B4	Belmont Co.		.H2	Hamilton Co. Mill Creek.
.B7	Boundaries. Toledo war,			Duck Creek.
	1836.		.H3	Hancock Co.
.B8	Brown Co.		.H4	Hardin Co.
.B86	Buckeye Lake.		.H5	Harrison Co.
.B9	Butler Co.		.H55	Henry Co.
.C2	Carroll Co.		.H6	Highland Co.
.C4	Champaign Co.		.H68	Hocking Co.
.C5	Clark Co.		.H7	Hocking River and Val-
.C53	Clermont Co.			ley.
.C55	Clinton Co.		.H8	Huron Co.
.C6	Columbiana Co.		.J4	Jefferson Co.
.C7	Coshocton Co.		.K7	Knox Co.
.C8	Crawford Co.		.L2	Lake Co.
.C9	Cuyahoga Co.		.L6	Licking Co.
.D2	Darke Co.			Cf. F 497.B86.
.D3	Delaware Co.		.L7	Little Miami River and
.E6	Lake Erie region, O.			Valley.
	Cf. F 555, F 497.O8.			Cf. F 497.M64.

Table of subdivisions (a), (b), (c), or (d) under each state may be found on pages 85–87.

486-500   **Ohio.**

497   **Regions. Counties. Boundaries—Continued.**

.L86	Lorain Co.	.P9	Preble Co.
.L9	Lucas Co.	.R5	Richland Co.
.M14	Madison Co.	.R7	Rocky River and Valley.
.M18	Mahoning Co.	.R8	Ross Co.
.M2	Mahoning River and Valley. Cf. F 157.M3.	.S2	Sandusky Co.
		.S23	Sandusky Bay, River and Valley.
.M3	Marion Co.	.S3	Scioto Co.
.M4	Maumee River and Valley. Cf. F 532.M62.	.S32	Scioto River and Valley.
		.S4	Seneca Co.
.M5	Medina Co.	.S7	Stark Co.
.M6	Miami Co.	.S9	Summit Co. The Portage path.
.M64	Miami (or Great Miami) River and Valley.	.T8	Trumbull Co.
.M7	Montgomery Co. Twin Valley.	.T9	Tuscarawas Co.
		.U5	Union Co.
.M8	Morrow Co.	.W2	Warren Co.
.M9	Muskingum Co.	.W3	Washington Co.
.O3	Ohio River and Valley, O. Cf. F 516-520.	.W4	Wayne Co.
		.W5	Western Reserve. Firelands.
.O8	Ottawa Co. Put-in Bay.		Parsons, S. H. E 207.P2.
.P4	Perry Co. Cf. F 497.B86.	.W8	Wood Co.
.P5	Pickaway Co.	.W9	Wyandot Co.
.P8	Portage Co.		

500   **Topics.**

> Negroes E 185.93.O2.

516-520   **Ohio River and Valley.**

> Mississippi River and Valley F 351-354.
> Old Northwest F 476-485.
> Ohio River and Valley, Pa. F 157.B2.
> Indians of the Ohio Valley. E 78.O4.

516   **General works. Collections, etc.**

517   **Before 1795. Celoron's expedition, 1749. Grant to Ohio company 1749. Biographies: Wetzel, Lewis; etc.**

> New France F 1030.
> Louisiana F 372.
> French and Indian war, 1755-1763 E 199.
> Vincennes F 534.V7.
> Clark's campaign, 1778 E 234.
> Wars with northwestern Indians, 1790-1795 E 83.79.

518   **1795-1865.**

> Civil war; military operations E 470.4, 471-478.

519   **1865-**

Table of subdivisions (a), (b), (c), or (d) under each state may be found on pages 85-87.

521–535 Indiana (d).

First explored from New France; the southwest portion set off to Louisiana 1712 as part of the Illinois country. Ceded to Great Britain 1763 and annexed to the province of Quebec 1774. Conquered by Clark for Virginia 1779 and British title surrendered to U. S. by treaty of 1783. On relinquishment of claims of certain states under their colonial charters,1781–1786, the "Territory of the United States Northwest of the Ohio" was created 1787. In 1800 Indiana Territory was formed by setting off the part west of the meridian of the Kentucky River, including nearly all of the modern Indiana, the western part of Mich. and all of Ill. and Wis. and northeast Minn. 1803, on the admission of Ohio, Indiana received an accession of a strip along her eastern border, and the rest of Mich. 1805 the Territory of Michigan was set off from Indiana (including the lower peninsula only) 1809 the Territory of Indiana was reduced to substantially its present limits, and the region of the west and northwest established as the Territory of Illinois. Indiana was admitted as a state 1816.

526   General works. Periods.

Harrison, W. H. E 392.
Tippecanoe campaign, 1811 E 83.81.
War of 1812; military operations E 355.
Colfax, Schuyler E 415.9.C68.
English, W. H. E 664.E58.
Hendricks, T. A. E 664.H49.
Lane, J. H. F 685.L.
War with Mexico E 409.5.I7.
Dunn, W. M. E 415.9.D9.
Hovey, A. P. E 467.1.H7.
Morton, O. P. ` E 506.M.
Civil war E 506.
  Military operations E 470.4, 471–478.
Kerr, M. C. E 664.K4.
Harrison, Benjamin E 702.
Fairbanks, C. W. E 664.F16.
War of 1898 E 726.I3.

532   Regions. Counties. Boundaries.

.A2	Adams Co.	.D18	Dearborn Co.
.A4	Allen Co.	.D2	Decatur Co.
.B2	Bartholomew Co.	.D3	Delaware Co.
.B4	Benton Co.	.D8	Dubois Co.
.B5	Blackford Co.	.E4	Elkhart Co.
.B6	Boone Co.	.F2	Fayette Co.
.B7	Boundaries.	.F9	Fulton Co.
.C3	Carroll Co.	.H2	Hamilton Co.
:C4	Cass Co.	.H3	Hancock Co.
.C5	Clark Co.	.H5	Hendricks Co.
.C6	Clay Co.	.H6	Henry Co.
.C8	Crawford Co. Wyandotte	.H8	Howard Co.
	cave.	.J4	Jay Co.

Table of subdivisions (a), (b), (c), or (d) under each state may be found on pages 85–87.

521–535   Indiana.

    532   Regions.   Counties.   Boundaries—Continued.

.J6	Johnson Co.		.P4	Perry Co.
.K2	Kankakee River and Valley.		.P6	Pike Co.
			.P9	Putnam Co.
	Cf. F 547.K27; F 532.S2.		.R3	Randolph Co.
.K8	Kosciusko Co.		.S2	St. Joseph Co. St. Joseph-Kankakee portage.
.L17	Lagrange Co.			
.L2	Lake Co.			Cf. F 572.S43.
.L3	Laporte Co.		.S3	St. Joseph River and Valley.
.M2	Madison Co.			
.M4	Marion Co.			Cf. F 572.S43.
.M6	Marshall Co.		.S5	Shelby Co.
.M62	Maumee River and Valley, Ind.		.S6	Spencer Co.
			.S7	Starke Co.
	Cf. F 497.M4.		.S8	Steuben Co.
.M67	Lake Michigan region, Ind.		.S9	Sullivan Co.
			.T6	Tippecanoe Co.
	Cf. F 553.		.V2	Vanderburgh Co.
.M7	Monroe Co.		.V5	Vermillion Co.
.M8	Morgan Co.		.V7	Vigo Co.
.N5	Newton Co. Beaver Lake.		.W18	Wabash Co.
.N6	Noble Co.		.W2	Wabash River and Valley.
.O3	Ohio Co.			
.O4	Ohio River and Valley, Ind.			Cf. F 547.W14.
			.W4	Warrick Co.
	Cf. F 516–520.		.W5	Wayne Co.
.O9	Owen Co.		.W55	Wells Co.
.P2	Parke Co.		.W6	Whitley Co.

    535   Topics.

       .G3   Germans.

536–550   Illinois (c).

      The Illinois country was explored and colonised by New France in the 17th century. A part of Louisiana 1712. Ceded to Great Britain 1763 and annexed to the province of Quebec 1774. Conquered by Clark for Virginia 1779 and confirmed to the U. S. by treaty 1783. The states with claims to the region under colonial charters having ceded them to the general government 1781–1786, the "Territory of the United States Northwest of the Ohio" was organised 1787. On the division of the Northwest Territory in 1800, Illinois became part of the Indiana Territory. 1809 the Territory of Illinois was organised, consisting of the present states of Illinois and Wisconsin, and the upper peninsula of Mich. and northeast Minn. 1818 Illinois was admitted as a state with boundaries substantially as at present, the remainder of the territory being annexed to Mich.

    544   Before 1775. The Illinois country.

       New France   F 1030.

       Mississippi River and Valley   F 352.

Table of subdivisions (a), (b), (c), or (d) under each state may be found on pages 55–57.

536-550 Illinois—Continued.
545   1775-1865. Biographies: Edwards, Ninian; Coles, Edward; Cartwright, Peter; Duncan, Joseph; Snyder, A. W.; etc.

        Clark's campaign, 1778-1779   E 234.
        War of 1812; military operations   E 355.
        Cook, D. P.   E 340.C7.
        English settlement in Edwards Co.   F 547.E3.
        Black Hawk war, 1832   E 83.83.
        Lincoln, Abraham   E 457.
        Douglas, S. A.   E 415.9.D73.
        Baker, E. D.   E 467.1.B16.
        Mormons at Nauvoo   B —, F 549.N3.
        Judd, N. B.   E 415.9.J9.
        War with Mexico   E 409.5.I4.
        Palmer, J. M.   E 664.P2.
        Civil war   E 505.
          Military operations   E 470.4, 471-478.

546   1865– Biographies: Madden, M. B.; Altgeld, J. P.; etc.
        Palmer, J. M.   E 664.P2.
        War of 1898   E 726.I2.

547   Regions. Counties. Boundaries.

.A2	Adams Co.	.J2	Jackson Co.
.B6	Bond Co.	.J3	Jasper Co.
.B7	Boundaries.	.J4	Jefferson Co.
.B8	Bureau Co.	.J5	Jersey Co.
.C15	Calhoun Co.	.J6	Jo Daviess Co.
.C2	Carroll Co.	.K2	Kane Co.
.C3	Cass Co.	.K25	Kankakee Co.
.C4	Champaign Co.	.K27	Kankakee River and Valley, Ill.
.C5	Christian Co.		
.C55	Clay Co.		Cf. F 532.K2.
.C57	Clinton Co.	.K4	Kendall Co.
.C6	Coles Co.	.K7	Knox Co.
.C7	Cook Co.	.L2	Lake Co.
.C9	Cumberland Co.	.L3	La Salle Co.
.D3	De Kalb Co.	.L4	Lawrence Co.
.D5	De Witt Co.	.L5	Lee Co.
.D7	Douglas Co.	.M13	McDonough Co.
.D9	Du Page Co.	.M14	McHenry Co.
.E3	Edwards Co. English settlements.	.M16	McLean Co.
		.M18	Macoupin Co.
.E4	Effingham Co.	.M2	Madison Co.
.F8	Fulton Co.	.M3	Marion Co.
.G7	Greene Co.	.M34	Marshall Co.
.G8	Grundy Co.	.M37	Mason Co.
.H2	Hancock Co.	.M4	Massac Co.
.H3	Hardin Co.	.M5	Menard Co.
.H4	Henderson Co.	.M56	Lake Michigan region, Ill.
.I2	Illinois River and Valley.		
.I7	Iroquois Co.		Cf. F 553.

Table of subdivisions (a), (b), (c), or (d) under each state may be found on pages 35-37.

536–550   Illinois.

547   Regions.   Counties.   Boundaries—Continued.

.M6	Military lands (between Miss. and Ill. rivers). Cf. E 359.4.	.S3	Sangamon Co.
		.S4	Schuyler Co.
		.S6	Shelby Co.
.M7	Montgomery Co.	.S7	Stark Co.
.M8	Morgan Co.	.S8	Stephenson Co.
.M9	Moultrie Co.	.T2	Tazewell Co.
.O3	Ogle Co.	.V2	Vermilion Co.
.P4	Peoria Co.	.W12	Wabash Co.
.P5	Piatt Co.	.W14	Wabash River and Valley, Ill. Cf. F 532.W2.
.P6	Pike Co.		
.P8	Putnam Co.		
.R2	Randolph Co.	.W2	Warren Co.
.R5	Richland Co.	.W4	Whiteside Co.
.R6	Rock Island Co.	.W5	Will Co.
.R7	Rock River and Valley. Cf. F 587.R63.	.W6	Williamson Co.
		.W7	Winnebago Co.
.S2	St. Clair Co.	.W8	Woodford Co.

548   Chicago.   (Metropolis subdivisions.)

    .4   Before 1875.
         Fort Dearborn massacre 1812   E 356.C53.
    .42   1865–1875.   Great fire of 1871.
    .45   1875–1892.
    .5   1892–
         World's Columbian exposition   T.
    .67   Streets.
    .68   Suburbs.   Sections of the city.

.I7	Irving Park.	.W8	Wolf's Point.
.N	North Shore.	.W82	Woodlawn.

    .9   Topics.

.F8	French Canadians.
.N3	Negroes.

550   Topics.

.C3	Catholics.	.S2	Scandinavians.
.G3	Germans.	.S8	Swedes.
	Negro slavery E 445.I2.	.S9	Swiss.

551–556   The Lake Region.   Great Lakes.   Early French explorations.   British posts.   The portion of the northern boundary of the U. S. between the St. Lawrence River and Lake of the Woods.

       Physical geography   GB 1627.
       New France   F 1030.
       Old Northwest   F 476–485.

552   Lake Superior.

       Lake Superior region, Mich.   F 572.S9.
       Lake Superior region, Wis.   F 587.S9.
         Apostles Islands and Chequamegon Bay   F 587.A8.
       Lake Superior region, Minn.   F 612.S9.
       Lake Superior region, Ontario   F 1059.S9.
         Thunder Bay region   F 1059.T5.

Table of subdivisions (a), (b), (c), or (d) under each state may be found on pages 36–67.

551–556   The Lake Region.   Great Lakes—Continued.

553   Lake Michigan.

        Lake Michigan region, Ind.   F 532.M67.
        Lake Michigan region, Ill.   F 547.M56.
        Lake Michigan region, Mich.   F 572.M57.
        Lake Michigan region, Wis.   F 587.M57.
          Green Bay   F 587.G6.
        Mackinac straits and region   F 572.M16.

554   Lake Huron.

        Lake Huron region, Mich.   F 572.H92.
          Saginaw Bay   F 572.S15.
        Lake Huron region, Ontario   F 1059.H.
          Georgian Bay   F 1059.G3.
        Lake St. Clair   F 572.S34.

555   Lake Erie.

        Lake Erie region, N. Y.   F 127.E65.
        Niagara region   F 127.N6.
        Lake Erie region, Penn.   (Erie Co.)   F 157.E6.
        Lake Erie region, O.   F 497.E6.
          Western Reserve   F 497.W5.
        Lake Erie region, Ontario   F 1059.E6.

556   Lake Ontario.

        Lake Ontario region, N. Y.   F 127.O72.
        Lake Ontario region, Ontario   F 1059.O6.
        St. Lawrence River   F 1050.

561–575   Michigan (d).

        For early political history of this region see note under F 476. The present Michigan formed part of the original Northwest Territory in 1787; was divided in 1800, with its western part in Indiana Territory. 1803 the eastern part also was annexed to Indiana Territory. In 1805 the territory of Michigan was set off from Indiana, consisting at that time of the lower peninsula only (the upper peninsula continuing a part of Indiana Territory till the organization of Illinois Territory in 1809). 1818, on the admission of Illinois as a state, the northern portion of the former Illinois Territory (including the northern peninsula, all of Wis. and northeast Minn.) was added to Mich. In 1834, all the region west, bounded by Missouri, the Missouri River and the Canadian line, was annexed, including the rest of Minn., Iowa and parts of the Dakotas. This was followed by agitation for the erection of a new state east of Lake Michigan and the organization of the region west of that lake as a new territory. The matter was complicated by a controversy between O. and Mich. over their boundary, (the Toledo war). Congress took action by organizing Wisconsin Territory under an act approved April, 1836, and offering statehood to Mich. in June, 1836, on her acceptance of the northern peninsula in compensation for the tract in dispute with Ohio. Michigan, which had already organized a state government in 1835, accepted statehood on these terms in December, 1836.

Table of subdivisions (a), (b), (c), or (d) under each state may be found on pages 86–87.

561-575 Michigan—Continued.

566   General works. Periods.

Pontiac's war, 1763–1765   E 83.76.
Clark's campaign against Detroit, 1781   E 237.
Tippecanoe campaign, 1811   E 83.81.
Hull, William   E 353.1.H9.
War of 1812; military operations   E 355.
Cass, Lewis   E 340.C3.
Toledo war, 1836   F 497.B7.
Chandler, Zachariah   E 664.C4.
Civil war   E 514.
Williams, A. S.   E 467.1.W72.
War of 1898   E 726.M6.

572   Regions. Counties. Boundaries.

.A3	Allegan Co.	.K2	Kalamazoo Co.
.A4	Alpena Co.	.K3	Kent Co.
.B15	Baraga Co.	.L3	Lapeer Co.
.B2	Barry Co.	.L5	Lenawee Co.
.B3	Bay Co.	.L7	Little Traverse Bay region. Cf. F 572.G5.
.B36	Bean Creek Valley (Tiffin River), Mich.		
	Cf. F 497.B3.	.L8	Livingston Co.
.B5	Berrien Co.	.M14	Mackinac Co. Les Cheneaux Islands.
.B7	Boundaries.	.M16	Mackinac region. Straits
	Ohio boundary F 497 .B7.	.M2	Macomb Co.
		.M3	Manistee Co.
.B8	Branch Co.	.M33	Marquette Co.
.C2	Calhoun Co.	.M36	Mason Co.
.C3	Cass Co.	.M4	Mecosta Co.
.C5	Cheboygan Co.	.M5	Menominee Co.
.C7	Clinton Co.	.M52	Menominee River and Valley. Cf. F 587.M5.
.E2	Eaton Co.		
.G3	Genesee Co.	.M57	Lake Michigan region, Mich.
.G46	Grand River and Valley.		Cf. F 553.
.G5	Grand Traverse Bay region. The Traverse region. Cf. F 572.L7.	.M6	Midland Co.
		.M7	Monroe Co.
.G6	Grand Traverse Co.	.M8	Montcalm Co.
.G8	Gratiot Co.	.M9	Muskegon Co.
.G87	Green Bay region, Mich. Cf. F 587.G6.	.N5	Newaygo Co.
		.N8	Northern or Upper Peninsula.
.H6	Hillsdale Co.		
.H8	Houghton Co.	.O2	Oakland Co.
.H9	Huron Co.	.O3	Oceana Co.
.H92	Lake Huron region, Mich. Cf. F 554.	.O7	Osceola Co.
		.O8	Ottawa Co.
.I5	Ingham Co.	.S15	Saginaw Bay region.
.I6	Ionia Co.	.S17	Saginaw Co.
.I7	Isabella Co.	.S2	Saginaw River and Valley.
.J2	Jackson Co.	.S3	St. Clair Co.

Table of subdivisions (a), (b), (c) or (d) under each state may be found on pages 35–65.

561–575 Michigan.

572   Regions. Counties. Boundaries—Continued.

.S34	Lake St. Clair region.	.S9	Lake Superior region,
	Cf. F 1059.S3.		Mich.
.S4	St. Joseph Co.		Cf. F 552.
.S43	St. Joseph River and		Traverse region F 572.G5.
	Valley, Mich.	.T9	Tuscola Co.
	Cf. F 532.S3.	.V3	Van Buren Co.
.S5	Sanilac Co.	.W3	Washtenaw Co.
.S7	Shiawassee Co.	.W4	Wayne Co.

575   Topics.

.D9	Dutch.	.G3	Germans.
.F8	French Canadians.	.J5	Jews.

576–590 Wisconsin (c).

Explored by the French from New France. Ceded to Great Britain with other French territory east of the Mississippi, 1763, and annexed to Quebec 1774. Transferred to the U. S. by the peace of 1783 and included in Northwest Territory 1787, in Indiana Territory 1800, in Illinois Territory 1809, in Michigan Territory 1818. Wisconsin Territory was organized 1836, to include the modern states of Wis., Iowa and Minn. and eastern North and South Dakota. In 1838 the Territory of Iowa was set off, taking the region between the Mississippi and Missouri rivers. Wisconsin was admitted as a state with substantially its present limits, 1848 (the northwestern part of the territory forming part of Minnesota Territory organized 1849).

584   Before 1848. Biographies: Burnett, T. P.; etc.
         Jones, G. W.   E 415.9.J6.
         Martin, M. L.   F 586.M.
         Dodge, Henry   E 340.D7.

585   1836–1848. Wisconsin Territory.

586   1848– Biographies: Martin, M. L.; Hubbell. Levi; Hopkins, B. F.; etc.
         Dodge, Henry   E 340.D7.
         Carpenter, M. H.   E 664.C29.
         Schurz, Carl   E 664.S39.
         Civil war   E 537.
         Payne, H. C.   E 664.P34.

587   Regions. Counties. Boundaries.

.A2	Adams Co.	.C8	Crawford Co.
.A8	Ashland Co. Apostles	.D3	Dane Co.
	Islands. Chequamegon	.D6	Dodge Co.
	Bay.	.D7	Door Co.
.B7	Boundaries.	.F6	Fond du Lac Co.
.B9	Buffalo Co.	.F7	Fox River and Valley.
.C2	Calumet Co.	.G5	Grant Co.
.C5	Chippewa River and	.G6	Green Bay region.
	Valley.		Cf. F 572.G87.
.C6	Clark Co.	.G7	Green Co.
.C7	Columbia Co.	.G74	Green Lake Co.

Table of subdivisions (a), (b), (c), or (d) under each state may be found on pages 85–87.

576–590 **Wisconsin.**
   587 Regions. Counties. Boundaries—Continued.

.16	Iowa Co.	.P8	Portage Co.
.J2	Jackson Co.	.R2	Racine Co.
.J4	Jefferson Co.	.R4	Richland Co.
.J9	Juneau Co.	.R6	Rock Co.
.K3	Kenosha Co.	.R63	Rock River and Valley, Wis.
.K4	Kickapoo River and Valley.		Cf. F 547.R7.
.L14	La Crosse Co.	.S14	St. Croix River and Valley.
.L2	Lafayette Co.		Cf. F 612.S2.
.M2	Manitowoc Co.		
.M5	Menominee Valley, Wis.	.S2	Sauk Co.
	Cf. F 572.M52.	.S5	Sheboygan Co.
.M57	Lake Michigan region, Wis.	.S9	Lake Superior region, Wis.
			Cf. F 552.
	Cf. F 553.	.V5	Vernon Co.
.M6	Milwaukee Co.	.W18	Walworth Co.
.M63	Mississippi River and Valley, Wis.	.W2	Waukesha Co.
		.W3	Waupaca Co.
	Cf. F 351–354, 597.	.W5	Winnebago Co.
.M7	Monroe Co.	.W8	Wisconsin River and Valley. Dalles of the Wisconsin.
.P6	Pierce Co.		
.P7	Polk Co.		

   590 Topics.

.B4	Belgians.		Negro slavery E 445.W8.
.B8	British.	.S9	Swedes.
.G3	Germans.		

591–595 **The West. Trans-Mississippi region.**
        Mississippi River and Valley F 351–354.
        Louisiana (Province) F 372–373.
        The "Indian country," 1803–1854 F 697.
        The Northwest (Upper Mississippi Valley) F 597.
        Missouri River and Valley F 598.
        Rocky Mountains F 721.
        The Southwest F 799–800, 786.
        Pacific coast F 851.
        Pacific Northwest F 852.
        Indian wars (General) E 81.

   591 General works. History.
        Indians of the West E 78.W5.

   592 Before 1848. U. S. exploring expeditions: Lewis and Clark; Pike; Fremont, etc. Biographies: Pike, Z. M.; Carson, Christopher; etc.
        Spanish discoveries E 123.
           Vásquez de Coronado E 125.V3.
           Nuñez Cabeça de Vaca E 125.N9.
           Peñalosa F 799.P.
        Cibola F 799.
        Quivira F 799.

Table of subdivisions (a), (b), (c), or (d) under each state may be found on pages 55–57.

591–595   **The West.**

592   Before 1848—Continued.

New Mexico (Spanish and Mexican) F 799–800.

The Indian country (unsettled part of La. purchase, 1821–1854) F 697.

California F 864.

Texas F 390.

Mormons and Utah F 826.

Fremont, J. C. E 415.9.F8.

Oregon question F 880.

War with Mexico E 401–415.

Donner party F 868.N5.

Mexican cession of 1848 F 800, 864.

593   1848–1860. Later U. S. expeditions. Overland journeys to the Pacific. Biographies: Beale, E. F.; Gilpin, William; etc.

Wars with Pacific coast Indians, 1847–1865 E 83.84.

Texas cession of 1850 F 801.

Gadsden purchase F 786.

Spirit Lake massacre, 1857 E 83.857.

Mill Creek war, 1857–1865 E 83.858.

Fremont, J. C. E 415.9.F8.

Carson, Christopher F 592.C.

Warren, G. K. E 467.1.W4.

594   1860–1880. Biographies: Cody, W. F.; James, Frank; James, Jesse; Younger, Cole; etc.

Civil war, military operations E 470.9, 471–478.

Carson, Christopher F 592.C.

Dakota Indian war, 1862–1863 E 83.86.

Indian wars, 1863–1865 E 83.863.

Indian wars, 1863–1895 E 83.866.

Beecher Island battle, 1868 E 83.868.

Modoc war, 1872–1873 E 83.87.

Dakota Indian war, 1876 E 83.876.

Custer, G. A. E 467.1.C99.

Nez Percés war, 1877 E 83.877.

Ute war, 1879 E 83.879.

595   1880–

Dodge, G. M. E 467.1.D6.

Indian wars, 1866–1895 E 83.866.

Apache war, 1883–1886 E 83.88.

Dakota Indian war, 1890–1891 E 83.89.

597   **The Northwest.** Upper Mississippi Valley. Sources of the Mississippi. Northern boundary of the U. S. (from Lake of the Woods to Rocky Mountains).

Old Northwest F 476–485.

Pacific Northwest F 852.

Canadian Northwest F 1060.

Indians of the Northwest E 78.N8.

Lake Itasca and park F 612.I8.

598   **Missouri River and Valley.**

Table of subdivisions (a), (b), (c), or (d) under each state may be found on pages 85–87.

601-615 **Minnesota** (d).

The entire state was visited by explorers in the 17th century and embraced in French Louisiana. That portion west of the Mississippi was ceded to Spain in 1762 and shared in the fortunes of Louisiana till the latter was purchased by the U. S. from France in 1803. The eastern part was ceded to Great Britain 1763, annexed to Quebec 1774, surrendered to the U. S. by treaty in 1783, and formed part of the Northwest Territory 1787. It belonged to Indiana Territory 1800-1809, Illinois Territory 1809-1818, Michigan Territory, 1818-1836. In the meantime, the western part of the present state of Minnesota had been included in Louisiana District (later Territory) 1804-1812, Missouri Territory 1812-1821, and after latter date in the unsettled northwestern residue of the Louisiana purchase usually known as the "Indian country." In 1834, so much of the region as lay east of the Missouri River was added to Michigan Territory. In 1836 Minnesota was included in the new Wisconsin Territory. Two years later it was divided on the old Mississippi River line, the western part being set off to Iowa Territory. 1849 Minnesota Territory was organized consisting of the present state, and the Dakotas, east of the Missouri River. It was admitted as a state 1858 with substantially its present limits.

606   General works.   Periods.
Civil war E 515.
Dakota Indian war, 1862-1863   E 83.86.
War of 1898   E 726.M7.

612   Regions.   Counties.   Boundaries.

.A6	Anoka Co.		.M9	Mower Co.
.B7	Boundaries.		.N7	Nobles Co.
	International boundary		.O5	Olmsted Co.
	F 597.		.P7	Polk Co.
.D2	Dakota Co.		.R2	Ramsey Co.
.F2	Faribault Co.		.R27	Red River of the North and
.F4	Fillmore Co.			Valley (in the U. S.).
.G6	Goodhue Co.			Cf. F 642.R3; F1064.R3.
.H5	Hennepin Co. Lake Minnetonka.		.R3	Redwood Co.
			.R5	Rice Co.
.H8	Houston Co.		.R7	Rock Co.
.I8	Itasca Lake. State park.		.S2	St. Croix River and Valley, Minn.
.J2	Jackson Co.			
.K2	Kandiyohi Co.			Cf. F 587.S14.
.L9	Lyon Co.		.S8	Steele Co.
.M3	Meeker Co.		.S9	Lake Superior region, Minn.
.M4	Minnesota River and Valley.			
				Cf. F 552.
.M5	Mississippi River and Valley, Minn.		.W17	Waseca Co.
			.W2	Washington Co.
	Cf. F 351-354, 597.		.W7	Winona Co.

614   Towns and cities.
.M5   Minneapolis.
.M6   "The twin cities," Minneapolis and St. Paul.
.S4   St. Paul.

615   Topics.
.S9   Swedes.   .W4   Welsh.

Table of subdivisions (a), (b), (c), or (d) under each state may be found on pages 86-87.

616-630   Iowa (d).

Part of the province of Louisiana down to 1805. (See note under F 366.) Included in District (later Territory) of Louisiana 1804–1812, Missouri Territory 1812–1821 and after latter date, in the unsettled residue of the Louisiana purchase, usually known as the "Indian country." In 1834 it was annexed to Michigan Territory with the rest of the region between the Mississippi and Missouri Rivers, and 1836 formed part of the new Wisconsin Territory. In 1838 Iowa Territory was created, including Minnesota west of the Mississippi and the eastern part of the Dakotas as well as modern Iowa. The state of Iowa was admitted 1846, with substantially its present limits (after a territorial convention had refused to accept an act of admission passed by Congress in 1845 which left out the western third of the present state and included a section now part of southeast Minn.). The remainder of the territory, with adjacent part of old Wisconsin Territory, was organized as the territory of Minnesota in 1849.

621   General works. Periods. Biographies: Lucas, Robert; Chambers, John; etc.

Grimes, J. W.   E 415.9.G85.
Dodge, A. C.   E 415.9.D68.
Jones, G. W.   E 415.9.J6.
Harlan, James   E 664.H27.
Grinnell, J. B.   E 415.9.G86.
Spirit Lake massacre, 1857   E 83.857.
Dodge, G. M.   E 467.1.D6.
Civil war   E 507.
Henderson, D. B.   E 664.H48.
War of 1898   E 726.I4.

627   Regions. Counties. Boundaries.

.A2	Adair Co.	.C8	Crawford Co.
.A6	Appanoose Co.	.D14	Dallas Co.
.A8	Audubon Co.	.D2	Davis Co.
.B4	Benton Co.	.D26	Decatur Co.
.B5	Big Sioux River and Valley, Ia.	.D3	Delaware Co.
		.D4	Des Moines Co.
	Cf. F 657.B5.	.D43	Des Moines River and Valley.
.B6	Black Hawk Co.		
.B67	Boone Co.		Cf. F 472.D4.
.B7	Boundaries.	.D5	Dickinson Co. Spirit Lake.
	Missouri boundary F 472.B7.		Cf. E 83.857.
.B8	Bremer Co.	.D8	Dubuque Co.
.B9	Butler Co.	.F2	Fayette Co.
.C25	Carroll Co.	.F5	Floyd Co.
.C3	Cass Co.	.F8	Fremont Co.
.C4	Cedar Co.	.G7	Greene Co.
.C5	Chickasaw Co.	.G75	Grundy Co.
.C54	Clay Co.	.G8	Guthrie Co.
.C56	Clayton Co.	.H3	Hardin Co.
.C6	Clinton Co.	.H5	Henry Co.

Table of subdivisions (a), (b), (c), or (d) under each state may be found on pages 85-87.

616–630 Iowa.

  627   Regions. Counties. Boundaries—Continued.

.H7	Howard Co.		.M8	Monroe Co.
.H8	Humboldt Co.		.M83	Montgomery Co.
.I2	Ida Co.		.M9	Muscatine Co.
.J2	Jackson Co.		.O2	O'Brien Co.
.J3	Jasper Co.		.O6	Osceola Co.
.J4	Jefferson Co.		.P2	Page Co.
.J6	Johnson Co.		.P3	Palo Alto Co.
.J7	Jones Co.		.P5	Plymouth Co.
.K3	Keokuk Co.		.P6	Pocahontas Co.
.L4	Lee Co.		.P7	Polk Co.
.L7	Linn Co.		.P8	Pottawatamie Co.
.L8	Louisa Co.		.R5	Ringgold Co.
.L9	Lyon Co.		.S2	Sac Co.
.M13	Madison Co.		.S4	Scott Co.
.M2	Mahaska Co.		.S5	Shelby Co.
.M3	Marion Co.		.S8	Story Co.
.M4	Marshall Co.		.U5	Union Co.
.M6	Mills Co.		.V2	Van Buren Co.
.M64	Mississippi River and Valley, Ia.		.W2	Wapello Co.
	Cf. F 351–354, 597.		.W25	Warren Co.
			.W3	Webster Co.
.M66	Missouri River and Valley, Ia.		.W7	Winneshiek Co.
			.W8	Woodbury Co.
	Cf. F 596.		.W86	Worth Co.
.M7	Mitchell Co.			

  630   Topics.

.D9	Dutch.		J5	Jews.
.G3	Germans.		.S3	Scandinavians.

631–645 North Dakota (d).

      The northern part of Dakota Territory, admitted as a state 1889.
      See note under South Dakota, F 646–660.

  636   General works. Periods.

      Dakota Territory F 655.

  642   Regions. Counties. Boundaries.

.B7	Boundaries.		.R3	Red River of the North and Valley, N. D.
	International boundary F 597.			Cf. F 612.R27; F 1064
.B9	Burleigh Co.			.R3.
.M6	Missouri River and Valley, N. D.		.R5	Richland Co.
	Cf. F 596.			

Table of subdivisions (a), (b), (c), or (d) under each state may be found on pages 86–87.

646–660 South Dakota (c).

The old Dakota Territory was a part of the Louisiana purchase 1803; included in the Louisiana District (later Territory) 1804–1812, Missouri Territory 1812–1834. In 1834, so much as lay east of the Missouri River was annexed to Michigan Territory, included in Wisconsin Territory 1836–1838, Iowa Territory 1838–1849, Minnesota Territory 1849–1858. Meanwhile the part of modern Dakota west of the Missouri remained part of the unorganised "Indian country" till 1854, when it was included in the new territory of Nebraska. In 1861 the territory of Nebraska was reduced in size and the northern part, with the part of old Minnesota Territory not admitted as a state in 1858, organised as Dakota Territory. This was greatly reduced in size by the creation of Idaho Territory in 1863. Divided in 1889 and admitted to the union as North and South Dakota.

655 The Dakota region before 1861. Dakota Territory 1861–1889.

Indian wars 1863–1865   E 83.863.

656 1889–   State of South Dakota.

Dakota Indian war, 1890–1891   E 83.89.

657 Regions.   Counties.   Boundaries.

.B5	Big Sioux River and Valley.	.M6	Minnehaha Co.
	Cf. F 627.B5.	.M7	Missouri River and Valley, S. D.
.B6	Black Hills.		Cf. F 598.
.B7	Boundaries.	.P8	Potter Co.
.C9	Custer Co.	.W7	Wind cave. Wind cave national park.
	Cf. F 657.W7.		
.H8	Hughes Co.	.Y2	Yankton Co.

661–675 Nebraska. (d).

The entire state was embraced in the old province of Louisiana, purchased by the U. S. 1803. It formed part of the District (later Territory) of Louisiana 1804–1812, and part of Missouri Territory 1812–1821, and after 1821 constituted part of the unorganised region usually known as the "Indian country." In 1854 Nebraska Territory was organised to include the northern part of this region, containing, besides the modern Nebraska, the western parts of the Dakotas, Montana, Wyoming, and part of Colorado. 1861 the northern part was set off as Dakota Territory, and 1863 the western part of the remainder was added to the new Idaho Territory. Nebraska was admitted to the union in 1867, with substantially its present limits.

666 General works.   Periods.

Kansas-Nebraska bill, 1854   E 433.

Table of subdivisions (a), (b), (c), or (d) under each state may be found on pages 85–87.

661–675 **Nebraska—Continued.**
672   Regions.   Counties.   Boundaries.

.B6	Boone Co.	.M6	Missouri River and Valley, Neb.
.B7	Boundaries.		Cf. F 598.
.B85	Buffalo Co.		
.B9	Butler Co.	.N8	North Platte River and Valley. Cf. F 767.N8.
.C3	Cass Co.		
.C6	Clay Co.	.O8	Otoe Co.
.C9	Custer Co.	.P3	Pawnee Co.
.D6	Dodge Co.	.P5	Phelps Co.
.F9	Furnas Co.	.P6	Platte River and Valley.
J6	Johnson Co.	.P7	Polk Co.
.K7	Knox Co.	.S2	Sarpy Co.
.L2	Lancaster Co.	.S5	Seward Co.
.L8	Loup River and Valley.	.S7	South Platte River and Valley. Cf. F 782.S7.

676–690 **Kansas.** (c).

Nearly all of Kansas belonged to the Louisiana purchase of 1803. It was included in the District (later Territory) of Louisiana 1804–1812, part of Missouri Territory 1812–1821 and after 1821 formed part of the unorganized region usually known as the "Indian country." In 1854 the Kansas-Nebraska bill was passed, and Kansas Territory was organized, consisting of the present Kansas and a portion of Colorado (the southwestern portion of modern Kansas being a part of the territory purchased by the U. S. from Texas 1850). In 1861 Kansas was admitted as a state, with substantially its present limits, the western portion of the former territory forming part of the new territory of Colorado the same year.

685   Before 1860.   Struggle between pro-slavery and anti-slavery parties.   New England emigrant aid company.   Armed bands from Missouri.   Lecompton constitution.   Biographies: Robinson, Charles; Lane, J. H.; etc.

Quivira F 799.
Kansas-Nebraska bill, 1854 E 433.
Pomeroy, S. C. E 415.9.P78.
Geary, J. W. E 467.1.G29.
Walker, R. J. E 415.9.W2.
Brown, John E 451.

686   1860–

Pomeroy, S. C. E 415.9 P78.
Robinson, Charles F 685.R.
Ingalls, J. J. E 664.I4.
Civil war E 508.
  Military operations E 470.9,471–478.
  Quantrill's raid, 1863 E 474.97.
War of 1898 E 726.K2.

Table of subdivisions (a), (b), (c), or (d) under each state may be found on pages 36–37.

676–690   Kansas—Continued.
  687   Regions.   Counties.   Boundaries.

.A4	Allen Co.	.L4	Leavenworth Co.
.A7	Arkansas River and Val-ley, Kan. Cf. F 417.A7.	.L7	Lincoln Co.
		.M6	Missouri River and Valley, Kan. Cf. F 598.
.B2	Barton Co.		
.B5	Big Blue River. Blue Val-ley.	.M7	Montgomery Co.
		.N3	Nemaha Co.
.B7	Boundaries.	.N4	Ness Co.
.B8	Brown Co.	.N8	Norton Co.
.C5	Cheyenne Co.	.P8	Pottawatomie Co.
.C6	Cloud Co.	.R4	Republic Co.
.D6	Doniphan Co.	.R5	Riley Co.
.D7	Douglas Co.	.R7	Rooks Co.
.E3	Ellis Co.	.S4	Sedgwick Co.
.E4	Ellsworth Co.	.S5	Shawnee Co.
.G3	Geary Co. (formerly Davis Co.)	.S9	Sumner Co.
		.W2	Wabaunsee Co.
.L2	Labette Co.		

  690   Topics.
              .82 Scandinavians.

691–705   Oklahoma (a).

All of the present state of Oklahoma, except the westernmost strip, was included in the Louisiana purchase 1803. It formed part of the District (later Territory) of Louisiana 1804–1812, and territory of Missouri 1812–1819. In 1819 it was included in the new Arkansas Territory, but by acts of Congress in 1824 and 1828 was detached from Arkansas and thenceforth formed part of the Indian country, or the unsettled region west of Arkansas and Missouri. It was not till after the close of the civil war that the government succeeded in bringing to it all the Indian tribes destined to occupy the territory; no territorial government in the ordinary sense was granted. In 1890 the northwestern part, having been purchased by the government from its Indian owners, was organized as Oklahoma Territory; No-man's land, north of Texas and west of 100° being added to the new territory. Meanwhile the Indian Territory continued its existence till the two territories were reunited and admitted as the state of Oklahoma in 1907.

  696   Antiquities.
              Indians of Indian Territory and Oklahoma E 78.O45.
              The Five civilized tribes (collectively) E 78.I5.

  697   The "Indian country" (that part of the Louisiana pur-
              chase, west of Ark., Mo. and the Missouri River).
              Indian Territory before division in 1890.

  698   Indian Territory, 1890–1907.

  699   Oklahoma Territory, 1890–1907.

  700   1907- State of Oklahoma.

Table of subdivisions (a), (b), (c), or (d) under each state may be found on pages 86–87.

691–705   **Oklahoma—Continued.**

702   **Regions. Counties. Boundaries.**

.A7   Arkansas River and Valley, Okl.
     Cf. F 417.A7.

.B7   Boundaries.
     Colorado boundary F 782.B7.
     Texas boundary F 392.B7.

.C2   Canadian River and Valley. Cf. F 802.C2.

.M84   Murray Co.
     Cf. F 377.R3.
     Cf. F 702.P7.

.M9   Muskogee Co.

.N8   Noble Co. Otoe and Missouria reservation.

.P7   Platt national park.

.R3   Red River and Valley, Okl.

721   **Rocky Mountains. Rocky Mountains in the U. S.**
Rocky Mountain region of Col., etc. F 782.R6, etc.
Rocky Mountain region, Canada F 1090.

722   **Yellowstone national park. Its boundaries.**
Yellowstone River F 737.Y4.

726–740   **Montana (d).**

The greater part of Montana belonged to the Louisiana purchase 1803; the western portion being part of the Oregon country (for many years in dispute between Gt. Brit. and U. S. and organised as the Territory of Oregon 1846–48). The former and larger part was included in the District (later Territory) of Louisiana 1804–1821, in the "Indian country" 1821–1854, Nebraska Territory 1854–1861, Dakota Territory 1861–1863. In 1863 the Territory of Idaho was organised, including the western parts of Dakota and Nebraska territories, and the eastern part of Washington Territory (the present Montana, Wyoming and Idaho) The Territory of Montana was organized 1864 with substantially its present limits; and admitted as a state 1889.

731   **General works. Periods.**
Meagher, T. F.   E 467.1.M4.
Dakota Indian war, 1876   E 83.876.
Nez Percés war, 1877   E 83.877.

737   **Regions. Counties. Boundaries.**

.B6   Bitter Root River and Valley.

.B7   Boundaries.
     International boundary F 597.
     Idaho boundary F752.B7.
     Yellowstone national park boundary F 722.

.C5   Chouteau Co.

.C8   Crow Indian reservation.

.C9   Custer Co.

.F3   Fergus Co.

.G2   Gallatin Valley. East and West Gallatin rivers.

.G5   Glacier national park, Lake McDonald.

.J6   Jocko or Flathead Indian reservation.

.M2   Madison Co.

.M6   Missoula Co.

.M7   Missouri River and Valley, Mont.
     Cf. F 598.

.R8   Rocky Mountain region, Mont.
     Cf. F 721.

.Y4   Yellowstone River and Valley.
     Cf. F 722.

Table of subdivisions (a), (b), (c), or (d) under each state may be found on pages 55–57.

741–755   Idaho (d).

> The present state of Idaho was a part of the Oregon country, jointly occupied by Gt. Brit. and U. S.; divided between the two countries, and the American portion organized as Oregon Territory 1846–1848. On the formation of Washington Territory in 1853, the northern part of Idaho was included in it, and on the admission of Oregon as a state in 1859, the remainder of the present Idaho was annexed to Washington Territory. In 1863 the Territory of Idaho was organized from portions of the territories of Nebraska, Dakota and Washington, so as to include what is now Idaho, Montana and Wyoming. Montana Territory was cut off in 1864 and Wyoming Territory in 1868. Idaho was admitted as a state 1890.

746   General works. Periods.

> Nes Percés war, 1877   E 83.877.

752   Regions. Counties. Boundaries.

.B6   Bingham Co.

.B67   Boise Co.

.B7   Boundaries.
> International boundary F 597, 880.
> Washington boundary F 897.B7.
> Yellowstone national park boundary F 722.

.F8   Fremont Co.

.I2   Idaho Co.

.K8   Kootenai Co.
> Cf. F 752.S5.

.S5   Shoshone Co. Coeur d'Alene mining district.

.S7   Snake River and Valley.
> Cf. F 882.S6; F 897.S6.
> Yellowstone national park F 722.

756–770   Wyoming (d).

> The east and northeast parts (about two thirds of the area) of the present state of Wyoming formed a part of the Louisiana purchase of 1803. This was included in the District (later Territory) of Louisiana 1804–1812, in Missouri Territory 1812–1821, in the "Indian country" 1821–1854, and Territory of Nebraska 1854. The western part of Wyoming was part of the Oregon country (cf. note under F 871) and the southwest a part of the Mexican cession of 1848 (cf. note under F 791) while a small area in the south belonged to the Texas cession of 1850. In 1863 all the territory of which Wyoming is composed, previously belonging to the territories of Nebraska, Dakota, Washington and Utah, was included in the new Idaho Territory. Wyoming was organized as a separate territory in 1868 and admitted as a state in 1890.

761   General works. Periods.

> Ute war, 1879   E 83.879.

767   Regions. Counties. Boundaries.

.B7   Boundaries.
> Yellowstone national park boundary F 722.

.F8   Fremont Co.

.N8   North Platte River and Valley, Wy.
> Cf. F 672.N8.

.U3   Uinta Co. Jackson's Lake.
> Yellowstone national park F 722.

Table of subdivisions (a), (b), (c), or (d) under each state may be found on pages 95–97.

771–785   Colorado (c).

> The present state of Colorado includes territory from three sources: the Louisiana purchase of 1803, the Mexican cession of 1848 and the Texas purchase of 1850. It was organised as a territory in 1861 from parts of the territories of Kansas, Nebraska, Utah and New Mexico, and admitted as a state 1876.

780   Before 1876.   Biographies: Hall, B. F.; etc.

> Gilpin, William   F 593.G.
>
> Battle of Beecher Island, 1868   E 83.868.

781   1876—

> Ute Indian war, 1879   E 83.879.

782   Regions.   Counties.   Boundaries.

.A7	Arkansas River and Valley, Col. Cf. F 417.A7.	.L3	Las Animas Co.
		.M5	Mesa Co.
.B7	Boundaries.	.M52	Mesa Verde National Park.
.B8	Boulder Co.	.M7	Montezuma Co. Mancos River and Valley.
.C6	Clear Creek Co.		
.C8	Costilla Co. Sangre de Cristo grant.	.M8	Montrose Co. Uncompahgre Valley.
		.O6	Otero Co.
.E3	El Paso Co. Manitou. Crystal Park. Stratton Park.	.P9	Pueblo Co.
		.R6	Rocky Mountain region, Col. Cf. F 721.
.F8	Fremont Co.		
.G7	Grand River and Valley, Col. Cf. F 832.G6.	.S18	San Juan Mountains.
		.S2	San Luis Park. Cf. F 782.C8.
.G9	Gunnison Co.	.S7	South Platte River and Valley, Col. Cf. F 672.S7.
.J4	Jefferson Co.		
.L3	Larimer Co. Estes Park		

785   Topics.

.D9	Dutch.	.W4	Welsh.

786   The New Southwest (since 1848).   The region of the Mexican cession of 1848, the Texas purchase of 1850 and the Gadsden purchase of 1853. Mexican boundary. Santa Fe trail. The Gadsden purchase. Frontier troubles with Mexico.

> Accounts of this region before 1848   F 799–800.
>
> Mexican war   E 401–415.
>
> Mexican frontier troubles (General)   F 1232–1234.
>
> Civil war, military operations   E 470.9, 471–478.

788   Colorado River, Cañon and Valley.

791–805 **New Mexico (c).**

> A part of the province of New Spain and later empire and republic
> of Mexico down to 1836, when the eastern part was included in
> Texas and won its independence. The remainder was transferred
> to the U. S. by purchase in 1848, as a result of the Mexican war.
> This cession included the whole of California, Utah, Nevada, and
> parts of Arizona, New Mexico, Colorado and Wyoming. In 1850
> the part of Texas northwest of its present limits was purchased from
> that state by the U. S. and from the whole of this former Mexican
> territory, the two territories of New Mexico and Utah and the state
> of California were formed the same year. In 1853 the Gadsden
> purchase was added to the first named. New Mexico, as thus
> organized, included the whole of the present New Mexico and
> Arizona, the southern extremity of Nevada and part of southern
> Colorado. The formation of the territory of Colorado in 1861,
> the territory of Arizona in 1863 and the state of Nevada in
> 1864–66 reduced New Mexico to its present limits. Admitted as
> a state 1912.

799   **Before 1822. Spanish discoveries and settlements in
the Southwest between the Mississippi River and
California. Cibola. Quivira. Nuevo Mexico. Spanish province. Peñalosa.**

> Vásquez de Coronado E 125.V3.
> Núñez Cabeza de Vaca E 125.N9.
> General works on the Spaniards in North America F 1410.

800   **1822–1848. Mexican state. The region between Texas
and California.**

> Texas F 389.
> Santa Fe trail F 786.
> Utah F 826.
> Texan Santa Fe expedition, 1841 F 390.
> Conquest by U. S. troops E 405.2.

801   1848– **Purchase of northwest Texas by U. S., 1850.**

> The New Southwest since 1848 F 786.
> Compromise of 1850 E 423.
> Gadsden purchase F 786.
> Civil war E 522.
>   Confederate E 571.
>   Military operations E 470.9, 471–478.
> Apache war, 1883–1886 E 83.88.

Table of subdivisions (a), (b), (c), or (d) under each state may be found on pages 86–87.

791–805 New Mexico—Continued.

    802   Regions. Counties. Boundaries.

.B5	Bernalillo Co.	.L7	Lincoln Co.
.B7	Boundaries.	.L9	Luna Co.
	International boundary	.P3	Pecos River and Valley,
	F 786.		N. M.
	Texas boundary F 392		Cf. F 392.P3.
	.B7.	.Q2	Quay Co.
	Colorado boundary	.R5	Rio Grande River and Val-
	F 782.B7.		ley, N. M.
.C2	Canadian River and Val-		Cf. F 392.R5.
	ley, N. M.	.S18	San Juan Co.
	Cf. F 702.C2.	.S2	San Miguel Co.
.C5	Chaves Co.	.S3	Sandoval Co.
.C7	Colfax Co.	.S4	Santa Fe Co.
.D6	Doña Ana Co.	.S5	Sierra Co.
.E2	Eddy Co.	.S6	Socorro Co.
.G9	Guadalupe Co. (1903–1904	.T2	Taos Co.
	named Leonard Wood		Cf. F 782.C2.
	Co.)		

806–820   Arizona (d).

          For early ownership and transfers of this region see note under New Mexico (F 791.) Arizona was cut off from New Mexico and organ- ized as a separate territory in 1863. The following year it was reduced to present limits by the transfer of its northern extremity to Nevada. Admitted as a state 1912.

    811   General works. Periods.

          Gadsden purchase F 786.

          Fremont, J. C. E 415.9.F8.

          Apache war, 1883–1886 E 83.86.

    817   Regions. Counties. Boundaries.

.B7	Boundaries.	.P5	Pima Co. Quijotoa Moun-
	International boundary		tains.
	F 786.	.P6	Pinal Co.
.C7	Colorado River, Cañon	.S2	Salt River and Valley.
	and Valley, Ariz.	.Y3	Yavapai Co.
	Cf. F 786.	.Y9	Yuma Co. Mohawk Val-
.M3	Maricopa Co.		ley.

Table of subdivisions (a), (b), (c), or (d) under each state may be found on pages 65–67.

821–835   Utah (d).

> The entire territory comprising the state of Utah was Spanish and Mexican property till embraced in the Mexican cession of 1848. The Mormons had settled this region in 1847 and two years later formed the state of Deseret, which, however, was not recognized. The Territory of Utah as organized in 1850 included not only the modern Utah but parts of Wyoming and Colorado on the east, and on the west all of Nevada except the southern extremity. It was reduced in size in 1861, by the formation of Colorado Territory, the extension of Nebraska Territory westward, and the formation of Nevada Territory on the west. It was reduced to present limits by the cutting out of the northeast corner on formation of territory of Idaho in 1863 and the admission of the state of Nevada on the west in 1864, with boundary line moved eastward to the 115th and later to the 114th meridian. Utah was admitted as a state in 1896.

826   General works. Mormon settlement. State of Deseret. Mountain Meadows massacre. Mormon rebellion, 1857–1859.

> Mormon church and Mormonism   B.
> Compromise of 1850   E 423.
> Johnston, A. S.   E 467.1.J73.
> Smoot, Reed   E 664.S66.

832   Regions. Counties. Boundaries.

.B7	Boundaries.	.G7	Great Salt Lake region.
.B8	Boxelder Co. Bear River and Valley.	.S2	Sanpete Co.
		.U4	Uintah Co.
.C7	Colorado River and Valley, Utah.		Cf. F 832.U5.
	Cf. F 788.	.U5	Uncompahgre Indian reservation.
.E5	Emery Co.		
.G6	Grand River and Valley.		
	Cf. F 782.G7.		

836–850   Nevada (d).

> Under Mexico, this region was considered a part of Upper California. Ceded to the U. S. 1848, as a result of the Mexican war. On the division of the cession in 1850 all but the southern extremity of the present state of Nevada fell within the new territory of Utah. In 1861 Nevada Territory was organized. It was admitted as a state in 1864, receiving an extension to the east to the 115th meridian at the expense of Utah. Two years later the eastern line was moved still farther to the 114th meridian and the part of the modern Nevada south of 37° added at the expense of Arizona.

841   General works. Periods.

847   Regions. Counties. Boundaries.

Table of subdivisions (a), (b), (c), or (d) under each state may be found on pages 85–87.

851   **The Pacific states.**   Pacific coast of North America.

> Indians of the Pacific states   E 78.P2.
> Wars with the Pacific coast Indians, 1847–1865   E 83.84.

.5   Exploring expeditions to the Pacific coast before 1769. Early accounts.

> Cabrillo   E 125.C12.
> Drake   E 129.D7.
> Explorations since 1769   F 864, F 850, F 1088, F 907.

852   **The Pacific Northwest** (Washington, Oregon, Idaho, Montana) since 1859.

> The region before 1769   F 851.5.
>   1769–1859   F 880.
> Indians of the Pacific Northwest   E 78.N77.

853   Columbia River and Valley.

854   Northwest boundary of the U. S. (Rocky Mountains to Pacific) since 1846.

> Boundary controversy previous to 1846   F 880.
> Pickett, G. E.   E 467.1.P57.

856–870   **California** (c).

> A part of the Spanish colony of New Spain and later empire and republic of Mexico. It was the "Upper California" of the Mexicans, first settled about 1769. American settlers declared their independence of Mexico about the same time that expeditions arrived from the east in connection with the Mexican war. The whole region was embraced in the Mexican cession of 1848. California was admitted as a state in 1850.

864   Before 1869. Spanish explorers after 1769. Spanish California, including Lower and Upper California. Indian missions. American and European intrigues before 1846. Fremont in California, 1846. Bear flag war, 1846. Biographies: Terry, D. S., etc.

> Explorations before 1769   F 851.5.
> Old Spanish mission buildings now standing   F 870.M6.
> Lower California   F 1246.
> Nootka Sound controversy, 1789–1790   F 1089.N8.
> Fremont, J. C.   E 415.9.F8.
> American military conquest, 1846   E 405.2.
> Sloat, J. D.   E 403.1.S6.
> Kearney, S. W.   E 403.1.K2.
> Halleck, H. W.   E 467.1.H18.
> Donner party   F 868.N5.
> Wars with Pacific coast Indians, 1847–1865   E 83.84.
> Broderick, D. C.   E 415.9.B84.
> Geary, J. W.   E 467.1.G29.

Table of subdivisions (a), (b), (c), or (d) under each state may be ound on pages 86–87.

856–870   **California.**

864   **Before 1869—Continued.**
> Field, S. J.   E 664.F46.
> Baker, E. D.   E 467.1.B16.
> Beale, E. F.   F 593.B.
> Question of admission; Compromise of 1850   E 423.
> Mill Creek war, 1857–1865   E 83.858.
> Civil war   E 497.

865   **1848–1856. Gold discoveries. Argonauts. Voyages to Cal. by the Cape Horn or Central American isthmus routes. Vigilance committees. Biographies: Sutter, J. A.; etc.**
> Overland journeys from the east   F 593

866   **1869–**
> Modoc war, 1872–1873   E 83.87.
> War of 1898   E 726.C1.

867   **Southern California.**
> Early Spanish missions   F 864.
> Spanish mission buildings   F 870.M6.

868   **Other regions. Counties. Boundaries.**

.A3	Alameda Co. Livermore Valley.	.L2	Lake Co.
.A4	Amador Co.	.L8	Los Angeles Co. Mount Lowe. San Antonio Cañon. Monica Bay region. Santa Catalina Island. Cf. F 868.S232.
.B7	Boundaries.		
.B8	Butte Co.		
.C14	Calaveras big tree national forest.		
.C16	Calaveras Co.	.M3	Marin Co.
.C6	Colorado River and Valley, Cal. Cf. F 788.	.M4	Mariposa Co. Fremont land grant.
		.M5	Mendocino Co.
.C7	Colusa Co.	.M7	Monterey Co.
.C76	Contra Costa Co.	.N2	Napa Co.
.D4	Del Norte Co.	.N5	Nevada Co. Donner Lake. Donner party.
.E3	El Dorado Co.		
.F3	Feather River and Valley.	.O6	Orange Co.
		.P7	Placer Co.
.F8	Fresno Co. Panoche Grande rancho (Gomez-McGarrahan claim).	.R6	Riverside Co. Coachella Valley.
		.S12	Sacramento Co.
.G3	General Grant national park.	.S13	Sacramento River and Valley.
.G5	Glenn Co.	.S136	San Benito Co. San Juan Valley.
.H8	Humboldt Co.		
.I6	Inyo Co. Death Valley.	.S14	San Bernardino Co. Bear Valley. Ontario colony.
.K3	Kern Co.		
.K5	Kings Co.		

Table of subdivisions (a), (b), (c), or (d) under each state may be found on pages 86–87.

856-870 California.

868   Other regions. Counties. Boundaries—Continued.

.815   San Diego Co. Colorado Desert. Escondido Valley. Imperial Valley.

.8156   San Francisco Bay region.

.817   San Joaquin Co.

.8173   San Joaquin River and Valley.

.818   San Luis Obispo Co.

.819   San Mateo Co.

.822   Santa Ana River and Valley.

.823   Santa Barbara Co.
      Cf. F 868.8232.

.8232   Santa Barbara Islands (Channel Islands) collectively. The individual islands belong to Santa Barbara, Ventura and Los Angeles cos.

.825   Santa Clara Co. Santa Clara Valley.

.83   Santa Cruz Co. California redwood park.

.84   Sequoia national park.

.849   Shasta Co.

.8495   Shasta Mountains.

.85   Sierra Nevada Mountains. (Donner party F 868 .N5.)

.86   Siskiyou Co. Butte Valley.

.866   Solano Co.

.87   Sonoma Co.

.88   Stanislaus Co.

.89   Sutter Co.

.T3   Tehama Co.

.T8   Tulare Co. Mt. Whitney. Cf. F 868.84.

.T9   Tuolumne Co. Cf. F 868.C14.

.V5   Ventura Co.

.Y6   Yosemite national park. Yosemite Valley.

.Y8   Yuba Co.

870   Topics.

.C5   Chinese.

.F8   French.

.I6   Irish.

.J3   Japanese.

.M6   Mission buildings.

.P8   Portuguese.

871-885 Oregon (c).

The "Oregon country" in the later 18th and early 19th century comprised the region between New Spain (Upper California) and Russian America (Alaska); from 42° to 54° 40'. Both Spanish and British claimed it by right of discovery and exploration. In 1792 Capt. Gray explored the Columbia River, laying the basis of the American claim. In 1818 a treaty of joint occupation between the U. S. and Gt. Brit. was made. The Spanish treaty of 1819 (Florida treaty) also surrendered to the U. S. all Spanish claim to the Pacific coast above 42°. The joint occupancy of the two countries was terminated in 1846 by agreement to divide the territory on the line of 49° and the Straits of Fuca. The territory of Oregon was organized 1848, consisting of all the region north of 42° not included in the old Louisiana purchase (Oregon, Washington and Idaho and parts of Montana and Wyoming). The northern part of the region was organized as Washington Territory in 1853, and when Oregon was admitted as a state in 1859, the eastern part of Oregon Territory was added temporarily to Washington Territory.

Table of subdivisions (a), (b), (c), or (d) under each state may be found on pages 35-67.

871–885   Oregon—Continued.
     879   Before 1792.

> Exploration of the coast before 1769   F 851.5.
> Explorations in the Canadian Northwest   F 1060.7.
> Nootka Sound controversy, 1789–1790   F 1089.N8.

     880   1792–1859.   The Oregon country.   Joint occupation. The Oregon question. Northwest boundary to 1846. Biographies: Whitman, Marcus; Applegate, Jesse; etc.

> The northern part of the Oregon country since 1846 (British Columbia)   F 1086–1089.
> Hudson's Bay company   F 1060.
> Lewis and Clark expedition   F 592.L.
> International boundary since 1846   F 854.
> Wars with the Pacific coast Indians, 1847–1865   E 83.84.
> Lane, Joseph   E 415.9.L2.
> Shields, James   E 403.1.S5.

     881   1859–   Biographies: Meacham, A. B., etc.

> Applegate, Jesse   F 880.A.
> Wars with Pacific coast Indians   E 83.84.
> Baker, E. D.   E 467.1.B16.
> Civil war   E 526.
> Modoc war, 1872–1873   E 83.87.
> Nez Percés war, 1877   E 83.877.

     882   Regions.   Counties.   Boundaries.

.B2	Baker Co.	L7	Linn Co.
.B4	Benton Co.	.M2	Malheur Co.
.B7	Boundaries.	.M8	Morrow Co.
	International boundary	.P7	Polk Co.
	controversy F 880, 854.	.S5	Sherman Co.
.C5	Clackamas Co.	.S6	Snake River and Valley,
.C6	Columbia Co.		Or.
.C63	Columbia River and Val-		Cf. F 752.S7.
	ley, Or.	.T5	Tillamook Co.
	Cf. F 853.	.U4	Umatilla Co.
.C7	Coos Co.	.U5	Union Co.
.C8	Crater Lake national park.	.W2	Wallowa Co. Wallowa
.D4	Deschutes River and Val-		Lake.
	ley.	.W3	Wasco Co. Hood River.
.D7	Douglas Co.		Mosier Hills.
.J14	Jackson Co.	.W4	Washington Co.
.J8	Josephine Co.	.W6	Willamette River and Val-
.L2	Lane Co.		ley.
.L6	Lincoln Co.	.Y2	Yamhill Co.

Table of subdivisions (a), (b), (c), or (d) under each state may be found on pages 85–87.

886–900   **Washington (d).**

> The state of Washington was included in the Oregon country and the U. S. territory of Oregon (cf. note under F 871) down to 1853 when Washington Territory was organized. It originally included Idaho north of 46° and a strip of western Montana, and on the admission of Oregon to statehood in 1859, received an addition of all the rest of the original Oregon Territory outside the state of Oregon (the rest of Idaho and a part of Wyoming). It was reduced to its present limits in 1863 on the formation of Idaho Territory, and admitted as a state in 1889.

891   General works. Periods.

> Wars with Pacific coast Indians, 1847–1865   E 83.84.

897   Regions. Counties. Boundaries.

.A2	Adams Co.	.P6	Pierce Co. Mt. Tacoma.
.B4	Benton Co.	.P9	Puget Sound region.
.B7	Boundaries.	.R2	Mount Rainier. Mount
	International boundary		Rainier national park.
	F 880, 854.	.S2	San Juan Co. San Juan
.C5	Chehalis Co.		Islands.
.C6	Clarke Co.	.S5	Skagit Co.
.C7	Columbia River and Val-	.S6	Snake River and Valley,
	ley, Wash.		Wash.
	Cf. F 853.		Cf. F 752.S7.
.D7	Douglas Co.	.S66	Snohomish Co.
.F8	Franklin Co.	.S7	Spokane Co. Medical
.H8	Hood's Canal region.		Lake.
J9	Juan de Fuca Strait re-	.S9	Stevens Co.
	gion. Cf. F 1069.V3.	.T5	Thurston Co.
.K4	King Co.	.W18	Walla Walla Co.
.K48	Kitsap Co.	.W2	Walla Walla River and
.K5	Kittitas Co.		Valley.
.K6	Klickitat Co.	.W6	Whitman Co.
.L6	Lewis Co.	.Y18	Yakima Co. Natches
.L7	Lincoln Co.		River and Valley.
.M4	Mason Co.	.Y2	Yakima River and Val-
.O4	Okanogan Co.		ley.

901–915   **Alaska (a).**

> Explored and settled by Russia. Sold to the U. S. 1867.

907   Before 1867. Settlement. Purchase by U. S.

> Early voyages to Northwest   F 851.5.
> Polar voyages   G 600–830.

908   1867–1894.

909   1894–

Table of subdivisions (a), (b), (c), or (d) under each state may be found on pages 65–67.

901–915   Alaska—Continued.
  912   Regions. Boundaries.

	Aleutian Islands F 951.	.N7	Cape Nome region.
.B2	Point Barrow.	.P9	Pribilof Islands.
.B7	Boundaries.	.S15	Mount St. Elias.
.C7	Copper River region.	.S3	Seward Peninsula.
	Klondike gold fields F 931.	.Y9	Yukon River and Valley.
.M2	Mount McKinley.		Cf. F 1091.
.M9	Muir glacier.		

  931   Klondike region.
                 Yukon Territory   F 1091.

  951   Bering Sea and Aleutian Islands.

  970   Insular possessions of the U. S. as a whole.
                 Hawaiian Islands   DU 620–629.
                 Tutuila, Samoan Islands   DU 810–819.
                 Porto Rico   F 1951–1989.
                 Philippine Islands   DS 651–689.
                 Guam   DU 690.
                 Panama canal zone   F 1569.C2.

Table of subdivisions (a), (b), (c), or (d) under each state may be found on pages 85–87.

AMERICA, EXCLUSIVE OF THE UNITED STATES.

British North America.   Dominion of Canada   F 1001-1199.
Spanish or Latin America   F 1401-1413.
  Mexico   F 1201-1391.
  Central America   F 1421-1577.
  West Indies   F 1601-2151.
  South America   F 2201-3891.

BRITISH POSSESSIONS.

Canada   F 1001-1199.
Newfoundland and Labrador   F 1121-1139.
The thirteen North American colonies (before 1776)   E 186-199.
British East and West Florida (1763-1783)   F 301, 314.
British Honduras   F 1441-1456.
Bermudas   F 1631-1639.
Bahamas   F 1651-1659.
British West Indies   F 2131.
British Guiana   F 2361-2391.
Falkland Islands   F 3031.

DANISH POSSESSIONS.

Greenland   G 730-770.
Iceland   D 301-398.
Danish West Indies   F 2141.

DUTCH POSSESSIONS.

New Netherland to 1664   F 122.1.
New Sweden 1629-1664   F 167.
Dutch West Indies   F 2141.
Dutch Guiana   F 2401-2431.
Colony in Brazil 1625-1662   F 2532.

FRENCH POSSESSIONS.

New France and Acadia 1600-1763   F 1030, 1038.
Colony in Florida   1562-1565   F 314.
Louisiana 1698-1803   F 372.
St. Pierre and Miquelon   F 1170.
French West Indies   F 2151.
French Guiana   F 2441-2471.
Colony in Brazil 1555-1567   F 2529.

PORTUGUESE POSSESSIONS.

Brazil before 1821   F 2501-2659.

RUSSIAN POSSESSIONS.

Alaska before 1867   F 901–915.

SPANISH POSSESSIONS.

General   F 1401–1413.

SWEDISH POSSESSIONS.

New Sweden 1638–1655   F 167.

POLAR REGIONS.

Arctic regions   G 575–830.
Antarctic regions   G 850–890.

Though this region was visited by the Norse and other seamen,
the first extended explorations were those of Cartier in 1534.
No attempts at colonization were made till the next century,
when Champlain, Monts and the "Company of New France"
(1629-1663) established various settlements. From Quebec
as centre, explorers penetrated far to the south and west,
the sway of New France extending over not only eastern
Canada, but eastern Maine, western New York and Pennsylvania, the Old Northwest, the Great Lake region, the Mississippi Valley and beyond.

Meanwhile by virtue of discovery by Frobisher and Hudson the
British crown had, in 1670, established the Hudson's Bay
company with almost unlimited powers over the region about
the Hudson Bay and to the westward. This territory was
definitely recognized as British by France in 1713, after years
of conflict. Of the company's holdings, British Columbia was
surrendered to the Crown in 1858, while the remainder known
as Rupert's Land and the Northwest territories or Canadian
Northwest, was sold to the new Dominion of Canada in 1869.

In 1712 the province of Louisiana was formed, cutting off the
southern part of New France, so as to include the Illinois
country and all beyond. The record of the next half century
is one of conflict between the French and English in America.
The result of the final struggle (the French and Indian war of
1755-1763) was to dispossess France of her entire domain
in North America; the older parts of modern Canada and
Louisiana east of the Mississippi being surrendered to Great
Britain, and the rest of Louisiana to Spain. Under British
rule New France became Quebec, and to it there was annexed,
by the Quebec act of 1774, all the territory between the
settled parts of the 13 English colonies and the Mississippi
River north of the Ohio. Of the maritime provinces, Nova
Scotia and its dependencies continued to maintain their individual existence for a century more, and Newfoundland to
the present day. In 1791 Quebec was subdivided into the
provinces of Lower and Upper Canada, there being no central
government in British North America till 1841, when they
were reunited.

In 1867 the Dominion of Canada was organized by the federation
of the various provinces of British North America. The provinces came into the union from time to time, till now the only
one remaining outside is Newfoundland, with its dependency
Labrador.

1001   Periodicals.   Societies.
       Canadian geographical societies   G 4.

1003   Collections.
1004   Gazetteers. Geographic names.
1005   Biography. Genealogy.
    The old French Canadian families   F 1030, 1051–1053.
1006   Dictionaries. Encyclopedic works.
1008   Comprehensive works.
1009   Handbooks. Guide books.
   Description and travel.
    Before 1763   F 1030.
1013   1763–1867.
1015   1867–
1019   Antiquities.
    Indians of Canada   E 78.C2; E 92.
     Special tribes   E 99. e. g. Huron Indians.   E 99.H9.
1021   Social antiquities. Manners and customs.
   History.
1026   Comprehensive works.
1027   Miscellaneous. French Canadians.
    Boundaries (international), cf. E 398, F 42.B7, F 57.B7,
     F 127.B7, F 551, F 597, F 880, F 854, F 912.B7.
    French Canadians in the U. S., etc.   E 184.F85, etc.
1030   1603–1763. New France. History and description.
    English conquest of 1629. "Company of New
    France" 1629–1663. Royal province 1663.
    Company of the West Indies, 1665–1674. Mis-
    sionary activities and labors of the Catholic orders
    except the Jesuits. French explorers before 1760.
    Biographies: Monts, Pierre de Guast, sieur de;
    Laval de Montmorency, F. X. de; Bourdon, Jean;
    Talon, Jean; Frontenac, Louis de Buade, comte
    de; Bigot, François; etc.
      Discovery and explorations before 1603   E 101–135.
       Cartier   E 133.C3.
      Acadia (Nova Scotia)   F 1036–1039.5.
      Louisiana   F 366–380.
      Mississippi River and Valley   F 351–352.
      Hudson's Bay company and Rupert's Land   F 1060.
      Indian wars   E 81–83.
      Intercolonial wars   E 196–199.
      La Verendrye, P. G. de Varennes, sieur de   F 1060.7. L.
      Le Moyne d'Iberville, Pierre   F 372. L.
      Radisson, P. E.   F 1060.7. R.
      Chouart, Médard, sieur des Groseilliers   F 1060.7. C.
      Montcalm-Gozon, L. J. de   E 199.M.
   .1   Champlain. Champlain tercentenary,1908.
      Lake Champlain tercentenary, 1909   F 127.C6.
   .13   Brulé.

History.

1030   1603–1763.   New France—Continued.

     .15   Nicollet.

     .2   Marquette.
         Exploration of the Mississippi   F 352.

     .3   Joliet.
         Exploration of the Mississippi   F 352.

     .4   Hennepin.
         Exploration of the Mississippi   F 352.

     .5   La Salle.
         Exploration of the Mississippi   F 352.

     .7   Jesuits in New France and adjacent regions. Jesuit relations, Collected.

     .8   Single relations.

1031   1754–1763.   Last years of French rule. The English conquest.
         French and Indian war   E 199.

1032   1759–1867.   Province of Quebec, 1760; enlarged by Quebec act 1774; divided into Lower and Upper Canada 1791. The Canadian rebellion 1837: Burning of the "Caroline"; Alexander McLeod case. The reunion of Upper and Lower Canada, 1841. Fenian raid, 1866. The union of British North America, 1867. Biographies: Dorchester, Guy Carleton, baron; Haldimand, Sir Frederick; Papineau, L. J.; Mackenzie, W. L.; Lafontaine, Sir L. H.; Sydenham, C. E. P. Thomson, baron; Brown, George; etc.
         American revolution   E 201–298.
         British North America   E 263.C2; E 263.N9.
         Quebec campaign, 1775–76   E 231.
         American loyalists in Canada   E 277, F 1036–1039.5, 1041–1044.5, 1056–1059.5.
         Brock, Sir Isaac   E 353.1.B8.
         War of 1812.   E 359.5.C2; 359.8.
         Military operations   E 355.
         Selkirk, Thomas Douglas, earl of, and Red River settlement   F 1063.
         Confederates in Canada. St. Alban's raid   E 470.95.
         MacDonald, Sir J. A.   F 1033.M.
         Cartier, G. E.   F 1033.C.

1033   1867–   Annexation question. Fenian invasion of 1870–71. Biographies: MacDonald, Sir J. A.; Cartier, G. E.; Tupper, Sir Charles; Dufferin and Ava, F. T. H. T. Blackwood, marquis of; Strathcona and Mount Royal, D. A. Smith, 1st baron; Laurier, Sir Wilfrid, etc.
         Howe, Joseph   F 1038.H.

History—Continued.

1035   Topics.   Foreign elements.

        .C3   Catholics.   .I6   Irish.
        .F8   French.   .S4   Scotch.
        .I2   Icelanders.

PROVINCES. TERRITORIES. REGIONS.

1035.8   Maritime provinces.   Atlantic coast of Canada.

       Cf. F 106 (Atlantic coast of North America)

1036–1039.5 **Nova Scotia. Acadia.**

Visited by early explorers—perhaps by Norsemen; by Cabot, Verrazzano, etc. Cape Breton visited by French fishermen as early as 1504. Province of Acadia, 40° to 46° north latitude, granted to Monts by French king; and explored and settled 1604–1607 by Monts, Poutrincourt, Champlain and others. St. Croix and Port Royal settlements. Jesuit station on Mt. Desert Island 1609.

In its broadest extent, Acadia included not only the peninsula of Nova Scotia, but Maine as far as the Penobscot, New Brunswick, Gaspé Peninsula, Cape Breton and Prince Edward Island. 1613 the French settlements were broken up by an English expedition from Virginia, and 1621 King James granted the region (now first called Nova Scotia) to Sir William Alexander. Attempts at colonization proved abortive and 1632 Acadia was surrendered to France. It was parcelled into two districts separated by the St. Croix River, and the next twenty years were marked by the feud of their two governors, La Tour and Aulnay. Acadia was conquered under Cromwell's orders in 1654 but again returned to France 1667. It was the seat of almost continuous fighting for a century: conquered by the English in 1690, returned to France 1691; conquered again in 1710 and all claims formally relinquished by France in 1713, France still reserving Cape Breton Island. The French fortress of Louisburg on Cape Breton was captured by New Englanders in 1745 but restored to France in 1748. Meanwhile the disputes over the limits of Acadia were one of the causes bringing on the French and Indian war. The French would restrict it to the peninsula of Nova Scotia, the English claiming old Acadia in its largest sense. Halifax was founded 1749 and extensive English colonization begun. The French Acadians still loyal to their mother country were expelled in 1755. Louisburg was again captured in 1758 and the limits of Acadia ceased to have any international significance with Cape Breton Island and all Canada in English hands by the treaty of 1763.

1769 Prince Edward Island was made a separate colony.

During the American revolution there was a large influx of loyalists from the U. S. to whom extensive grants of land were made, especially in the north; and New Brunswick was set off in 1784. Cape Breton Island also became independent of Nova Scotia the same year, but was restored to the older province in 1820.

In 1867 Nova Scotia entered the Dominion.

Nova Scotia. Acadia—Continued.

1036   Periodicals. Societies. Collections.
 .5   Directories.
1037   Comprehensive works. Description.
1038   History. Biographies: Stirling, William Alexander, 1st earl of; Haliburton, Sir Brenton; Howe, Joseph; etc.

> Indians   E 78.N9; E 78.C2.
> Monts, Pierre de Guast, sieur de   F 1030.M
> Early settlements
> > Cf.   F 1030.
> > St. Croix Island   F 27.W3.
> > Maine   F 16–30.
> Wars with the eastern Indians, 1722–1726   E 83.72.
> Acadians in the U. S.   E 184.A2.
> Acadians in Louisiana, etc.   F 380.F8, etc.
> American revolution   E 263.N9.
> > Loyalists   E 277.
> Tupper, Sir Charles   F 1033.T.

1039   Regions. Counties. Boundaries.

.A16	Annapolis Co.	.C6	Colchester Co.
.B7	Boundaries (including old boundaries of Acadia).	.F9	Bay of Fundy.
		.K5	Kings Co.
		.L9	Lunenburg Co.
	International boundary since 1783 E 398.	.P6	Pictou Co.
			Prince Edward Island F 1046–1049.
.C2	Cape Breton Island.	.Q3	Queens Co.
	Capture of Louisburg, 1745 E 198.	.S13	Sable Island.
	Capture of Louisburg, 1758 E 199.		Gulf of St. Lawrence F 1050.
		.Y3	Yarmouth Co.
.C5	Chignecto Isthmus.		

1039.5   Towns. Cities.

1041–1044.5 New Brunswick.

> Largely settled by American loyalists. Set off from Nova Scotia 1784. Entered the Dominion of Canada 1867.

1041   Periodicals. Societies. Collections.
 .5   Directories.
1042   Comprehensive works. Description.
1043   History.

> American revolution   E 263.N9.
> > Loyalists   E 277.
> Boundary troubles with U. S.   E 398.

1044   Regions. Counties. Boundaries.

.A7	Aroostook River and Valley, N. B. Cf. F 27.A7.	.C2	Campobello Island.
		.C4	Chaleurs Bay.
.B7	Boundaries.		Chignecto Isthmus F 1039.C5.
	International boundary. Aroostook war E 398.	.D3	Deer Island. Bay of Fundy F 1039.F9.

PROVINCES. TERRITORIES. REGIONS.

New Brunswick.

1044 Regions. Counties. Boundaries—Continued.

.N7 Nepisiguit River and Val- .S17 St. Croix River and Valley.   ley, N. B.

.P3 Passamaquoddy Bay re-   Cf. F 27.S2.
gion, N. B.   .S2 St. John River and Valley.
Cf. F 27.P3.   .T6 Tobique River and Valley.

1044.5 Towns. Cities.

1046–1049.5 Prince Edward Island.

Set off from Nova Scotia 1769.

1046 Periodicals. Societies. Collections.
1046.5 Directories.
1047 Comprehensive works.
1048 History.
1049 Regions. Counties.
1049.5 Towns. Cities.

1050 St. Lawrence Gulf, River and Valley.

St. Lawrence Valley, Que. F 1054.S3.
St. Lawrence Valley, Ont. F 1059.S4.
St. Lawrence Valley, N. Y. F 127.S23.
Thousand Islands F 127.T5.
Anticosti F 1054.A6.
Newfoundland F 1121–1124.5.
St. Pierre and Miquelon F 1170.
Isle of Orleans F 1054.O7.
St. Helen's Island F 1054.S26.

1051–1054.5 Quebec.

The present province of Quebec is the successor of the old
province of New France, comprising within its limits practically all the region actually settled by the French (except
Acadia) and continuing to this day predominantly French.
On the conquest of New France in 1760 the English changed
the name to Quebec and in 1774 added to it, by the Quebec
act, substantially all the territory earlier in dispute between
France and England, lying westward of the maritime colonies (Nova Scotia, Newfoundland, and the 13 continental
colonies) as far as the Mississippi and Rupert's Land. The
American revolution stripped Quebec of all the southern
part of this vast area by the establishment of the international boundary. In 1791 it was further reduced by division
into Lower Canada (now Quebec) and Upper Canada (Ontario).
The rebellion of 1837 in Lower Canada, under L. J. Papineau
(F 1032), was a revolt of the French against the English
government, having no real connection with the contemporary outbreak in Upper Canada. In 1867 Lower Canada
came into the Dominion under her old name Quebec.

Quebec—Continued.

1051   Periodicals. Societies. Collections.

  .5   Directories.

1052   Comprehensive works. Description.

1053   History. Biographies: Bedard, Pierre; etc.

        History before 1791   F 1030–1032.
          American revolution   E 263.C2.
            Quebec campaign   E 231.
            American loyalists   E 277, F 1058.
        War of 1812   E 359.5.C2; E 359.8.
          Military operations   E 355.
     . Papineau, L. J.   F 1032.P.
        Lafontaine, Sir L. H.   F 1032.L.
        Rebellion of 1837   F 1032.
        Cartier, G. E.   F 1033.C.
        Laurier, Sir Wilfrid   F 1033.L.
        French Canadians (general)   F 1027.
          In the U. S., etc.   E 184.F85, etc.

1054   Regions. Counties. Boundaries. Seigneuries.
        Parishes.

.A6	Anticosti Island.	.M6	Missisquoi Co.
.B6	Bonaventure Co.	.M8	Montmorency Co.
.B7	Boundaries.	.O7	Isle of Orleans.
	International boundary E 398.	.O9	Ottawa River and Valley.
	New York boundary F 127.B7.		Cf. F 1059.O91.
		.P8	Pontiac Co.
	New Hampshire boundary F 42.B7.	.P85	Portneuf Co.
		.Q4	Quebec Co.
.B8	Brome Co. Missisquoi River and Valley, Quebec Cf. F 57.F8.	.S14	Saguenay River and Valley.
		.S26	St. Helen's Island.
.C7	Compton Co.	.S264	St. Hyacinthe Co.
.C8	Crane Island (Isle aux Grues).	.S267	Lake St. John.
		.S3	St. Lawrence River and Valley, Quebec.
.D4	Deux Montagnes Co.		Cf. F 1050.
.G2	Gaspé Peninsula.		
.H9	Huntingdon Co.	.S7	Stanstead Co.
.K2	Kamouraska Co.	.T3	Lake Temiscaming.
.L2	L'Assomption Co.	.T4	Terrebonne Co.
.M5	Lake Memphremagog region, Quebec Cf. F 57.M5.		Thousand Islands F 127.T5.
		.Y3	Yamaska Co.

1054.5   Towns. Cities.

PROVINCES. TERRITORIES. REGIONS—Continued.

1056–1059.5 **Ontario.**

A part of the province of New France, but not settled by the French; save for a few forts and trading posts this region was left to the Indians. After the English conquest in 1760 it formed part of the province of Quebec, still remaining practically unsettled till the coming of the American loyalists, during and immediately after the American revolution. On the division of Quebec in 1791, this part took the name Upper Canada. It was a battle ground during the war of 1812. A large immigration, especially Scotch, poured in during the next few years. Popular discontent over administrative abuses known as the "Family compact" and the "Clergy reserves" led to the outbreak of the rebellion of 1837 under W. L. Mackenzie. (The literature of this rebellion as well as the contemporary troubles in Lower Canada is classed in F 1032) As a result of the rebellion, certain abuses were corrected, and Upper and Lower Canada reunited under one government, 1841. Upper Canada was a leader in the movement for federation of the British colonies in North America, which brought about the formation of the Dominion of Canada in 1867. At that time she assumed the name Ontario.

1056   Periodicals. Societies. Collections.

.5   Directories.

1057   Comprehensive works. Description.

1058   History. United empire loyalists in Ontario. Biographies: Simcoe, J. G.; Cartwright, Richard; Mowat Sir Oliver; Robinson, Sir J. B.; etc.

Early history to 1791 F 1030–1032, 1053.
American loyalists (general) E 277.
Indians E 78.O5; E 78.C2.
War of 1812 E 359.5.C2; E 359.8.
  Military operations E 355.
  Brock, Sir Isaac E 353.1.B8.
Mackenzie, W. L. F 1032.M.
Canadian rebellion of 1837 F 1032.
Brown, George F 1032.B.
MacDonald, Sir J. A. F 1033.M.

1059   Regions. Counties. Boundaries.

.A2	Addington Co.	.L2	Lake of the Woods region.
.A3	Algoma District.		Cf. F 1064.L2.
.B7	Boundaries.	.L5	Lenox Co.
.B95	Bruce Co.	.M6	Middlesex Co.
.E4	Elgin Co.	.M88	Muskoka District.
.E6	Lake Erie region, Ont.	.M9	Muskoka Lake region.
	Cf. F 555.	.N4	Lake Nepigon.
.F9	Frontenac Co.	.N48	Niagara Co.
.G3	Georgian Bay region.	.N5	Niagara peninsula.
.G5	Glengarry Co.		Cf. F 127.N6; F 1059.Q3.

Ontario.

1059   Regions.   Counties.   Boundaries—Continued.

.05	Ontario Co.	.83	Lake St. Clair region, Ont.
.06	Lake Ontario region, Ont.		Cf. F 572.834.
	Cf. F 556.	.84	St. Lawrence River and Valley, Ont.
.091	Ottawa River and Valley, Ont.		Cf. F 1050.
	Cf. F 1054.09.	.86	Simcoe Co.
.P3	Perth Co.	.89	Lake Superior region.
.P4	Peterborough Co.		Cf. F 552.
.Q3	Queen Victoria Niagara Falls park.	.T5	Thunder Bay region.
		.W4	Wentworth Co.
	Cf. F 127.N8.	.Y6	York Co.

1059.5   Towns.   Cities.

1060   The Canadian Northwest (Region to the west and northwest of the ancient New France). Hudson Bay. Hudson's Bay company. Rupert's Land. Northwest company of Canada. Northwest Territories.

> This region, though visited in its southern parts by French explorers was never colonized or actually governed by that power. By virtue of discovery by Frobisher and Hudson it was claimed by Great Britain and in 1670 the crown chartered the Hudson's Bay company to control the region about Hudson Bay and to the west, and this claim was ultimately recognized by the French, early in the 18th century. Outside the company's own domain, Rupert's Land or the region watered by the rivers flowing into Hudson Bay, it received temporary renewable leases of the western territory to the U. S. and the Pacific (the Northwest Territories). British Columbia was lost to the Company on its organization as a Crown colony in 1858, and in 1869 all the rest of the Company's holdings outside certain reservations were surrendered to the Dominion of Canada. In 1870 this region, excluding the district of Keewatin, was made a separate government as the "Northwest Territories." In 1882 it was subdivided by the formation of the provisional districts of Assiniboia, Saskatchewan, Alberta and Athabasca. (In 1905 these four districts were consolidated and admitted to the Dominion as the provinces of Saskatchewan and Alberta.) In 1895–97 the remaining unorganized territory in British North America was subdivided into the districts of Ungava, Franklin, Mackenzie and Yukon, of which the last was made a territory the following year. The present Northwest Territories, so-called, include Mackenzie, Keewatin, Ungava and Franklin.
>
> Boundaries.
> > U. S. boundary   F 597, 880, 854.
> > Alaska boundary   F 912.B7.
> > Ontario boundary   F 1059.B7.
> > Canadian Rocky Mts.   F 1090.
> > Polar regions   G 575–720.
> > Northwest passage   G 640–665.

PROVINCES. TERRITORIES. REGIONS.

The Canadian Northwest—Continued.

.4   General works.

.7   Before 1821. Explorers: Radisson, P. E.; Chouart, Médard, sieur des Groseilliers; La Verendrye, P. G. de Varennes, sieur de; Henry, Alexander (the elder); Hearne, Samuel; Cocking, Matthew; McKenzie, Alexander; Henry, Alexander (the younger); Harmon, D. W.; etc.

> Hudson, Henry   E 129.H8.
> New France and early French explorations in general F 1030.
> Le Moyne d'Iberville, Pierre   F 372.L.
> Nootka Sound controversy, 1789–1790   F 1089.N8.
> Red River settlement, 1815–1816   F 1063.

.8   1821–1867. Explorers: Simpson, Thomas; etc.

> Oregon question and international boundary   F 880.
> British Columbia   F 1086–1089.5.
> Vancouver Island   F 1089.V3.

.9   1867–   Riel rebellion 1885.

> Red River rebellion, 1869–1870   F 1063.
> Manitoba   F 1061–1064.5.

1061–1064.5 Manitoba.

> Part of the territory of the Hudson's Bay company (Rupert's Land). Lord Selkirk, a Scotch nobleman prominent in that company, colonized large numbers of his countrymen here, 1811–1818, but the settlement was broken up by the opposition of the rival Northwest company. Known as the Red River Settlement. Sold to the Dominion of Canada 1869 by the Hudson's Bay company with the rest of its land holdings. This sale was resented by the Canadian halfbreeds under Louis Riel who set up a government of their own but were quickly overthrown. Manitoba was admitted as a province of the Dominion 1870 and has since been greatly enlarged in territory.

1061   Periodicals. Societies. Collections.

.5   Directories.

1062   Comprehensive works. Description.

1063   History. Lord Selkirk. Red River settlement. Red River rebellion, 1869–70.

> Moundbuilders   E 74.M3.
> Hudson's Bay company; Rupert's Land   F 1060.
> Fenian raid, 1870–71   F 1033.
> Riel and his rebellion of 1885   F 1060.9.

1064   Regions. Boundaries.

> .B7   Boundaries.
>   Ontario boundary F 1059.B7.
> .L2   Lake of the Woods region, Manitoba. Cf. F 1059.L2.
>
> .R3   Red River of the North and Red River Valley. Cf. F 612.R27; F 642.R3
> .W5   Lake Winnipeg region.

1064.5   Towns. Cities.

1071 **Saskatchewan.**

> Province formed 1905 from eastern portions of provisional districts of Assiniboia, Saskatchewan and Athabasca.

1076 **Alberta.**

> Province formed 1905 from provisional district of Alberta and western portions of Assiniboia, Saskatchewan and Athabasca.

1086–1089.5 **British Columbia.**

> The coast was visited by Spanish and English seamen in the 18th century, and the interior by traders of the Northwest company. The southern portion formed part of the "Oregon country" concerning which Gt. Brit. and the U. S. made a treaty of joint occupation in 1818. On the union of the Northwest company with the Hudson's Bay company in 1821 the region was administered by the latter: the treaty of 1846 with the U. S. defining the southern limit. In 1849 Vancouver Island was made a British colony. And in 1858 owing to the large influx of population following the discovery of gold, British Columbia became a crown colony. In 1866 Vancouver Island was annexed. British Columbia joined the Dominion of Canada in 1871.

1086   Periodicals. Societies. Collections.

.5   Directories.

1087   Comprehensive works. Description.

> Pacific coast of North America F 851.

1088   History. Biographies: Douglas, Sir James; etc.

> Indians E 78.B9; E 78.C2.
> Exploring expeditions before 1769 F 851.5.
> Nootka Sound controversy, 1789–1790 F 1089.N8.
> Hudson's Bay and Northwest companies F 1060.
> The entire northwest coast between Alaska and New Spain (California), 1769–1846, including the Oregon question F 879–880.

1089   Regions. Counties. Boundaries.

> .B7 Boundaries.
>   International boundary F 880, F 854.
>
> .K7 Kootenai River and Valley.
>
> .N8 Nootka Sound. Nootka Sound controversy, 1789–1790.
>
> .Q3 Queen Charlotte Island.
> .S2 Salt Spring Island.
> .S4 Selkirk range.
> .V3 Vancouver Island.

1089.5 Towns. Cities.

1090   Rocky Mountains of Canada.

> Cf. F 721.

1091   Yukon.

> District created 1897, made a territory 1898.
> Klondike F 931.
> Alaska boundary F 912.B7.
> Yukon River and Valley as a whole F 912.Y9.

PROVINCES. TERRITORIES. REGIONS—Continued.

1096 Mackenzie.

District created 1897.
Polar regions   G 575–830.

1101 Franklin.

The Arctic regions at the northern extremity of the continent.
District created 1897.
Polar regions   G 575–830.

1106 Keewatin.

District created 1876; and at first annexed to Manitoba for
governmental purposes.
Ontario boundary   F 1059.B7.

1111 Ungava.

The northwestern part of the Labrador peninsula. District
created 1897.
Cf. F 1140.

1121–1124.5 Newfoundland.

Visited by Cabots and other early explorers. The cod fishery
attracted many seamen but few settlers. Various grants of
land were made by the British crown, but no permanent
settlements made under them. Newfoundland became a
British crown colony in 1728. In 1876 the eastern shore of
Labrador was annexed to the government of Newfoundland.
The colony has never joined the Dominion.

1121   Periodicals. Societies. Collections.

.5   Directories.

1122   Comprehensive works. Description.

1123   History. Baltimore's colony of Avalon.

1124   Regions. Counties.

1124.5   Towns. Cities.

1136 Labrador.

The eastern coast of the Labrador peninsula was annexed to
Newfoundland as a dependency in 1876.

1140 The Labrador peninsula.

The peninsula is at present divided into three regions for governmental purposes: The eastern coast as "Labrador" is a
dependency of Newfoundland, the southern part belongs to
Quebec, and the northwest portion, as the district of Ungava
is one of the Northwest Territories.

1170 St. Pierre and Miquelon.

French colony.

Conquered and settled by Cortés and his companions 1519-1540. Known as New Spain during the colonial period. It was governed by audiencias at first and after 1535 by viceroys, down to the end of the Spanish rule in 1821. Its greatest extent was from the bounds of the Audiencia or Captain generalcy of Guatemala on the south (including Yucatan but not the modern Mexican state Chiapas) nearly to the Mississippi on the northeast and to Vancouver Island on the north. The civil divisions of New Spain varied from time to time. The following were important during a large part of the colonial period:

1. Reyno de Mexico (including modern Mexico from the northern limits of Michoacan, Guanajuato and Vera Cruz to the extremity of Yucatan, but excluding Chiapas and part of Tabasco).
2. Nuevo reyno de Leon (the modern Nuevo Leon).
3. Nuevo Santander (Tamaulipas and southern Texas).
4. Nuevo reyno de Galicia (including in its smallest extent present states of Jalisco, Zacatecas and part of San Luis Potosi and in a large sense, for a time at least, all the provinces following).
5. Nueva Viscaya (Chihuahua).
6. Durango.
7. Sonora and Sinaloa.
8. Coahuila.
9. Texas.
10. The two Californias.

The first and fourth divisions named had each its own audiencia, at Mexico and Guadalajara respectively; the other provinces had governors. In 1786 the provinces and kingdoms named were abolished and New Spain divided into 12 intendencias. In addition to his rule over this vast region, the viceroy of New Spain had some rather vague supervision over the Audiencia of Santo Domingo (The West Indies), the Audiencia of Guatemala (Central America) and the Philippine Islands. In 1810 there broke out a rebellion against the Spanish crown which was generally unsuccessful. Independence was finally won by a combination of conservative and progressive factions in 1820. Then came Itúrbide of the former group and his brief empire 1822-1823, followed by a half century of almost continual revolution. After the election of Díaz to the presidency for the second time in 1884, Mexico enjoyed peace down to the successful revolt against him in 1910, which led to his expulsion.

General works on the Spaniards in North America F 1410.
Pacific coast of North America F 851.

1201   Periodicals. Societies.
Mexican geographical societies G 5.

MEXICO—Continued.

1203   Collections. Collected works.

1204   Gazetteers. Geographic names. Dictionaries.

   .5   Directories, General.

   .7   Business directories.

1205   Biography. Genealogy.

1208   Comprehensive works.

1209   Handbooks. Guide books.

1210   Miscellaneous.

          Description and travel.

1211   1516–1810.

           Early discoveries   E 101–141.

1213   1810–1867.

1215   1867–

1219   Antiquities. Native races. Indian history. Aztecs. Toltecs. Chichimecs. Zapotecs. Mexican calendar. Codexes.

           Mayas   F 1435.

   .1   Local.

           Cibola   F 799.

   .3   Topics.

1220   Modern Indian tribes.

           Mexican tribes belonging to the linguistic families of the northern part of the continent in   E 99.

             Tarahumare Indians   E 99.T3.

             Yaqui Indians   E 99.Y3.

1226   History. Comprehensive works.

1227   Miscellaneous.

          Periods.

1229   To end of Spanish rule in 1824.

           Early descriptive works on America   E 141–143.

           Spanish explorers before 1600 in parts of New Spain beyond the settled regions (Grijalva, Núñez Cabeza de Vaca, Marco da Nizza, Vásquez de Coronado, etc.)   E 123–125.

1230   1516–1535. The conquest. Cortés and companions; Díaz del Castillo, etc.

1231   1535–1810. The viceroys. Church and state. Expulsion of the Jesuits. Biographies: Palafox y Mendoza, Juan de; Lombardo, Guillén; Iturrigaray, José de; Talamantes Salvador y Baeza, Melchor de; etc.

History.
    Periods—Continued.

1231.5   1810–

1232   1810–1849. Wars of independence 1810–1821.
                  Hidalgo. Morelos. Empire of Itúrbide.
                  Santa Anna. Troubles with France 1838–
                  1839.
                      Secession of Central America F 1438.
                      Poinsett, J. R. E 340.P77.
                      Revolt and independence of Texas F 390.
                      Texan Mier expedition, 1842 · F 390.
                      War with U. S.; loss of N. Mex. and Cal. E 401–415.

1233   1849–1867. Juárez. European intervention.
                  French army in Mexico. Empire of
                  Maximilian 1864–1867.
                      Gadsden treaty, sale of territory south of the
                          Gila to U. S. F 786.

1234   1867– Díaz. Frontier troubles with· U. S.
                  Revolution of 1910–1911. Madero.
                      Local frontier troubles with U. S. F 391, 786.
                      Apache war, 1883–1886 E 83.88.

      States and Territories. Regions.
          The literature of the ecclesiastical subdivisions of New Spain,
          bishoprics, etc., including the provinces of the religious
          orders, is to be classed with provinces of same name, even
          if they are not identical as to limits.

1241   Aguascalientes.

1246   Baja California (Territory). Gulf of California.
          General works on the Spanish province of California F 864.
          Colorado River F 788.

1249   Boundaries. Ancient boundary between New Spain
            and Louisiana.
          Boundary of the Republic of Texas F 392.B7.
          U. S. boundary F 786.
          Nootka Sound controversy with Great Britain, 1789–1790
            F 1089.N8.
          Gadsden purchase, 1853 F 786.
          Rio Grande River F 392.R5.
          British Honduras boundary F 1449.B7.
          California (Spanish and Mexican province to 1848)
            F 864.

1251   Campeche.

1256   Chiapas.
          Formed one of the Central American states under the Audiencia
          of Guatemala during the colonial period.
          Cf. F 1437.

MEXICO.

States and Territories—Continued.

1261   Chihuahua.   (Province of Nueva Viscaya in colonial period.)
> International boundary   F 786.
> Rio Grande River   F 392.R5.

1266   Coahuila.
> International boundary   F 786.
> Rio Grande River   F 392.R5.
> Frontier troubles   F 391, F 1234.

1271   Colima.

1276   Durango.

1279   Grijalva River.

1281   Guanajuato.

1286   Guerrero.

1291   Hidalgo.

1296   Jalisco.   Nuevo reyno de Galicia (Audiencia de Guadalajara) including in its broadest extent not only the present states of Jalisco and Zacatecas but the provinces to the north.   Nayarit.

1301   Mexico (State).
> Mexico (Federal district, and city)   F 1386.

1306   Michoacan.

1311   Morelos.

1316   Nuevo Leon.   (Nuevo reyno de Leon of colonial times.)
> International boundary   F 786.
> Rio Grande River   F 392.R5.
> Frontier troubles   F 391, F 1234.

       Nuevo Mexico (Spanish and Mexican province to 1848)   F 799–800.

1321   Oaxaca.
> Isthmus of Tehuantepec   F 1359.

1326   Puebla.

1331   Queretaro.

1333   Quintana Roo (Territory).
> British Honduras boundary   F 1449.B7.

1334   Rio Grande River and Valley, Mexico.   Cf. F 392.R5.

1336   San Luis Potosi.

1341   Sinaloa.

1346   Sonora.

1351   Tabasco.

1356   Tamaulipas.   (Nuevo Santander of colonial times.)
> International boundary   F 786.
> Rio Grande River   F 392.R5.
> Frontier troubles   F 391, F 1234.

States and Territories—Continued.

1359	Tehuantepec, Isthmus of.
1361	Tepic (Territory)
	Texas (Mexican province to 1836) F 389.
1366	Tlaxcala.
1371	Vera Cruz (State)
	Vera Cruz (City) F 1391.V4.
1376	Yucatan. Indian ruins (General).
	British Honduras boundary F 1449.B7.
	Local Maya antiquities F 1435.1.
1381	Zacatecas. (Part of Nuevo reyno de Galicia in colonial times. Cf. F 1296)

Towns.   Cities.   Cf. F 1219.1.

1386	Mexico (Federal district and city).
1391	Other places (alphabetically).

1401-1418	Spanish America. Latin America.

Mexico, Central America, West Indies and South America; all or three of them combined. Spanish or Latin influence in America. Spaniards in North America (general).

Florida, to 1819   F 314, 301.
Louisiana, 1764–1803   F 373.
Texas, to 1836   F 389.
New Mexico, to 1848   F 799–800.
California, to 1848   F 864.
Mexico   F 1201–1391.
Central America   F 1421–1577.
West Indies   F 1601–2171.
South America   F 2201–3899.

1401	Periodicals. Societies. Collections.

Geographical societies of Mexico, Central America, West Indies and South America   G 5.

1403	Pan-American union (formerly Bureau of the American republics, and International bureau of the American republics).
1404	Pan-American conferences. Early congresses. Panama congress, 1826.
1405	International American conferences, 1889–
1406	Gazetteers.
.5	Directories.
1407	Biography.
1408	Comprehensive works.
1409	Description and travel since 1810.
	Earlier descriptive works E 141–143.
1409.5	Antiquities.
	Indians of Spanish America E 65.

SPANISH AMERICA—Continued.

1410   History. Spain's government of her American colonies.

1411   To 1600. Treatment of the Indians. Las Casas tracts.
> Biography of Las Casas   E 125.C4.
> Early accounts of America   E 141.

1412   1600–1830.
> Wars of independence   F 1232, F 1437, F 2235.

1413   1820–1898.

1414   1898– Relations of Spain with Spanish America; cultural, commercial, etc.

1418   Relations of the U. S. with Latin America.
> Cf. F 1403–1405.

CENTRAL AMERICA   F 1421–1577.

Discovered and conquered by Spaniards, partly from Mexico, in the early part of the 16th century. During the colonial period it formed a separate provincial government, under an audiencia established 1542, which had its seat usually at Guatemala. The Reyno de Guatemala did not include Panama, which belonged to New Granada, but did take in Chiapas, now a state of Mexico. It comprised the present states of Costa Rica, Nicaragua, Salvador, Honduras and Guatemala (the territory now covered by the last named being usually subdivided into three or more provinces). The early colonial history of the southern part of modern Central America belongs rather with South America than with the Reyno de Guatemala. The southwestern shore of the Caribbean, from Cape Gracia a Dios to the South American mainland was sparsely settled, and, as a whole, very early bore the names of Tierra Firma and Castilla del Oro. Its provinces or districts of Darien, Panama and Veragua were dependencies of the Audiencia of Santa Fe and later Viceroyalty of New Granada. Great Britain exercised control over sections of the coast, through actual settlement in the present British Honduras, and a protectorate over Mosquitia, both dating from the 17th century. On the attainment of independence from Spain the Central American states joined themselves to Mexico under the empire of Itúrbide. After its overthrow, they seceded, and formed a federal republic of their own. It was shortlived, as have been several successors down to our own day.

1421   Periodicals. Societies. Collections.
> Central American geographical societies   G 5.

1424   Gazetteers. Dictionaries.

1425   Directories.

1426   Biography.

1428	Comprehensive works.
1429	Handbooks. Guides.
	Description and travel.
1431	To 1821.
	Earliest voyages and explorations E 101–141, F 1230.
1432	1821–
1434	Antiquities.
	Aztecs F 1219.
1435	Mayas.
	Cf. F 1376; F 1465; etc.
.1	Local.
.3	Topics.
	History.
1436	General works.
1437	To 1821. Audiencia of Guatemala.
	Early explorations and discoveries E 101–141.
	English aggressions on the coast F 1441–1457, 1529.M9.
	Mexican war of independence F 1232.
	Chiapas F 1256.
1438	1821– Separation from Mexico. Attempts to form Central American union. Clayton-Bulwer treaty, 1850. Filibuster wars.
	Walker in Nicaragua F 1526.
1440	Topics.

British Honduras.

The coast of the Bay of Honduras occupied by British wood-choppers in the 17th century without any claim to the soil. After many years of hostility, it was recognized by Guatemala as a British colony. Early known as Belize or Balize.

1441	Periodicals. Societies. Collections.
1442	Gazetteers.
.3	Directories.
.7	Biography.
1443	Comprehensive works.
1444	Travel and description.
1445	Antiquities.
1446	History.
1447	Miscellaneous.
1449	Regions. Boundaries
	.B7 Boundaries.
1456	Cities and towns.
1457	Topics.
	.B4 Belgians.

CENTRAL AMERICA—Continued.

Guatemala.

Audiencia or captain generalcy of Guatemala before 1821
F 1437.

1461   Periodicals. Societies. Collections.
1462   Gazetteers.
   .3   Directories.
   .7   Biography.
1463   Comprehensive works.
1464   Travel and description.
1465   Antiquities.

Maya antiquities F 1435.

1466   History. Biographies: Molina, Luis; Sánchez, Caye-
        tano; etc.
1467   Miscellaneous.
1469   Regions. Departments. Boundaries.

.B7 Boundaries.	.I9 Isabal.
Mexican boundary	Cf. F 1469.S2.
F 1249.	.P4 El Peten.
British Honduras	.S2 St. Thomas (District).
F 1441-1457.	

1476   Cities and towns.

Maya local antiquities F 1435.1.

1477   Topics.

Salvador.

1481   Periodicals. Societies. Collections.
1482   Gazetteers.
   .3   Directories.
   .7   Biography.
1483   Comprehensive works.
1484   Travel and description.
1485   Antiquities.
1486   History. Biographies: Pérez, Estanislao; etc.
1487   Miscellaneous.
1489   Regions. Departments. Boundaries.

.S2 San Salvador.
.U8 Usulutan.

1496   Cities and towns.
1497   Topics.

Honduras.

1501   Periodicals. Societies. Collections.
1502   Gazetteers.
  .3   Directories.
  .7   Biography.
1503   Comprehensive works.
1504   Travel and description.
1505   Antiquities.
1506   History.
1507   Miscellaneous.
1509   Regions. Departments. Boundaries.

.B3   Bay Islands.   .O4   Olancho.
.B7   Boundaries.   .T2   Tegucigalpa (Province).
.M9   Mosquitia (District). .U4   Ulua River and Valley.

1516   Cities and towns.
1517   Topics.

Nicaragua.

1521   Periodicals. Societies. Collections.
1522   Gazetteers.
  .3   Directories.
  .7   Biography.
1523   Comprehensive works.
          Nicaragua canal TC.
1524   Travel and description.
1525   Antiquities.
          Mosquito Indians F 1529.M9.
1526   History. Walker and the Filibuster war. Biographies: Zelaya, J. S.; etc.
          Mosquito shore and the English protectorate F 1529.M9.
          General works on filibusters in Central America F 1438.
          Bombardment of Greytown, 1854 F 1536.S2.
1527   Miscellaneous.
1529   Regions. Departments. Boundaries.

.B7   Boundaries.   .M9   Mosquito Reservation.
      Honduras boundary   (Department of Zelaya).
      F 1509.B7.   Mosquito Indians.
.J4   Jinotega.

1536   Cities and towns.
1537   Topics.

CENTRAL AMERICA—Continued.

Costa Rica.

1541   Periodicals. Societies. Collections.
1542   Gazetteers.
  .3   Directories.
  .7   Biography.
1543   Comprehensive works.
1544   Travel and description.
1545   Antiquities.
1546   History.
1547   Miscellanous.
1549   Regions. Provinces. Boundaries.

.B7 Boundaries. Ancient	.D8 Golfo Dulce.
Costa Rica–Colombia	.H5 Heredia.
boundary.	.S15 San Jose.
Nicaragua boundary	
F 1529.B7.	

1556   Cities and towns.
1557   Topics.

Panama.

The isthmus of Panama. During the Spanish period and down to the revolution of 1903 Panama was connected rather with South America than with New Spain or Central America, forming a part of New Granada and its successor Colombia. The present republic comprises the ancient provinces of Panama, Darien, and Veragua. It was temporarily independent in 1841 and 1857, and its present state as a nation dates from 1903.

1561   Periodicals. Societies. Collections.
1562   Gazetteers.
  .3   Directories.
  .7   Biography.
1563   Comprehensive works.

Panama canal TC.

1564   Travel and description.
1565   Antiquities.
1566   History.

Scotch colony at Darien, 1699–1700 F 2281.D2.

1567   Miscellaneous.
1569   Regions. Provinces. Boundaries.

.B6 Bocas del Toro.	.C2 Canal Zone.
Chiriqui Lagoon.	Panama canal TC.
.B7 Boundaries.	.C5 Chiriqui.
The old Colombia-	.P3 Panama (Province).
Costa Rica bound-	Scotch at Darien
ary F 1549.B7.	F 2281.D2.
	.P4 Pearl Island.

1576   Cities and towns.
1577   Topics.

THE WEST INDIES.　F 1601-2161.

Discovered by Columbus in his early voyages; and certain
islands, notably Haiti, at once colonized by Spaniards.
Only the Greater Antilles and a few islands near the coast
were occupied, though the claims of Spain to the other islands
were not called in question for a century. The Audiencia
of Santo Domingo (Haiti) was in the early 16th century the
center of Spanish rule in America, and even after the establishment of viceroyalties in Mexico and Peru its sway covered
not only the West Indies but northern South America till
late in the 18th century. The West Indies became the
resorts of pirates and buccaneers, and early in the 17th century colonizing began on the part of other nations unfriendly
to Spain; notably English, French and Dutch. Especially
during the Seven years war, 1756-1763, the American revolution, 1775-1783 and the French wars of 1793-1815 were these
islands the victims of frequent change of masters.
Caribbean Sea and Spanish Main　F 2161.

1601	Periodicals.　Societies.　Collections.
1604	Gazetteers.
1606	Directories.
1607	Biography.　Genealogy.
1608	Comprehensive works.

　　　　Cf.　F 1741; 2001-2016; 2131-2151.

1609	Handbooks.　Guide books.

　　Description and travel.

1610	Before 1810.

　　　　Much of the descriptive literature is in E 141-143.

1611	1810–
1619	Antiquities.　Indians.

　　Works on the aborigines and antiquities of a special island or
　　group are classed in F 1631-2151.
　　　　Carib Indians　F 2001.

1621　History (General histories and histories of the
　　　　Spanish West Indies) Audiencia of Santo Do-
　　　　mingo. English West Indian expeditions of
　　　　1654–5, and 1695. Rodney and other com-
　　　　manders in the Seven years' war, 1756–1763.
　　　　Expeditions and campaigns of 1793–1815.

　　Despite changes in ownership of particular islands or groups,
　　the literature of British, Danish, Dutch and French West
　　Indies, at any period, is classed in F 2131-2151.
　　　　Early discoveries　E 101-141.
　　　　Spanish America in general　F 1411-1412.
　　　　Buccaneers and pirates in the West Indies　F 2161.
　　　　English West Indian expedition, 1739-1742　F 2272.5.
　　　　Capture of Havana, 1762　F 1781.
　　　　Naval operations in the American revolution　E 263.W5;
　　　　　E 271.
　　　　Rodney at St. Eustatius, 1781　F 2097.
　　　　Spanish West Indies in 19th century　F 1783.

1623　　Miscellaneous.

THE WEST INDIES—Continued.

1631–1639   **Bermudas. Somers Islands.**
> First settled by English in the 17th century. Granted in 1612 to an offshoot of the Virginia company of London.

     1631   General works. Travel.

     1636   History.
> American revolution   E 263.W5.

     1639   Local.

1651–1659   **Bahamas.**
> Columbus first saw land somewhere in the Bahama group (probably either Samana Cay or Watlings Island). The islands were colonized by the English from the Bermudas in the middle of the 17th century, and granted by the crown to the Duke of Albemarle and others, 1670. They were the seat of anarchy, misrule and inroads of pirates and Spaniards till a royal governor was sent out in 1718. New Providence was captured by Commodore Hopkins of the American navy in 1776 but not held. The Spaniards from Cuba conquered the islands in 1781 but they were retaken by the English in 1783. The proprietary titles were finally extinguished in 1786. During the American civil war New Providence was a depot for blockade running.
> British West Indies   F 2131.

     1651   General works. Travel.

     1656   History.

     1659   Local.
> .N3 New Providence. Nassau. .T9 Turks and Caicos Islands.

GREATER ANTILLES.

1741–1991   Cuba, Haiti, Porto Rico and Jamaica, and outlying islands. The Windward passage.

     1741   General works. Antiquities.

1751–1849   **Cuba.**
> The island was discovered by Columbus, and largely settled before 1515. Havana was captured by the English in 1762, but returned to Spain in the next year in exchange for Florida. Beginning with the middle of the 19th century discontent among the Cubans led to frequent insurrections against Spanish rule. About the same time there arose a strong movement, within and without, for annexation to the U. S. The Ostend manifesto of 1854 was one evidence of this. The last insurrection of 1895–96 led to the interference of the U. S. and independence. The Cuban republic was organized in 1902, but internal troubles caused a military occupation by the U. S., 1906–1909.

     1751   Periodicals. Societies. Collections.

Cuba—Continued.

1754	Gazetteers. Dictionaries.
.5	Directories.
1755	Biography, Collected. Genealogy.
1758	Comprehensive works.
	Description and travel.
1761	To 1810.
1763	1810–1898.
1765	1898–
1769	Antiquities.
	History.
1776	Comprehensive.
1777	Miscellaneous.
	By periods.
1779	1492–1810. English attacks. Admirals Vernon and Knowles.
	Discovery and exploration E 101–135.
1781	1762–1763. Siege of Havana and English control.
	Cf. E 199; DD 400.
1783	1810–1899. Question of annexation to U. S.
	Ostend manifesto, 1854 E 431.
1784	Insurrection, 1849–1851. Filibusters. López.
1785	1868–1880. Ten years war, 1868–1878. Filibusters. The Virginius. The "Little war" 1879–1880.
1786	1895–1899. Insurrection of 1895–1898. Question of intervention to Feb. 15, 1898.
	Spanish-American war E 714–735.
1787	1898– Cuban republic, 1902. Revolution of 1906. American occupation, 1906–1909. Biographies: Quesada, Gonzalo de; etc.
1789	Topics.
	.N3 Negroes.
	Provinces.
	Subdivided (1) Comprehensive.
	(5) History.
	(9) Local.
1791	Havana (Province).
1799	Local.
	e. g. .H3 Havana (City)
1801	Pinar del Rio.
1809	Local.
1811	Matanzas.
1819	Local.

GREATER ANTILLES.

Cuba.

    Provinces—Continued.

1821	Santa Clara.
1829	Local.
1831	Puerto Principe.
1839	Local.
1841	Santiago de Cuba.
1849	Local.

1861–1891 Jamaica.

> Discovered by Columbus in 1494 and early colonized by Spain. The English conquered the island in 1596 but did not hold it. It was again captured by an English fleet in 1655 and has since remained an English colony. Was a headquarters for buccaneers till the middle of the 18th century.
> British West Indies F 2131.

1861	Periodicals. Societies. Collections.
1864	Gazetteers.
1865	Biography. Genealogy.
1868	Comprehensive works.
1869	Handbooks. Guide books.
	Description and travel.
1870	To 1810.
1871	1810–
1881	History.

        Slavery in Jamaica HT.

1884	To 1810. Earthquake of 1692. Maroons; insurrection of 1795–1796.

        Admiral Vernon and the English West Indian expedition of 1739–1742 F 2272.5.

1886	1810– Negro emancipation. Gov. Eyre. Negro insurrection 1865. Earthquake of 1907.
1891	Regions. Counties. Parishes.

    .C3 Cayman Islands.   .S2 St. Mary Parish.

    .H2 Hanover Parish.   Turks and Caicos Islands F 1659.T9.

1895	Towns. Cities.

1901–1981 **Haiti (Island).**

> Discovered by Columbus in 1492, named Hispaniola or Española and at once settled by the Spaniards. It was the seat of the Audiencia of Santo Domingo and the centre of the Spanish colonial empire in America in the early 16th century. Even after the erection of separate governments in Mexico and Peru, it was still the capital for the West Indies and northern South America for a century more. In the early part of the 17th century bands of adventurers, chiefly French, obtained a foothold in the northwest of the island and out of this grew the French colony of Saint Domingue, occupying the western end of the island (corresponding to the republic of Haiti today). This was formally recognized as a French possession by Spain in 1697. Early in the French revolution, in 1791, the home government passed and then repealed an act granting civil rights to negroes in Saint Domingue. This caused a revolution which the French were unable to put down. The situation was further complicated by the incursion of an English force (that country being at war with France) which maintained itself on the western end of the island from 1793 till its final expulsion in 1798. In 1795 Spain withdrew from the island, ceding to France her colony in the east, which the latter power was unable to hold. By 1801 the native leader Toussaint Louverture had succeeded in restoring order in all parts and inaugurated a constitutional government, which he desired to have recognized and guaranteed by France. He was treacherously seized and taken to France, but Dessalines his successor (who had himself proclaimed emperor as Jacques I) finally expelled the French in 1803, declared the island independent 1804, under the aboriginal name of Haiti, and maintained his supremacy till his death in 1806. His empire was divided between the rival generals: Christophe who maintained himself in the north 1806–1820 and proclaimed a monarchy as King Henry I; and Pétion who ruled in the south 1806–1818, and was succeeded by Boyer. The latter annexed the dominion of Christophe in 1820 and in 1822 drove out the Spaniards who had regained their foothold in the east a few years before. He continued ruler of the entire island till 1843.
>
> The eastern or Spanish part of the island then asserted its independence and organized the Dominican Republic the following year. About 1869 there was a strong movement toward annexation to the U. S.
>
> The French or western end of the island, the Republic of Haiti, was a prey to anarchy for several years, one of her rulers, Soulouque, proclaiming himself king, as Faustin I, in 1849.

1901 Comprehensive works. Description of the whole island.

1909 Antiquities.

1911 History (of the island). Spanish colony, 1492–1795.
> Spanish colony 1804–1822 F 1931.
> Union of the whole island 1822–1843 F 1924.

GREATER ANTILLES—Continued.

1921	**Haiti (Republic).**
1923	French settlement and colony of Saint Domingue. Insurrection of 1791–1804. Toussaint Louverture. English invasion 1793–1798. Withdrawal of Spain from the island 1795. Independence.
1924	1804–1843. (Independence to final division of the island). Dessalines. Christophe. Pétion. Boyer.

Spanish colony revived in eastern end of island 1804–1822 F 1931.

1926	Republic of Haiti, 1844– Soulouque.
1929	Local.

.B7   Boundaries between Haiti and Dominican Republic.

1931	**Dominican Republic.** Spanish colony of Santo Domingo 1804–1822. Dominican Republic 1844.

Proposed annexation to U. S.   E 673.

1939	Local.

Porto Rico.

Discovered by Columbus 1493. Repeatedly attacked by English and others. Spain's rule, however, continued till the conquest of the island in 1898 by the U. S.

1951	Periodicals. Societies. Collections.
1954	Gazetteers.
.5	Directories.
1955	Biography. Genealogy.
1958	Comprehensive works.
1959	Handbooks. Guide books.
	Description and travel.
1961	To 1898.
1965	1898–
1969	Antiquities.
1971	History.
1973	To 1898. Biographies: Tapia y Rivera, Alejandro; etc.
1975	1898–

MacLeary, J. H.   F 391.M

1981	Local.

———

Minor unattached islands in this group.

1991	Navassa.

LESSER ANTILLES. F 2001-2129.

2001	**General works. Carib Indians.** Cf. F 2161.
2006	**Leeward Islands.** St. Thomas, St. John, Virgin Islands, St. Croix, Anguilla, St. Martin, St. Bartholomew, St. Eustatius, St. Christopher, Nevis, Barbuda, Redonda, Montserrat, Guadeloupe, Marie Galante, Dominica, Antigua, etc.
2011	**Windward Islands.** Martinique, St. Lucia, St. Vincent, Grenadines, Grenada, Barbados.
2016	**Islands along the Venezuela coast.** Tobago, Trinidad, Buen Ayre, Curaçao, Aruba.

SEPARATE.

2033	Anguilla (British).
2035	Antigua (British).
2038	Aruba (Dutch).
2041	Barbados (British).
2046	Barbuda (British).
2048	Buen Ayre (Dutch).
2049	Curaçao (Dutch).
2051	Dominica (British).
2056	Grenada (British).
2061	The Grenadines (British).
2066	Guadeloupe (French).
2076	Marie Galante (French).
2081	Martinique (French).
2082	Montserrat (British).
2084	Nevis (British).
2085	Redonda (British).
2088	Saba (Dutch).
2089	St. Bartholemew (French).
2091	St. Christopher (British).
2096	St. Croix (Danish).
2097	St. Eustatius (Dutch).
2098	St. John (Danish).
2100	St. Lucia (British).
2103	St. Martin (Dutch and French).
2105	St. Thomas (Danish).
2106	St. Vincent (British).
2116	Tobago (British).
2121	Trinidad (British).
2129	Virgin Islands (British).

LESSER ANTILLES—Continued.

2131   **British West Indies.**[1]

Bermudas, Bahamas, Jamaica, the Leeward Islands of Anguilla, St. Christopher, Nevis, Barbuda, Antigua, Redonda, Montserrat and Dominica; Windward Islands of St. Lucia, St. Vincent, Grenadines, Grenada, Barbados; also Tobago and Trinidad. The neighboring colonies of British Honduras and British Guiana are sometimes included in British West Indies.

General works on English colonies in America before 1775 E 162; E 188.

American revolution   E 263.W5.

British protectorate of Mosquito coast   F 1529.M9.

2136   **Danish West Indies.**[2]

St. Croix, St. John and St. Thomas.

2141   **Dutch West Indies.**[3]

The Leeward Islands of Saba, St. Eustatius, and part of St. Martin; also the islands of Curaçao, Aruba and Buen Ayre off the Venezuela coast. The neighboring colony of Dutch Guiana is sometimes included in the Dutch West Indies. 1828–1845 Dutch Guiana and the Dutch West Indies were united under a governor residing in the former.

2151   **French West Indies.**[4]

The Leeward Islands of Guadeloupe, Marie Galante, St. Bartholomew, and part of St. Martin; and the Windward island of Martinique. The neighboring colony of French Guiana is sometimes included in the French West Indies.

French colony of St. Domingue, Haiti   F 1923.

St. Pierre and Miquelon   F 1170.

Spanish West Indies   F 1601–1623.

2161   **Spanish Main.** The Caribbean Sea with coasts and islands adjoining. Buccaneers.

2171   Modern descriptive works, since 1810.

---

[1] The British West Indies consist of the following colonies: Bermuda; Bahamas; Jamaica; Leeward Islands (Antigua, Barbuda, Redonda, Montserrat, St. Christopher, Nevis, Anguilla, Dominica, and the Virgin Islands); Windward Islands (St. Lucia, St. Vincent, Grenada and the Grenadines); Barbados; Trinidad and Tobago (one colony).

[2] The Danish West Indies are united into one colony under that name.

[3] All the Dutch West Indies form a single colony under the name of Curaçao.

[4] The French West Indies consist of two colonies: Guadeloupe and dependencies (Guadeloupe, Marie Galante, St. Bartholomew, part of St. Martin, and certain smaller islands), and Martinique.

SOUTH AMERICA. F 2201–2239.

The coasts were visited by Spanish and Portuguese discoverers
in the years following 1492. Under the bull of demarcation
of Pope Alexander VI, 1493–1494, all save the eastern extremity of the continent was allotted to Spain. The Portuguese speedily colonized their portion (Brazil). Other
European nations have temporarily obtained footholds, but
only in the Guianas have they held their own. In the
early colonial period, nearly all Spanish South America was
subject to the Viceroy of Peru. But separate governments
were organized, under royal audiencias or captains general,
usually corresponding approximately with the independent
nationalities of to-day, and largely independent of the viceroy.
In 1718 (temporarily and in 1739 permanently) the northern
part of the continent was made the seat of the Viceroyalty of
New Granada, and in 1776 the southeastern part also was
set off from Peru as the Viceroyalty of La Plata. In the
early part of the 19th century, following Napoleon's de-
thronement of King Ferdinand, the revolutionary movement broke out all over Spanish America. By 1830 the
European authority had been entirely overthrown, and independent governments organized everywhere, save in Guiana.

2201	Periodicals. Societies. Collections.
	South American geographic societies G 5.
2204	Gazetteers. Dictionaries.
2205	Biography.
2208	Comprehensive works.
2209	Miscellaneous.
	Regions.
2212	Andes Mountains.
	For the Andes in the various countries, see regions under each; e. g. the Andes in the Argentine Republic F 2851.
2213	Pacific coast.
	Galapagos Islands F 3741.G2.
2214	Atlantic coast.
-2216	Northern South America (Colombia, Venezuela, Guiana, Ecuador, Peru, Brazil)
	Amazon River F 2546.
	Spanish Main F 2161.
2217	Southern South America (Peru, Bolivia, southern Brazil, Paraguay, Uruguay, Argentine Republic, Chile)
	The La Plata region F 2801–3021.
	Falkland Islands F 3031.
	Description and travel, General.
2221	Before 1810.
2223	1810–
2229	Antiquities. Native races.

SOUTH AMERICA—Continued.

2231   History.
2233   Colonial period. To 1830.
         Early discoveries E 101–141.
2235   Wars of independence, 1806–1830. Bolívar. San
         Martin.
         Miranda F 2323.
         The revolution in Mexico F 1232.
         Morillo y Morillo, Pablo F 2324.M.
         Poinsett, J. R. E 340.P77.
2236   1806–
2239   Topics. Foreign elements.
      .B8 British.
      .G3 Germans.
      .J5 Jews.

COLOMBIA   F 2251–2299.

The coast was visited by Spaniards as early as 1499 and by
Columbus himself on his fourth voyage in 1502. The whole
south shore of the Caribbean seems to have received the name
of Tierra Firma very early. In 1508 the Spanish crown granted
the entire coast from Cape Vela, Goajiros, to Cape Gracias a
Dios to two adventurers, Ojeda and Nicuesa. The Gulf of
Darien was the dividing point, all the coast of modern Colombia, under the name of Nueva Andalucia falling to Ojeda and
the Atlantic coast of Central America south of Honduras to
Nicuesa, as Castilla del Oro. Both leaders failed; the former
founding San Sebastian on the east coast of the Gulf of Darien
and his followers establishing Antigua del Darien on the
west coast of the same gulf (in Nicuesa's province). Meanwhile Nicuesa had founded Nombre de Dios (near Colon)
and soon after perished. Balboa, one of Ojeda's party, discovered the Pacific in 1513 and was in control of the survivors
of both expeditions at Darien till superseded by Pedro Arias
Dávila in 1514. The last named removed his capital across the
isthmus to Panama in 1519.

These settlements were on the Isthmus, then as at present inac-
cessible by land from Colombia. The coast of the latter was
still unsettled till Santa Marta was founded in 1525, Coro (in
Venezuela) in 1527 and Cartagena in 1533. Within the next
decade the interior part of the country was conquered and
settled by expeditions from these coast towns and from Quito,
already subjugated by Pizarro's lieutenants. Santa Fe de
Bogote was founded in 1538 by Jiménez de Quesada, who gave
the name Nuevo reyno de Granada to the country. In 1550
the Audiencia of Santa Fe de Bogote was established to govern
the country. In 1564 it was made a presidency, and elevated
to a vice royalty for a brief period, 1718–1722. During this
period there was a presidency and audiencia at Quito which
governed modern Ecuador and the southwest of Colombia, an
audiencia at Panama for that province, and a governor, and
later captain-general in Venezuela (subject to the Audien-

cia of Santo Domingo). The viceroy of Peru had some sort of suzerainty over the whole region. 1586 Drake attacked Cartagena, and Delcasse took it in 1695. In 1698 a colony of Scotch settled on the Atlantic coast of the Isthmus of Panama, near Darien, on land nominally belonging to New Granada but long neglected. They were expelled two years later. In 1739 New Granada was again made a viceroyalty embracing Colombia (including Panama), Ecuador and Venezuela, the audiencias of Panama and Quito being abolished. In 1741, the English took Porto Bello and attacked Cartagena. 1777 Venezuela was cut off and made a separate government under a captain general. About 1780 a formidable revolution broke out in Santander, known as the rebellion of the communes. In 1808 the revolutionary movement began in Colombia, and open warfare in 1811. The tide of war surged back and forth in Colombia and Venezuela till 1821 when, under Bolívar, the Spanish forces were disastrously defeated. The republic of the United States of Colombia was organized to include New Granada, with the captain generalcies of Caracas and Quito (modern Venezuela and Ecuador). Venezuela withdrew in 1829 and Ecuador the following year, and the republic of New Granada was organized in 1831. The remainder of the 19th century saw many revolutions, and reorganizations of the government. In 1886 the present name, Republic of Colombia, was adopted. In 1903 Panama won its independence. In 1908 the republic was divided into 27 departments, the old state divisions being abolished.

COLOMBIA—Continued.

2281   Regions.   Departments.   Boundaries.

.A5 Andes Mountains.
Cf. F 2212.

.A6 Antioquia (State and Dept.).

.B6 Bolivar (State).

.B7 Boundaries.
Brazil boundary F 2554.
Costa Rica boundary F 1549.B7.

.B8 Boyaca (State).

.C3 Cauca (State).

.C9 Cundinamarca (State).

.D2 Darien. Scots' colony (For modern Darien, see Province of Panama F 1569.P3).

.M2 Magdalena (State).

.S3 Santander (State).

.T6 Tolima (State).

2291   Cities. Towns.

2299   Topics.

VENEZUELA F 2301-2349.

Though seen by Columbus and the Spaniards before 1500 it was several years before any settlement was made. Cumaná was founded in the east in 1520 and Coro in the west in 1527. Charles V granted the coast in 1527 to his creditors, the Welsers of Augsburg, under whom expeditions were despatched to the interior. The Welser grant was cancelled in 1547 and a royal governor appointed. 1595 Caracas was taken and destroyed by the English buccaneers; in 1669 Morgan sacked Maracaibo and in 1679 the French pillaged Caracas. Again in 1739 and 1741 British expeditions attacked La Guaira and Puerto Cabello, and captured Trinidad in 1798.

Down to the creation of the viceroyalty of New Granada, Venezuela was subject to the Audiencia of Santo Domingo. In 1777 the provinces of Caracas, Maracaibo and Cumana and other territory comprising modern Venezuela were separated from New Granada as the captain generalcy of Caracas, and 1786 the Audiencia of Caracas was created.

Early in the 19th century revolutionary activity began; under Miranda considerable successes were won between 1806 and 1812, when he finally withdrew. But one of his adherents, Bolívar, at once took up the contest. The second period of the struggle closed with Bolívar's overthrow in 1814. The next year the war broke out again under Paez, Bolívar returned and by 1823, with the aid of British and other foreign mercenaries, he had expelled the last Spaniard.

In 1822 the federal republic of Colombia was formed, of New Granada, Venezuela and Quito (Ecuador), from which Venezuela withdrew in 1829. Since that time the country has continued independent, with numerous internal revolutions.

2301   Periodicals. Societies. Collections.

2304   Gazetteers. Dictionaries.

.5   Directories.

2305   Biography.

2308   Comprehensive works.
2309   Miscellaneous.
         Description and travel.
2311   Before 1810.
2313   1810–
2319   Antiquities. Indians.
2321   History.
2322   Before 1810.
             The Welsers   E 135.G3.
    .8   1806–
2323   1806–1812. Miranda.
2324   1810–1830. War of independence. Biographies:
               Morillo y Morillo, Pablo; Montilla, Mariano; etc.
               Bolívar, Simón   F 2235.B.
2325   1830– Republic of Venezuela. Anglo-German
               blockade, 1902. Revolution, 1902–1903.
               Biographies: Vargas, J. M.; etc.
               British Guiana boundary dispute   F 2331.B7.
2331   Regions. States. Boundaries.
             .A5 Andes.   Islands off the coast, be-
             .A9 Los Aves Islands.   longing to other pow-
             .B6 Bolívar.   ers   F 2016.
             .B7 Boundaries.   .T2 Tachira.
                  Colombia boundary   .Z9 Zulia.
                  F 2281.B7.
2341   Cities. Towns.
2349   Topics.

GUIANA   F 2351–2479.

A general name applied to the region bounded by the Caribbean Sea, the Amazon, Rio Negro and Orinoco rivers, and
embracing Venezuelan (Spanish), British, Dutch, French,
and Brazilian (Portuguese) Guiana. It is at present usually
restricted to the 2d, 3d, and 4th named. Though visited
by Columbus and other explorers before 1500, little was
known of this region till the fame of the golden city of
El Dorado attracted adventurers. Between 1595 and 1617
Raleigh promoted three expeditions to Guiana. Early in
the 17th century the Dutch established settlements on the
Demerara and Essequibo and later at Berbice (all in
modern British Guiana). In 1621 these passed under control of the Dutch West India company. Meanwhile the
French had gained a foothold at Cayenne and the English at
first established themselves in the region of the Oyapok
River 1604–1629. The permanent English settlements came
later in the modern Dutch Guiana, where a grant between
the Copenam and Maroni rivers was made in 1663 to Wil-
loughby and Hyde. British claims in Guiana were, how-

GUIANA—Continued.

ever, all ceded to Holland in 1667 in exchange for New York,
leaving the Dutch in full control of all modern British and
Dutch Guiana; which was divided into the provinces Essequibo, Demerara, Berbice and Surinam, each taking the
name of its principal river. In 1781 the first three were
captured by British privateers, taken by France in 1782
and restored to Holland 1783. In 1796 the British took
possession of the four Dutch colonies, restoring them in 1802,
only to seize them again in 1803. The four provinces remained in British hands 1804-1816, the convention of London
1814 determining the ultimate ownership of these colonies,
when Surinam alone was restored to Holland. 1828-1845
Holland united all her American dependencies, including
Guiana and the West Indian islands, under a governor
residing at Paramaribo. 1809 French Guiana was conquered
by the Portuguese of Brazil and annexed to the latter till 1815.

2351   General works on the region between the Amazon and
               the Orinoco.
               Early voyages E 111-135.
               Raleigh E 129.R2.

2361–2391   British Guiana.
2361   Periodicals.   Societies.   Collections.
2364   Gazetteers.   Dictionaries.
2364.5   Directories.
2365   Biography.   Genealogy.
2368   Comprehensive works.
2369   Miscellaneous.
               Description and travel.
2370   Before 1803.
2371   1803–
2379   Antiquities.
2380   Indian tribes.
2381   History.
2383   Before 1803.   Dutch colonies of Essequibo, De-
                  merara and Berbice.   English conquests.
                  Cf. F 2423, 2461.
                  Raleigh's explorations E 129.R2.
2384   1803–
                  Boundary dispute with Venezuela F 2331.B7.
2387   Regions.   Districts.   Boundaries.
               .B7 Boundaries.
                  Brazil boundary F 2554.
                  Venezuela boundary F 2331.B7.
2389   Towns.   Cities.
2391   Topics.

BRAZIL   F 2501-2659.

Visited in 1499 by Pinzón, a companion of Columbus, and by the Portuguese Cabral, in 1500. It fell to Portugal according to the Bull of demarcation of Pope Alexander VI in 1493, as modified in 1494. In 1531 the Portuguese crown began to encourage colonization by parceling the coast into captaincies of 50 leagues each, and by the middle of the 16th century the seaboard from the La Plata to the Amazon was studded with independent settlements. In 1548 the governmental powers of the captains were revoked and a governor sent out from Portugal who established his capital at Bahia. Rio de Janeiro was occupied by a French colony, nominally Huguenot, in 1548; but these settlers were soon dispersed. Portugal being absorbed by Spain under the latter's king, there was very little colonial activity 1578-1640. But the enemies of Spain were watchful: the English made various attacks between 1586 and 1595, and the French founded and maintained a colony on the island of Marajo, at the mouth of the Amazon 1612-1618. The Dutch were the most troublesome. The Dutch West India company in 1625 took Bahia, which was quickly recaptured; but in 1630 they captured Olinda, near Pernambuco, which they made the capital of a Dutch province extending in time from the San Francisco River to Maranhao. The Dutch were finally expelled in 1654 and relinquished their claims by treaty in 1662.

Meanwhile the expulsion of the Spanish from Portugal in 1640 had been the signal for new activity in colonial affairs. The first effect was a movement for complete independence among the Portuguese colonists in South Brazil, but on the failure of this, all efforts were concentrated on the expulsion of the Dutch in north Brazil.

From early in the 17th century there was strife between the inhabitants of the back country of south Brazil and the Jesuit reductions in Paraguay, culminating in the War of the Seven reductions in 1754. In 1760 the Jesuits were expelled from Brazil.

In 1807 on the invasion of Portugal by Napoleon the royal family and court took refuge in Brazil. The Spanish colonial movement for independence scarcely spread to Brazil. In fact, advantage was taken of the disturbance to the south to annex the former Spanish colonies north of the La Plata in 1817. King John VI returned to Portugal to resume his crown in 1821, leaving his son Pedro in Brazil. The latter was crowned emperor of Brazil the next year, and the Portuguese expelled in 1823. Discontent at home and popular uprisings led to the loss of Uruguay, after a war with the La Plata provinces, and Pedro I abdicated the throne in favor of his son Pedro II, in 1831. In 1849-1852 Brazil joined with the provinces of Uruguay, Entre Rios, Corrientes and Paraguay to expel Rosas, governor of Buenos Aires and actual ruler of the La Plata region. And in 1864 Brazil was again at war, this time with Argentine Republic and Uruguay against López, ruler of Paraguay, who was overthrown in 1870.

In 1889 the empire was abolished, and after an interim government, a constitutional republic inaugurated in 1891. There was a wide-spread rebellion in 1893–94. Under the republic there has been special activity in the settlement of long-standing boundary disputes with all Brazil's neighbors. That with Bolivia was notable in transferring to Brazil in 1903 the disputed Acre Territory.

2501　Periodicals. Societies. Collections.
2504　Gazetteers. Dictionaries.
　.5　Directories.
2505　Biography. Genealogy.
2508　Comprehensive works.
2509　Miscellaneous.
　　　Description and travel.
2511　　Before 1821.
2513　　1821–1889.
2515　　1889–
2519　Antiquities.
　　　　Moxo Indians　F 3319.
　.1　　Local.
　.3　　Topics.
2521　History.
2524　　Colony, to 1821.
2526　　　To 1548.
　　　　　Cabral　E 125.C11.
2528　　　1549–1762. Expulsion of the Jesuits.
　　　　　Jesuit missions of Paraguay　F 2684.
　　　　　War of the Seven reductions, 1754　F 2684.
　　　　　Portuguese settlement at Colonia, Uruguay　F 2723.
2529　　　French colony at Rio de Janeiro 1555–1567. Villegagnon.
2530　　　Spanish control 1578–1640.
2532　　　Dutch colony 1625–1662.
2534　　　1763–1821. Portuguese court in Brazil.
　　　　　Expulsion of Brazilians from Colonia　F 2723.
　　　　　History of Portugal　DP 500–
　　　　　French Guiana　F 2461.
2536　　Empire, 1822–1889. Abdication of Pedro I. Revolution of 1889.
　　　　　War with Argentine over Uruguay, 1825–1828　F 2726.
　　　　　War with Argentine Republic, 1849–1852　F 2846.
　　　　　Paraguayan war, 1865–1870　F 2687.
2537　　Republic, 1889– Rebellion of 1893–94.
　　　　　Misiones award, 1894　F 2916, 2626.

BRAZIL—Continued.

Regions. States. Boundaries.

2540	Acre Territory.
2541	Alagoas.
2546	Amazonas. Amazon River. Madeira River. Marañion River. Purus River. Jauapiry River. Jurua River, etc.
2551	Bahia.
2554	Boundaries.
	Cf. F 2540.
2556	Ceara.
2561	Espirito Santo. German colonies.
2564	Fernando Noronha Island.
2566	Goyaz.
2571	Maranhao.
2576	Matto Grosso.
	Jesuit missions of Paraguay F 2684.
2581	Minas Geraes. Mucury colony.
	Espirito Santo boundary F 2561.
2586	Para.
	Cf. F 2546.
2591	Parahyba.
2596	Parana.
	Jesuit missions of Paraguay F 2684.
2601	Pernambuco.
2606	Piauhy.
2611	Rio de Janeiro (State).
	Rio de Janeiro (City) F 2646.
2616	Rio Grande do Norte.
2621	Rio Grande do Sul. German colonies.
2626	Santa Catharina. German colonies. Part of Misiones awarded to Brazil.
	Paraná boundary F 2596.
2629	São Francisco River and Valley.
2631	São Paulo. The Paulistas.
	Jesuit missions of Paraguay F 2684.
	War of the Seven reductions, 1754 F 2684.
2636	Sergipe.

Cities. Towns.

2646	Rio de Janeiro.
2651	Other places (alphabetically)
	The various "colonies" of immigrants are entered under state in which each is located.
2659	Topics. Foreign elements.
	.G3 Germans.

PARAGUAY   F 2661-2699.

Paraguay was visited by Sebastian Cabot in 1527. Asuncion was founded in 1535 and soon became the capital of the Spanish possessions in the La Plata region, which comprised not only modern Paraguay, but Uruguay, Rio Grande do Sul and Santa Catharina, Brazil, and the Argentine provinces of Misiones, Corrientes, Entre Rios, Buenos Aires and Santa Fé. The history of the La Plata region in these early days is classed in F 2841. In 1620 on the division of this large domain into the two provinces of Paraguay or Guaira, and Buenos Aires or La Plata, the real history of modern Paraguay begins. But it is only the part of Paraguay east of the Paraguay River that has a colonial history, the western portion of the country forming part of the Chaco region and remaining practically unsettled till late in the 19th century. The early colonists had been accompanied by Franciscan priests, who made some efforts to convert the natives, as did a band of Jesuits about 1586. But in 1608 Philip III of Spain granted the latter order permission to convert the Indians on the upper Parana. At the time, the boundaries between Spanish and Portuguese possessions were undefined, and as the Spanish kings had usurped the Portuguese crown, no conflict of jurisdiction was likely. These Jesuits gathered the natives into towns or "reductions", under a sort of military rule. Their influence spread rapidly on both sides of the Parana River above the Guaira Falls, in the modern Brazilian states of Parana, São Paulo and Matto Grosso. In 1629 the missions were raided and entirely broken up by the Portuguese from São Paulo, (Paulistas). No aid was given by the government of Paraguay; in fact the Jesuits were seldom on friendly terms with the civil authorities. The Jesuits moved their remaining followers down below the falls, and started anew in the country between the Parana and Uruguay rivers, with a centre in or near the modern Argentine territory of Misiones, but extending to the west far into modern Paraguay, and to the east and south into the Brazilian province of Rio Grande do Sul, Uruguay and Corrientes. Though nominally subject to the governor of Paraguay, the missions were virtually independent and the Jesuits now began to arm and drill their converts. In 1728 the missions were detached from Paraguay and placed under the government of Buenos Aires. The attempt of the Spanish crown in 1750 to transfer the "Seven reductions" east of the Uruguay to Portugal in exchange for Colonia, led to armed resistance on the part of the missions in 1754. They were defeated by the combined Spanish and Portuguese forces, and driven across the Uruguay River. But the proposed transfer of territory was abandoned. In 1769 the Jesuits were expelled from the Spanish dominions, and the missions entrusted to the civil authorities. They were soon given up, the Indians mostly withdrawing south into Uruguay and Entre Rios, and northwest into Paraguay proper. On the outbreak

PARAGUAY—Continued.

of the revolution in Buenos Aires, an expedition was despatched to Paraguay, which the Spanish governor easily defeated. But Spaniards were few in the country, and a revolutionary rising from within was successful almost without bloodshed. Dr. Francia easily dominated the country and was virtual dictator till his death in 1840. He was succeeded by C. A. López, 1841–1862, and by the latter's son, F. S. López, 1862–1870. The former was in conflict with neighbors and maritime nations over the right to navigate the Parana; and in 1864 the attempt of the younger López to interfere in the civil wars in Uruguay brought on the Paraguayan war, in which Uruguay, Argentine Republic and Brazil united against Paraguay and finally crushed and nearly annihilated her in 1870.

2661 · Periodicals. Societies. Collections.
2664   Gazetteers. Dictionaries.
.5   Directories.
2665   Biography. Genealogy.
2668   Comprehensive works.
2669   Miscellaneous.
     Description and travel.
2671   Before 1811.
2675   1811–
2681   History.
2683   Before 1811. Province of Paraguay 1620.
       Whole La Plata region before 1620   F 2841.
2684   Jesuit province. Missions or reductions, 1609–1769. War of the Seven reductions, 1754.
       Regions occupied by the missions   F 2621, 2723, 2891, 2916.
2686   1811– Francia. C. A. López. Navigation of the Parana. F. S. López.
2687   Paraguayan war, 1865–1870.

2691   Regions. Departments. Partidos. Colonies. Boundaries.
     .B7   Boundaries.
         Cf. F 2691.C4.
         Brasil boundary   F 2554.
     .C4   Paraguayan Chaco. El Chaco Boreal. Western Paraguay.
         Territory between the Paraguay and Pilcomayo rivers.
         Cf. El Gran Chaco   F 2876.
2695   Cities. Towns.
2699   Topics. Foreign elements.
     .G3   Germans.

URUGUAY F 2701-2799.

Though visited by Díaz de Solis and Cabot early in the 16th century, the native Charruas were successful in repelling all invaders. The Jesuit missions of Paraguay made some advances into the Uruguayan territory early in the 17th century. In 1680 the Brazilians erected a fort at Colonia, which was in dispute for over a century, changing hands repeatedly between Portuguese and Spanish. Montevideo was founded by Buenos Aires in 1726 and thenceforth Spanish influence was predominant. Like Buenos Aires it suffered from the English invasion of 1806–07. Early in the revolutionary movement the Spaniards were defeated in the province under the leadership of Artigas, but Brazil had never renounced her claim to the north shore of the La Plata. She invaded the country and annexed it, though the conquest was not completed. Brazil and Argentine went to war over the question of ownership, 1825–1828. The outcome was a renunciation of the claim of each, and the organization of the independent republic. The remainder of Uruguay's history, down to the present day, has consisted of a series of party struggles and civil wars between the "Blancos" and "Colorados." The interference of Rosas, ruler of Buenos Aires, in Paraguayan affairs in 1842 was the prelude to an alliance which overthrew him in 1852. Uruguay also joined the allies in the Paraguayan war of 1865–70, against the tyrant Lopez.

2701	Periodicals. Societies. Collections.
2704	Gazetteers. Dictionaries.
.5	Directories.
2705	Biography. Genealogy.
2708	Comprehensive works.
2709	Miscellaneous.
	Description and travel.
2711	Before 1810.
2713	1810–
2719	Antiquities.
2721	History.
2723	Before 1810. Contests over Colonia.

  Jesuit missions F 2684.
  War of the Seven reductions, 1754 F 2684.
  English invasions of the La Plata, 1806–07 F 2845.

2726 1810– War of independence. Brazilian occupation. War between Brazil and Argentine over Uruguay, 1825–1828. Civil wars of Blancos and Colorados.

  War against Rosas, 1849–1852 F 2846.
  Paraguayan war, 1865–1870 F 2687.

URUGUAY—Continued.

2731   Regions.   Departments.   Boundaries.
.B7   Boundaries.
     Brazil boundary   F 2554.
.C7   Colonia (Department).
     Portuguese settlement at Colonia   F 2723.
.P3   Paysandu.
.R6   Rocha.
     Cities.   Towns.
2781   Montevideo.
2791   Other places (alphabetically).
2799   Topics.   Foreign elements.

ARGENTINE REPUBLIC. THE LA PLATA REGION   F 2801–3021.

Unlike other countries in South America the present Argentine
Republic did not, in the settlement and early colonial history, form a geographical or political unit. Of the La Plata
provinces proper, Paraguay and Uruguay have won their independence, while the early history of the western states of the
republic belongs rather with Chile and Upper Peru (Bolivia)
than with the La Plata; and the territories to the south,
the old Patagonia, have no colonial history of importance.
The Rio de la Plata was first visited by Juan Díaz de Solis in
1516 and by Sebastian Cabot in 1526. In 1534 a colony set
out from Spain under Pedro de Mendoza as adelantado of
La Plata, and founded Buenos Aires the following year.
In 1538 Asuncion was made the capital and all colonists
removed thither. Under the lieutenant-governorship of
Garay, 1576–1584, many separate settlements were established and Buenos Aires again occupied. The La Plata
region was a dependency of the Viceroy of Peru, and immediately subordinate to the Audiencia of Charcas (otherwise
La Plata, the modern Sucre, Bolivia). About 1620 the
government was divided: all that part below the confluence
of the Parana and Paraguay rivers as the province of
Rio de la Plata or Buenos Aires, and the region around and
to the eastward of Asuncion, as Guaira or Paraguay. The
former province was almost entirely confined to the present
provinces of Buenos Aires and Santa Fe, the region between
the Uruguay and Parana rivers being held by Indians, and
the modern Uruguay not occupied at all till 1680, when the
Portuguese from Brazil erected a fort at Colonia opposite
Buenos Aires. This was the seat of frequent contests between
Spanish and Portuguese colonists. 1726 Montevideo was
founded by Spaniards, who thenceforth were predominant
on the northern bank, but the Colonia question remained
unsettled many years. Meanwhile, to the westward, in modern
Argentine territory, two separate governments had been organized: Cuyo (the modern Argentine provinces of Mendoza, San
Juan and San Luis) a dependency of Chile; and Tucuman (provinces of Cordoba, Rioja, Santiago del Estero, Tucuman, Cata-

marca, Salta and Jujuy) a part of Upper Peru or Charcas. The Jesuit missions of Paraguay, though largely in the
present Argentine territory of Misiones, belong rather with the
history of Paraguay, F 2684: though they were transferred to
the government of Buenos Aires in 1728. The same is true
of the War of the Seven reductions, which was an attempt
to dispossess such of these mission Indians as were east of
the Uruguay (in modern Rio Grande do Sul, Brazil). In 1776 the
Spanish crown established the Viceroyalty of La Plata, with
seat at Buenos Aires, transferring to its control all the territories
previously subject to the Audiencia of Charcas. And in 1782
there was also an audiencia established at Buenos Aires.
The viceroyalty comprised the following governments: 1.
Buenos Aires (the Argentine provinces of Buenos Aires,
Santa Fe, Entre Rios and Corrientes; and Uruguay); 2. Paraguay; 3. Upper Peru or Charcas (modern Bolivia); 4. Tucuman; 5. Cuyo, now detached from Chile. 1806 the city of
Buenos Aires was taken by an English expedition which held
it till defeated the following year. 1810 the revolution broke
out, in the formation of a governing junta in Buenos Aires.
The Spaniards were soon expelled, and expeditions under-
taken against the Spanish strongholds on the Pacific. A
constitutional government was organized in 1825, but for
many years there was anarchy or civil war within and
among the provinces, between the two factions of Unita-
rians or the party of centralization and Federalists, or those
who favored autonomy for the provinces. During these
conflicts Bolivia, Paraguay and Uruguay asserted their own
independence, the last named in 1828 after a war with its
Brazilian invaders. From 1829 to 1852 Rosas, though nominally a Federalist and governor of Buenos Aires, was virtual
dictator of the whole La Plata region. In 1843 a civil war
in Uruguay was the occasion of Rosas' interference, and he
was attacked at home by Urquiza, governor of Entre Rios.
The alliance of these enemies with Brazil resulted in the
expulsion of Rosas in 1852. Under Urquiza's government
the province of Buenos Aires maintained its independence
till 1859, when it reentered the confederation; but jeal-
ousies between the capital and the provinces were prominent
for many years. 1865 the Argentine provinces were drawn
into the war against López, ruler of Paraguay. Boundary
disputes with Chile caused much irritation and warlike
preparations on the part of both countries. The territory
involved was not merely the frontier of two countries, but
the vast unsettled regions of Patagonia and farther south.
Final agreement was made in 1902. Another boundary
adjustment, with Bolivia and Chile, gave to Argentina a
portion of the former's Atacama region, now the territory of
Los Andes, 1899–1900.

2801 Periodicals. Societies. Collections.

2804 Gazetteers. –Dictionaries.

.5 Directories.

ARGENTINE REPUBLIC. THE LA PLATA REGION—Continued.

2805   Biography.   Genealogy.
2808   Comprehensive works.
2809   Miscellaneous.
      Description and travel.
2811   Before 1806.
2815   1806–
2821   Antiquities.
   .1   Local.
   .3   Topics.
2831   History.
2841   Before 1806.   Viceroyalty of La Plata.
         Upper Peru and Audiencia of Charcas   F 3301–3359.
         Paraguay   F 2683.
         Brazilian claims to Colonia   F 2723.
         Jesuit province or reductions   F 2684.
         War of the Seven reductions, 1754   F 2684.
2845   1806–1817.   English invasions.   War of independence.
         San Martin   F 2235.8.
2846   1817–   Rosas.   Civil wars.   War with Brazil, 1849–1852.
         War with Brazil over Uruguay, 1825–1828   F 2726.
         Paraguayan war, 1865–1870   F 2687.
         Misiones award, 1894   F 2916.
      Regions.   Provinces.   Territories.   Boundaries.
2851   Andes Mountains (including Chilean boundary question).
2853   Los Andes (Territory).
2857   Boundaries.
         Cf. F 2853.
         Chile boundary   F 2851.
         Brazil boundary   F 2554, 2916.
         Paraguay boundary   F 2691.B7.
2861   Buenos Aires (Province).
         Buenos Aires (City)   F 3001.
         Martin Garcia (Island)   F 2909.
2871   Catamarca.
2876   El Chaco (Territory).   El Gran Chaco.
         Paraguayan Chaco   F 2691.C4.
2881   Chubut (Territory).
2886   Cordova.
2891   Corrientes.
2896   Entre Rios.
2901   Formosa (Territory).
2906   Jujuy.

Regions. Provinces. Territories, etc.—Continued.

2909   La Plata River and Valley. Parana River. Martin Garcia (Island).

2911   Mendoza. The ancient Chilean gobernación of Cuyo.

2916   Misiones (Territory). The Misiones question with Brazil (cf. F 2626).
     The Jesuit missions of Paraguay F 2684.

2921   Neuquen (Territory).

2924   Pampa (Territory).

2926   Pampas region. Region south of Mendoza and San Luis, and west of Buenos Aires, extending south to Patagonia.

2936   Patagonia.
     (Including collective works on Patagonia, Falkland Islands, Tierra del Fuego, Straits of Magellan, Cape Horn, etc.) Argentine Patagonia is now subdivided into territories of Neuquen, Rio Negro, Chubut and Santa Cruz. Chilean Patagonia is embraced in the Chilean province of Chiloe and territory of Magallanes.
     Falkland Islands F 3031.
     Tierra del Fuego F 2986.
     Straits of Magellan F 3191.

2951   Rio Negro (Territory).

2956   La Rioja.

2958   Salta.

2961   San Juan.

2966   San Luis.

2971   Santa Cruz (Territory).

2976   Santa Fe.

2981   Santiago del Estero.

2986   Tierra del Fuego (Territory). Tierra del Fuego (Island).
     The western part of the island forms part of the Chilean territory of Magallanes.
     Cf. F 3186.

2991   Tucuman (Province) The ancient gobernación of Tucuman.

     Cities. Towns.

3001   Buenos Aires (City).

3011   Other places (alphabetically). ·

3021   Topics. Foreign elements.
     .F8   French.
     .I8   Italians.

————

3031   Falkland Islands. Pepys Island (Imaginary).

CHILE   F 3051–3285.

At the time of the Spanish conquest of Peru, northern Chile was occupied by Indian tribes, which had been conquered by the Incas, while the region south of modern Valparaiso was held by warlike and independent tribes, the Araucanians and others. The country was invaded by Spaniards from Peru: in 1535 by Almagro, and in 1540 by Valdivia, who founded Santiago and other towns, and even despatched expeditions across the Andes to the east, where there was organized the province of Cuyo; now part of the Argentine Republic. In 1553 most of the Chilean settlements were destroyed in Indian inroads and for the next hundred years there was almost ceaseless fighting, often known as the Araucanian war. The difficulties of conducting a contest at such a distance from Peru, were such that a royal audiencia was established in Chile in 1567. This was abolished in 1575 and a royal governor and captain general substituted. The audiencia was revived in 1609. Finally in 1640 a treaty was made with the Indians which left them all the land south of the Biobío River. There were later Indian wars in 1655, 1724 and 1766. In 1776 the province of Cuyo, comprising the part of Chile east of the Andes, was transferred to the new viceroyalty of La Plata. The movement for independence which broke out in 1810 was crushed by the viceroy of Peru in 1814; but on the arrival of San Martín and his Argentine army in 1817 the royalists were finally overthrown. Chile was made a centre of military and naval operations against Peru until the final defeat of the Spaniards in 1824. The republic then organized was unstable at first, and there have been a number of risings against the government down to recent times. In 1836, Chile became involved in war with the Peru-Bolivian confederation, and in 1865 was drawn by Peru into a brief war with Spain. The Chile-Peruvian war of 1879–1882 was brought on by commercial troubles over the nitrate industry in the Bolivian province of Atacama. Peru took the side of Bolivia, and the result of the struggle was the loss by Bolivia of her entire seaboard. Territorial questions growing out of the war and transfer of territory have kept alive unfriendly feelings down to the present day. The Bolivian territory of Atacama (Chilean province of Antofagasta) and the Peruvian department of Tarapaca (Chilean province of the same name) were transferred outright, and, by the treaty of Ancon accepted Oct. 23, 1883, the Peruvian territories of Tacna and Arica temporarily transferred to Chile, pending ultimate decision ten years later. They are still retained by Chile. In 1891 there was a successful revolution against President Balmaceda. From 1898 to 1902 boundary disputes with the Argentine Republic led the country to the verge of war.

3051	Periodicals. Societies. Collections.
3054	Gazetteers. Dictionaries.
.5	Directories.

3055	Biography. Genealogy.
3058	Comprehensive works.
3059	Miscellaneous.
	Description and travel.
3061	Before 1810.
3063	1810–
3069	Antiquities.
.1	Local.

          Araucania and Araucanians   F 3126.

.3	Topics.
3072	Ciudad de los Cesares.
3081	History.
3091	Before 1810. Araucanian wars.
3094	War of independence, 1810–1824. Biographies: O'Higgins, Bernardo; etc.

          San Martín   F 2235.8.

3095	1824– War with Spain, 1865–1866. Biographies: Montt, Manuel; etc.

          War with Peru-Bolivian confederation, 1836–1839   F 3447.

3097	War with Peru and Bolivia, 1879–1882.
.3	Territorial questions, growing out of the war. Tacna and Arica.

          Cf. F 3116, 3231, 3241.

3098	Revolution of 1891.
	Regions. Provinces. Boundaries.
3106	Aconcagua.
3111	Andes Mountains in Chile.

          Cf. F 2212, 2851.

3116	Antofagasta. (Formerly Bolivian territory of Atacama.)
3126	Arauco. The ancient Araucania and Araucanians

          Cf. F 3069, 3091.

3131	Atacama.

          Cf. Easter Island   F 3169.

3136	Biobio.
3139	Boundaries.

          Cf. F 3097.3.
          Argentine boundary   F 2851, 2853.

3141	Cautin.
3146	Chiloe.

          Cf. F 2936.

3151	Colchagua.
3156	Concepcion.
3161	Coquimbo.
3166	Curico.

CHILE—Continued.

Cuyo (transferred to Viceroyalty of La Plata, 1776)
F 2911.

3169	Easter Island. (Isla de Pascua. Te Pito te Henua.)
3171	Juan Fernandez Islands.
3176	Linares.
3181	Llanquihue.
3186	Magallanes (Territory).

Cf. F 2936.
Island of Tierra del Fuego   F 2936.

3191	Straits of Magellan.

Magellan   G 286.M2; G 420.M2.

3196	Malleco.
3201	Maule.
3206	Ñuble.
3211	O'Higgins.
3221	Santiago (Province).

Santiago de Chile (City)   F 3271.

3231	Tacna. Peruvian territories of Tacna and Arica.

Cf. F 3097.3.

3236	Talca.
3241	Tarapaca.

Cf. F 3097.3.

3246	Valdivia.
3251	Valparaiso (Province).

Cf. Islas de Juan Fernández   F 3171.

Cities.   Towns.

3271	Santiago de Chile (City).
3281	Other places (alphabetically).
3285	Topics. Foreign elements.

.F8   French.
.G3   Germans.

BOLIVIA   F 3301–3359.

In early days the modern Bolivia was a part of Peru, both under
the Incas and for over two centuries following the Spanish
conquest. In 1559 a royal audiencia was established in
Charcas (otherwise the city of La Plata, now Sucre) having
jurisdiction over the region known as Upper Peru. This
included not only modern Bolivia, but the gobernación
of Tucuman (now the northwestern provinces of Argentine
Republic). The La Plata region (eastern Argentine, Paraguay and Uruguay) though having governors of its own, was
also subject to the Audiencia, while the whole acknowledged
the supremacy of the Viceroy of Peru at Lima. In 1776
the entire region subject to the Audiencia of Charcas was
detached from the Viceroyalty of Peru and by royal decree
became the Viceroyalty of La Plata, with capital at Buenos

Aires. From 1809 till the final expulsion of the Spaniards in 1825, the country was the scene of almost continual warfare. As the Argentines had not been able to conquer it, Bolívar, who was in command at the final conquest, succeeded in inducing the La Plata provinces and Peru to abandon their territorial claims, Upper Peru becoming independent as the republic of Bolivia, under his lieutenant Sucré. The Colombians were expelled in 1827. In 1835 President Santa Cruz of Bolivia took part in the civil wars of Peru and united the two countries, forming the "Confederación Perú-Boliviana." Chile considered her interests threatened and interfered, with the result that the confederation was dissolved in 1839. In 1841 Peru made an attempt to annex a part of Bolivia, which was successfully resisted. For the next generation, the country was the victim of many civil wars. In 1873 Peru and Bolivia entered a secret agreement to resist aggressions of Chile which had acquired extensive commercial interests in the seacoast provinces of the allies. War with Chile broke out in 1879, and resulted in the complete overthrow of the allies, and the loss by Bolivia of her entire coast. The Acre territory in the northern part of the country declared itself independent in 1900, and being claimed by Brazil, was ceded to that country in 1903 for certain considerations.

3301	Periodicals. Societies. Collections.
3304	Gazetteers. Dictionaries.
.5	Directories.
3305	Biography. Genealogy.
3308	Comprehensive works.
3309	Miscellaneous.
	Description and travel.
3311	Before 1809.
3313	1809–
3319	Antiquities. Moxo Indians.
3321	History.
3322	Before 1809. Upper Peru. Audiencia of Charcas.

Southern part of Upper Peru in colonial period; Tucuman F 2991.
Viceroyalty of Peru (before 1776) F 3444.
Viceroyalty of La Plata, 1776–1810 F 2841.
Insurrection of Tupac Amaru, 1780–1781 F 3444.

3323	War of independence, 1809–1825.
3324	1825–

Confederación Perú-Boliviana, 1835–1839 F 3447.
War with Chile, 1879–1882 F 3097.

3341	Regions. Departments. Boundaries.

Acre territory F 2540.

.A5	Andes Mountains, Bolivia.

Cf. F 2212.

BOLIVIA.

3341   Regions.   Departments.   Boundaries—Continued.

Atacama, (now Chilean province of Antofagasta F 3116, and Argentine territory of Los Andes F 2853).

.B7   **Boundaries.**
Argentine boundary   F 2837, 2853.
Brazil boundary   F 2554, 2540.
Chile boundary   F 3139, 3097.3, 3116.
Paraguay boundary   F 2631.B7.
Peru boundary   F 3451.B7.

.C6   Chuquisaca.

.C7   Cochabamba.

.L3   La Paz.
Acre territory   F 2540.
Lake Titicaca   F 3451.T6.

.O7   Oruro.

.S2   Santa Cruz.

.T3   Territorio Nacional de Colonias.

.T6   Lake Titicaca region, Bolivia.
Cf. F 3451.T6.

3351   Towns.   Cities.

3359   Topics.

PERU   F 3401–3619.

At the time of the Spanish conquest, 1531, the ruling family of Incas had recently consolidated its dominion, which included not only modern Peru, but Ecuador (province of Quito) on the north, Bolivia (Upper Peru) on the east and northern Chile on the south. Taking advantage of internal quarrels, Pizarro and his followers speedily overran the whole Inca empire. Quarrels arose among the conquerors,— Pizarro himself was assassinated in 1541 and Emperor Charles V sent out Núñez de Vela as 1st viceroy of Peru in 1544. Though the rule of the viceroy extended over practically all Spanish South America down to the erection of the Vice-royalties of New Granada in 1739 and La Plata in 1776; yet it was found necessary to establish local governments under audiencias or captains general. Such were the audiencia of Charcas, 1559, the presidency and audiencia of Quito, 1564, the audiencia (later captain generalcy) of Chile, 1567, etc. Peru itself remained the centre of Spanish power in America. While the revolutionary movement gained full strength in remoter regions it was only in 1820 that Peru itself was seriously threatened. San Martín from the south, and Bolívar from the north, concentrated their victorious forces, and the battle of Ayacucho, Dec. 1824, marked the end of the Spanish power in South America. After years of civil war, President Santa Cruz of Bolivia invaded Peru, 1835, and joined the two countries as the Confederación Perú-Boliviana. An invasion from Chile broke up their union in 1839. In 1865–66 there was a war with Spain in which Chile was also involved. War broke out between Chile and Bolivia in 1879 over the nitrate deposits on the coast, and Peru, as ally of the latter,

was drawn in. The disastrous defeat of the allies was followed
by the absolute loss of the Peruvian province of Tarapaca
to the victor, while the territories of Tacna and Arica were
conditionally surrendered for ten years, subject to a plebiscite
at the end of that period. Chile still holds them, as the province of Tacna, with ultimate status unsettled.

3401	Periodicals. Societies. Collections.
3404	Gazetteers. Dictionaries.
.5	Directories.
3405	Biography. Genealogy.
3408	Comprehensive works.
3409	Miscellaneous.
	Description and travel
3411	Before 1820.
3423	1820–
3429	Antiquities. Incas.
.1	Local.
.3	Topics.
3430	Indian tribes of modern Peru.
3431	History.
3442	Before 1548. Spanish conquest. Pizarro.

Indians of Peru and the Inca empire, before 1531 F 3429.

3444	1548–1825. Viceroyalty of Peru. Insurrection of Tupac Amaru, 1780–1781.
3446	War of independence, 1810–1825. Biographies: Miller, William; etc.
3447	1820– Civil wars. Confederación Perú-Boliviana. 1835–1839. War with Spain, 1865–1866.

War with Chile, 1879–1882 F 3097.

Putumayo atrocities F 3451.P94.

3451	Regions. Departments. Boundaries.	
	.A4	Amazonas.
	.A9	Ayacucho.
	.B7	Boundaries.
	.C9	Cuzco.
	.J9	Junin. German colony of Pozuzu.
	.L7	Lima.

Lima (City) F 3601.

	.L8	Loreto.
	.M8	Moquegua. Misti (Volcano).
	.P9	Puno. Inambari River.
	.P94	Putumayo River and Valley. Rubber atrocities.
	.T6	Lake Titicaca region.

Cf. F 3341.T6.

	Cities. Towns.
3601	Lima.
3611	Other places (alphabetically).
3619	Topics. Foreign elements.

ECUADOR   F 3701–3799.

At the time of the Spanish conquest of Peru the Incas had just recently completed the overthrow of the Caras, or Indians of this region. It was natural then to extend the Spanish control to the north. As early as 1535 Quito was made a centre for Spanish incursions into modern Colombia, to the north. In 1564 the old kingdom of Quito, with outlying Colombian and Peruvian provinces, was erected into a presidency, with a royal audiencia, nominally under the jurisdiction of the Viceroy of Peru till 1739, when the viceroyalty of New Granada was created. In 1809 the Spanish government was overthrown in favor of a native junta at Quito. This lasted but a short time, and under a prudent Spanish commander, Ecuador continued a royalist stronghold till 1819. In the latter year, the rebellion broke out afresh, encouraged by the successes of Bolívar in the north and San Martín in the south. The victory of Pichincha in May 1822 was decisive, and the four provinces forming modern Ecuador were absorbed into Bolívar's new republic of Colombia. After various smaller revolts, the old presidency of Quito declared itself independent, 1830, under the name of the republic of Ecuador.

3701	Periodicals. Societies. Collections.
3704	Gazetteers. Dictionaries.
3705	Biography. Genealogy.
3708	Comprehensive works.
3709	Miscellaneous.
	Description and travel.
3711	Before 1810.
3713	1810–1830.
3714	1830–
3721	Antiquities. Indians.
.1	Local.
.3	Topics.
3731	History.
3733	Before 1810.
3734	1810–1830.
3735	1830–
3741	Regions. Provinces. Boundaries.
.A6	Andes Mountains, Ecuador.
	Cf. F 2212.
.B7	Boundaries.
	Peru boundary F 3451.B7.
.G2	Galapagos Islands.
	Cities. Towns.
3881	Quito.
3891	Other places (alphabetically).
3899	Topics. Foreign elements.

References to these additions are preceded by "a" in index. The suggestion is made that additions be either entered in proper place by hand, or at least a check made to indicate where matter is to be inserted.

E 11-29   *Add as footnote.*

> These numbers are reserved for works which are actually comprehensive in scope. A book of travel would seldom, if ever, be classed here, but rather under U. S., Spanish-America, etc., whichever might be the main country or region covered.

E 29.F8   *Add* Huguenots.

E 31-50   *Add as footnote.*

> These numbers, like E 11-29, are to be assigned only to works professedly and actually comprehensive; *e. g.*, a book dealing principally with British America with a few pages at the end on the U. S. would be placed in F 1001-1035, regardless of title. Most works having United States in the title relate so largely to this country that they are classed E 151:—

E 83   *Refer* Indian wars and uprisings in Virginia 1609-1676 (Massacres 1622 and 1641, etc.) F 229.

.67   *Refer* Gookin, Daniel   F 67.G.

.77   *Refer* Logan, John, Indian chief   E 99.M64L.

.813   *Add* Jackson's execution of the Tennessee militiamen.

    Refer Pinckney, Thomas   E 302.6.P57.

.875   *Add* Cheyenne outbreak, 1875.

E 99   *Add* .M64   Mingo Indians.

E 121   *Add* Demarcation line of Alexander VI.

E 159   *Refer* Altitudes   GB 494-496; G 109.

E 162   *Add* Thanksgiving day and customs in the colonies (Cf. F 7; GT 4975).

E 175.4   *Add* The work of historical societies.

.5   *Add* Ropes, J. C.
      Squier, E. G.

E 182   *Add* Steedman, Charles: Rowan, S. C.; Roe, F. A.; Philip, J. W.

    Refer Bailey, Theodorus   E 467.1.B14.
      Porter, D. D.   E 467.1.P78.

E 184   *Add* .A8   Asiatics   Cf. E 184.O6.
      .B8   British   Cf. E 184.E5; .S3; .S4; .W4.

.F8   *Add* Cf. E 184.H9.

.F85   *Add* Cf. E 184.A2.

.G3   *Add* Cf. E 184.M8.

E 186   *Refer* under .99.
         Order of Washington   E 202.7.

E 195   *Refer* Ruggles, Timothy   F 67.R.

E 199   *Refer* Ruggles, Timothy   F 67.R.

E 202   *Add* .7   Order of Washington.
         .9   Other societies (alphabetically).

E 207   *Refer* Cornwallis, Charles Cornwallis, 1st marquis   DA 506.C8.
         Howe, Richard Howe, earl   DA 87.H8.

E 231   *Add* Patriot's day, Apr. 19.

E 239   *Add* Evacuation day.

E 241   *Add as footnote.*
         The Library of Congress at present classes battles here. A scheme will probably be worked out later for E 231–239, on lines somewhat similar to E 471–478.

E 263.M3   *Add* Eden, Sir Robert.

.M4   *Refer* Leonard, Daniel   E 278.L5.
         Paine, R. T.   E 302.6.P14.

.N84   *Add* Northwest, Old.

.P4   *Refer* Ross, George   E 302.6.R79.
         Rush, Benjamin   E 302.6.R85.

E 278   *Add* .L5   Leonard, Daniel.

E 302.6   *Add* .P14   Paine, R. T.
         .R61   Rodney, C. A.
         .R79   Ross, George.
         .R85   Rush, Benjamin.
         Refer Rodman, William   F 153.R.

E 335   *Add* Morris, R. V.

E 340   *Add* .M83   Morrow, Jeremiah.
         .P88   Prentiss, Samuel.
         .R7   Robertson, George.
         .R8   Ross, H. H.
         .R9   Rush, Richard.
         .V7   Vinton, S. F.
         Refer Murphy, H. C.   F 123.M.
         Prentice, G. D.   E 415.9.P85.
         Rodney, C. A.   E 302.6.R61.

E 356   *Add as footnote.*
         The Library of Congress at present classes battles here. A scheme will probably be worked out later for E 355, on lines somewhat similar to E 471–478.

E 382   *Refer* 1st Creek war; execution of Tennessee militiamen.   E 83.813.

E 401   *Add* .2   Guadalupe club.

E 403.1	*Refer* Bailey, Theodorus E 467.1.B14.
.P6	*Add* Cf. Pillow court-martial E 405.6.
E 405.6	*Add* Pillow court-martial.
E 406	*Add as footnote.*

> The Library of Congress at present classes battles here. A scheme will probably be worked out later for E 405, on lines somewhat similar to E 471–478.

E 415.6	*Add* Black, J. S.
.9	*Add* .B6 Black, J. S.
	.B63 Blair, F. P.
	.P5 Phillips, H. M.
	.P85 Prentice, G. D.
	.R75 Rollins, E. H.
	.R76 Rollins, J. S.
	.Y2 Yancey, W. L.

> *Refer* Peirpoint, F. H. E 534.P.
> Reed, R. R.   F 153.R.
> Reemelin, Charles F 496.R.
> Sherman, John E 664.S5.
> Watts, T. H. F 326.W.
> Under Phillips, Wendell, *Refer* Phillips' collected works in E 415.6.P.   .

E 436	*Refer* Paraguay expedition F 2686.
E 438	*Refer* Squatter sovereignty E 415.7.
E 442	*Refer* Murrell, J. A. F 396.M.
E 447	*Refer* New York negro plot, 1741 F 128.4.

> Richmond insurrection, 1800 (Gabriel's) F 234.R5.
> Charleston insurrection, 1822 (Denmark Vesey's) F 279.C4.
> Southampton insurrection, 1831 (Nat Turner's) F 232.S7.

E 463	*Refer* Loyal publication society's pamphlets (collected) E 458.L.
E 467.1	*Add* .B14 Bailey, Theodorus.
	.D87 Duffié, A. N.
	.E13 Early, J. A.
	.P78 Porter, D. D.
	.R2 Ramseur, S. D.

> Under .W4, *add* Cf. Warren court-martial E 477.675.
> *Refer* Blair, F. P. E 415.9.B63.
> Piatt, Donn F 496.P.
> Rowan, S. C. E 182.R.
> Rusk, J. M. E 664.R93.
> Watts, T. H. F 326.W.

E 472.17	*Add* (Battle of Rich Mountain).
.7	*Add* (Port Royal expedition, Nov. 1861).
E 473.2	*Add* (Merrimac and Monitor).
.3	*Add* (Capture of Elizabeth City).
.4	*Add* (Battle of Nueces River).
E 474.61	*Add* (Siege of Harper's Ferry).
E 475.1	*Add* (Streight's raid toward Rome, Ga., Apr.–May, 1863).
.5	*Add* (Battle of Middleburg).
.62	*Add* Siege of Charleston.
E 476.33	*Add* (Battle of Pleasant Hill).
.87	*Add* (Battle of Allatoona).
E 477.16	*Add* (Battle of Westport).
.52	*Add* (Battle of Spring Hill).
.67	*Add* (Battle of Gravelly Run).
.9	*Add* (Stoneman's raid, 1865).
E 482	*Refer* Confederate States almanacs AY 381.
E 487	*Refer* C. S. A. documents JK 9661–9799.
E 536	*Refer* Gov. Peirpoint E 534.
E 541	*Add* .P4 Pennsylvania. University
E 545	*Refer* Comparisons of the Union and Confederate armies E 491.
E 608	*Refer* Andrews' railroad raid, 1862 E 473.55.
E 621	*Add* National association of civil war nurses.
E 639	*Add* Southern relief agencies.
E 661.7	*Refer* Relations with Latin America F 1418.
E 664	*Add* .D4 Depew, C. M.
	.M85 Morton, L. P.
	.R93 Rusk, J. M.
	.S57 Sherman, John.
	Refer Black, J. S. E 415.9.B6.
	Piatt, Donn F 496.P.
	Rollins, E. H. E 415.9.R75.
E 702	*Refer* Harrison's collected works in E 660.H.
E 714.6	*Refer* Philip, J. W. E 182.P.
F	*Add* Thanksgiving day in New England Cf. E 162; GT 4975.
F 38	*Refer* Rollins, E. H. E 415.9.R75.
F 39	*Add* Rand, E. D.

F	53	*Refer* Prentiss, Samuel E 340.P88.
F	67	*Add* Winthrop, John, jr.; Gookin, Daniel; Russell, James; Read, John; Ruggles, Timothy.
F	68	*Add* Pilgrim society, Plymouth.
		Refer Old Colony historical society, Taunton F 74.T2O.
		Thanksgiving day F 7; E 162; GT 4975.
F	69	*Add* Phillips, Samuel; Phillips, William; Phillips, John; Pickering, John; Russell, Thomas.
		Refer Paine, R. T. E 302.6.P14.
		Prescott, William E 207.P75.
F	123	*Add* Murphy, H. C.
		Refer Ross, H. H. E 340.R8.
F	124	*Refer* Murphy, H. C. F 123.M.
F	127	*Add* .M4 Military tract (set off from Tryon Co., 1782; embracing the present counties of Onondaga, Cortland, Cayuga, Tompkins and Seneca, with parts of Oswego, Wayne and Schuyler)
	.P9	*Refer* Oblong tract F 127.D8.
	.W5	*Refer* Oblong tract F 127.D8.
F	128.9	*Add* .N3 Negroes.
F	152	*Refer* Ross, George E 302.6.R79.
F	153	*Add* Cooper, James; Reed, R. R.; Ritner, Joseph; Rodman, William.
		Refer Black, J. S. E 415.9.B6.
		Phillips, H. M. E 415.9.P5.
		Rush, Benjamin E 302.6.R85.
		Rush, Richard E 340.R9.
F	154	*Add* Ross, George; Crawford, J. W.; Durham, I. W.; Harper, T. B.
F	168	*Refer* Rodney, C. A. E 302.6.R61.
F	184	*Refer* Biographies: Sharpe, Horatio; etc.
F	213	*Refer* Murrell, J. A. F 396.M.
F	229	*Refer* Gookin, Daniel F 67.G.
F	230	*Add* Simms, Charles.
F	232	*Add* .E4 Elizabeth City Co.
		.H6 Highland Co.
		.R7 Rockingham Co.
		.W4 Westmoreland Co.
F	247	*Add* .B8 Brooke Co.
F	258	*Add* Ruffin, Thomas.
F	262	*Add* .S9 Surry Co. Fisher's River, N. C.

F 272   *Add* Biographies: Pinckney, Charles, etc.

F 277   *Add* .S18   St. James Parish.

F 290   *Add* Cession of western lands to U. S., 1802.

F 296   *Refer* Gulf coast before 1763; Louisiana   F 372.

F 314   *Add* Ribaut; Laudonnière.
             Refer Gulf coast before 1763   F 372.

F 326   *Add* Watts, T. H.
             Refer Yancey, W. L.   E 415.9.Y2.

F 353   *Refer* Murrell, J. A.   F 396.M.

F 389   *Add* Biographies: Rusk, T. J.; etc.

F 396   *Add* Murrell, J. A.
             Refer Ozark Mountain region   F 417.O9.

F 417   *Add* .O9   Ozark Mountain region   Cf. F 472.O9.
                    .S4   Sevier Co.

F 455   *Refer* Prentice, G. D.   E 415.9.P85.
                   Robertson, George   E 340.R7.

F 456   *Add* Biographies: Goebel, William; Powers, Caleb; Reid, Richard; etc.
             Refer Prentice, G. D.   E 415.9.P85.

F 466   *Refer* Blair, F. P.   E 415.9.B63.
                   Rollins, J. S.   E 415.9.R76.

F 472   *Add* .B3   Bates Co.
                    .O9   Ozark Mountain region, Mo.
                        Cf. F 417.O9.

F 495   *Refer* Morrow, Jeremiah   E 340.M83.
                   Vinton, S. F.   E 340.V7.
                   Piatt, Donn   F 496.P.
                   Reemelin, Charles   F 496.R.

F 496   *Add* Reemelin, Charles; Piatt, Donn.

F 546   *Add* Phillips, D. L.

F 548.45   *Refer* Haymarket square riot, 1886   HX 846.C4

F 586   *Add* Dewey, Nelson.
             Refer Rusk, J. M.   E 664.R93.

F 597   *Add* Explorers: Carver, Jonathan; etc.

F 697   *Refer* Kansas   F 685.
                   Nebraska   F 666.

F 752   *Add* .C2   Canyon Co.

F 864   *Add* Admission as state.

F 908   *Refer* Alaska commercial company   F 912.P9.

F 912.P9   *Add* Alaska commercial company.

F 1030.8   *Add* and other writings.

F 1054   *Add* .I8   Isle aux Coudres.
                 .R5   Richelieu River and Valley.
                 .T32   Temiscouata Co.

F 1390   *Add* Topics. Foreign elements.
                 .G3   Germans.

F 1409   *Add* National characteristics of the Latin Americans.
          Refer Voyages to the Pacific coast (following gold discovery) F 865.

F 1432   *Refer* Voyages to the Pacific coast (following gold discovery) F 865.

F 1619   *Refer* Lucayan Indians F 1655.

F 1621   *Add* Naval operations in West Indian waters.
          Refer Spanish West Indies in the 19th century F 1783.
                Ruyter's attack on Barbados, 1655 F 2041.
                English capture of Martinique, 1809 F 2081.

F 1655   *Add* Antiquities. Lucayan Indians.

F 1783   *Add* General works on the Spanish West Indies in the 19th century.

F 1973   *Refer* Spanish West Indies, 1810–1898 F 1783.

F 2223   *Refer* Voyages to the Pacific coast (following gold discovery) F 865.

F 2281   *Add* .G8 Goajira (Ter.)
          Refer Putumayo River and Valley F 3451.P94.

F 2526   *Refer* Demarcation line of Alexander VI E 121.

F 2626   *Refer* General works on Misiones award F 2916.

F 2686   *Add* U. S. Paraguay expedition, 1858–1859.

INDEX

Names of cities and towns, not being regularly brought out in the classification, are not entered in the index. A very few cities have special numbers in the scheme and a few others are entered for special reasons in the index. In cases where the same name is borne by a city and a state or department, the index is to be understood as referring to the latter, unless city is specially mentioned.

INDEX.

INDEX.

Coachella Valley, Cal.: F 868.R6.

Coahuila, Mexico: F 1266.

Cobb, David: F 69.C.

Cobb Co., Ga.: F 292.C6.

Cobbett, William
Collected works: E 302.C.

Cochabamba, Bolivia: F 3341.C7.

Cocking, Matthew: F 1060.7.C.

Cod, Cape: F 72.C3.

Cody, W. F.: F 594.C.

Coeur d'Alene mining district:
F 752.85.

Colchagua, Chile: F 3151.

Colchester Co., Nova Scotia: F 1089.C6.

Cold Harbor, battle of, 1864: E 476.52.

Colden, Cadwallader: F 122.C.

Coles, Edward: F 545.C.

Coles Co., Ill.: F 547.C6.

Colfax, Schuyler: E 415.9.C68.

Colfax Co., N. Mex.: F 802.C7.

Colima, Mexico: F 1271.

Collamer, Jacob: F 53.C.

Colleges: LD 9-6391.
Revolution: E 270.
Civil war: E 541; E 586.

Colombia: F 2251-2299.

Colombo, Cristoforo: E 111-120.

Colonia, Uruguay (City), Contests
over: F 2723.

Colonia, Uruguay (Dept.): F 2731.C7.

Colonial customs, U. S.: E 162.

Colonial dames of America: E 186.5.

Colonial daughters of the seventeenth
century: E 186.7.

Colonias, Territorio, Bolivia: F 3341.T3.

Colonies, The thirteen: E 186-199.

Colonization, Negro: E 448.

Colorado: F 771-785.
Civil war: E 498.
Indians: E 78.C6.

Colorado Desert, Cal.: F 868.815.

Colorado River, Tex.: F 392.C6.

Colorado River, Cañon, and Valley:
F 788.
Arizona: F 817.C7.
California: F 868.C6.
Utah: F 832.C7.

Colorados, Uruguay: F 2726.

Columbia, S. C., Burning of, 1865:
E 477.75.

Columbia Co., N. Y.: F 127.C8.

Columbia Co., Or.: F 882.C6.

Columbia Co., Pa.: F 157.C7.

Columbia Co., Wis.: F 587.C7.

Columbia Heights, D. C.: F 202.C6.

Columbia River and Valley: F 853.
Oregon: F 882.C63.
Washington: F 897.C7.

Columbian exposition, 1893: T 500.

Columbiana Co., Ohio: F497.C6.

Columbus, Christopher. See Colombo,
Cristoforo.

Columbus, Ky., demonstration upon,
1861: E 472.28.

Columbus, Ohio, Camp Chase: E 616.C4.

Colusa Co., Cal.: F 868.C7.

Comal Co., Tex.: F 892.C7.

Comanche Indians: E 99.C85.

Commerce, Indians of North America:
E 98.C7.

Commerce, Restrictions on, U. S.
Colonial period: E 215.1.
1800-1810: E 336.

Commerce during Civil war:
HF 3027.6.

Committees of correspondence and
safety: E 216.

Company of New France: F 1030.

Company of the West Indies: F 1030.

Compromise of 1850: E 423.

Compton Co., Quebec: F 1054.C7.

Conant, Roger: F 67.C.

Concepción, Chile: F 3156.

Concord, battle of, 1775: E 241.C7.

Concord River: F 72.M7.

Concordia Parish, La.: F 377.C7.

Conecuh Co., Ala.: F 332.C7.

Conemaugh River and Valley:
F 157.C73.

Conestoga Indians: E 99.C87.

Conewago Creek and Valley, Pa.:
F 157.C75.

Coney Island, N. Y.: F 129.C75.

Confederación Perú-Boliviana: F 3447.

Confederate memorial day: E 645.

Confederate memorial literary society:
E 483.75.

Confederate operations in Canada:
E 470.95.

Confederate States of America:
E 482-489; JK 9801-9993.
Army: E 545-548.
See also Army of Northern Vir-
ginia; Army of Tennessee.

INDEX.

INDEX.

INDEX.

INDEX.

Virginia—Continued.
Negroes: E 185.93.V8.
Slavery: E 445.V8.

Virginia, Army of: E 470.2.
Virginia, Valley of: F 232.V2.
Virginia and Tennessee railroad, expedition against, 1864: E 476.62.
Virginia company of London: F 229.
Virginia, Grand camp Confederate veterans: E 483.28.
Virginia military institute, Lexington: U 430.V7.
Civil war: E 586.V5.
Virginia military lands, Old Northwest: F 483.
Virginia resolutions, 1798: E 328.
Virginia. University: LD 5660–5689.
Civil war: E 586.V6.
Virginius affair: F 1785.
Voyages of discovery: E 101–135.
Voyages to California following gold discovery: F 865.

W

Wabash Co., Ill.: F 547.W12.
Wabash Co., Ind.: F 532.W18.
Wabash River and Valley: F 532.W2.
Illinois: F 547.W14.
Wabaunsee Co., Kans.: F 687.W2.
Wachovia, N. C.: F 262.F7.
Wachusett Mountain: F 72.W9.
Waddell, Hugh: F 257.W.
Wade, B. F.: E 415.9.W16.
Wadsworth, J. S.: E 467.1.W13.
Wagner, Battery, 1863: E 475.63.
Waldo patent, Me.: F 27.M95.
Walker, R. J.: E 415.9.W2.
Walker, William: F 1526.
Walla Walla Co., Wash.: F 897.W18.
Walla Walla River and Valley, Wash.: F 897.W2.
Wallace, W. H. L.: E 467.1.W3.
Wallowa Co., Oreg.: F 882.W2.
Wallowa Lake, Oreg.: F 882.W2.
Walton Co., Fla.: F 317.W24.
Walworth Co., Wis.: F 587.W18.
Wampanoag Indians: E 99.W2.
Wampum: E 98.M7.
Wapello Co., Iowa: F 627.W2.

War
For chronological list of wars see under Wars.
Ward, Artemas: E 207.W2.
Ware Co., Ga.: F 292.W2.
Warfare, Indian: E 98.W2.
Warren, G. K.: E 467.1.W4.
Court-martial: E 477.675.
Warren, Joseph: E 263.M4W.
Warren Co., Ill.: F 547.W2.
Warren Co., Iowa: F 627.W25.
Warren Co., Miss.: F 347.W29.
Warren Co., N. J.: F 142.W2.
Warren Co., N. Y.: F 127.W2.
Warren Co., Ohio: F 497.W2.
Warren Co., Pa.: F 157.W2.
Warrick Co., Ind.: F 532.W4.
Wars
Indian wars: E 81–83.
Chronological list under E 83.
Negro insurrections: E 447.
Chronological list under aE 447.
Slave riots: E 450.
Spanish conquest of Mexico, 1519–1540: F 1230.
Spanish conquest of Peru, 1522–1548: F 3442.
Destruction of Huguenot colony in Florida, 1565: F 314.
Dutch conquest of Brazil, 1624–1654: F 2532.
English conquest of New France, 1629: F 1030.
Dutch conquest of New Sweden, 1655: F 167.
English conquest of New Netherland, 1664: F 122.1.
Dutch conquest of New York, 1673: F 122.
Bacon's rebellion, 1676: F 229.
Spanish attack on Carolina, 1680: F 272.
King William's war, 1689–1697: E 196.
Revolution of 1689 in New England: F 7.5.
Queen Anne's war, 1702–1713: E 197.
Expedition against St. Augustine, 1740: F 314.
Cartagena expedition, 1741: F 2272.5.
King George's war, 1744–1748: E 196.